Philadelphia
Architecture
A GUIDE TO THE CITY

Third Edition

First Paul Dry Books Edition, 2009
Copyright © 2009 by the Center for Architecture
All rights reserved

Designed and typeset by Joel Katz Design Associates
Philadelphia, Pennsylvania

Printed in China

Cataloging-in-Publication Data is printed on the inside back
cover.

ISBN 978-1-58988-047-4

Philadelphia *Architecture*

A GUIDE TO THE CITY
Third Edition

John Andrew Gallery

Prepared for the
Center for Architecture
Philadelphia, Pennsylvania

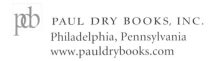

PAUL DRY BOOKS, INC.
Philadelphia, Pennsylvania
www.pauldrybooks.com

Introduction to the Third Edition

Acknowledgments

This third edition of *Philadelphia Architecture, A Guide to the City*, expands the catalog of buildings to include those completed between 1993, the date of the second edition, and early 2008. In keeping with the approach of earlier editions, buildings were selected to represent a range of building types and to illustrate the varied character of contemporary architectural design. Significant buildings by nationally prominent architects were automatically included, and a special effort was made to identify notable buildings by a new generation of architects whose work is just coming to public attention in this century.

In addition to including buildings constructed after 1993, some buildings that were overlooked in the previous editions have also been added and a few deleted that did not seem to stand the test of time. Only one building in the first edition was demolished prior to the second edition— the White Tower hamburger stand at Broad and Race streets, built in 1932. Between the second and third editions only four more were lost: the Ridge Avenue Farmers Market, 1875; the U.S. Naval Hospital, 1933-35; Mill Creek Public Housing, 1946-54, 1959-62; and Schuylkill Falls Public Housing, 1954-55. One remarkable difference between the second and third editions is the number of buildings that were rehabilitated and adapted to new uses. These changes and the architects responsible for them are noted in the building descriptions.

Although this guide focuses on Philadelphia, it seemed appropriate to include a few of the many outstanding buildings outside the city that are within easy reach. The eleven buildings included were selected to cover a range from the colonial period to the current day and because they are generally open to the public.

The choice of buildings to be added to this edition was aided by suggestions from many people, for whose advice I am grateful. Over the years many people also provided comments and corrections to previous editions. I have appreciated those comments and tried to incorporate them as much as possible.

A few individuals deserve special mention. John Claypool, executive director of the Center for Architecture, offered thoughtful advice and generous patience for the length of time it took me to complete this project.

Joel Katz created the graphic format of the first edition, and Peter Olson took virtually all the photographs for both the first and second editions. Although much of their work is now 25 years old, it is a testament to their exceptional talent that both the graphic design and the photographs seem as outstanding to me now as they did originally. Joel has also been a personal mentor for me on each edition of *Philadelphia Architecture*, providing good advice and guidance well beyond graphic design.

For this edition I am grateful to Mary Torrieri for her contributions to the graphic design. It was a special pleasure for me to work with my son, Wyatt Gallery, who took most of the color photographs. I am also grateful to the architects and photographers who provided material about the new buildings. Elise Vider served as editor for new text. Ben Katz was very helpful in obtaining final photographs and photo credits. Paul Dry was an enthusiastic publisher who gave us a free hand to create the best book we could, while providing many suggestions to help us achieve that.

Much of this edition is based on the earlier editions and it seems appropriate to acknowledge those individuals not already mentioned who contributed in the past. Nancy Williams, Christine Cavajal, and Caroline Piven were responsible for much of the original research, writing and editing. Jerome Cloud contributed to the original graphic design; Peter Lapham and Joanne Hepp helped prepare the final manuscript. Many institutions contributed visual material. The Philadelphia Historical Commission, the Free Library, the Historical Society of Pennsylvania, the Library Company, the Athenaeum of Philadelphia, and the Philadelphia Museum of Art deserve special recognition.

It has been a pleasure for me to work with all of these individuals and the many others who have contributed to *Philadelphia Architecture* over the past twenty-five years.

John Andrew Gallery

Contents

Introduction and How to Use the Book

More than any other American city, Philadelphia represents the history of architecture in the United States. As the leading city of the colonies and the nation's first capital, Philadelphia was the center of cultural, scientific and civic leadership in the 18th century. It was a principal channel through which changing architectural tastes in England were introduced to the United States.

In the 19th century, Philadelphia's important scientific community placed the city in the forefront of industrial change. At one time, Philadelphia was the largest manufacturing center in the country. New building types and the thousands of houses built for the rapidly growing population made the 19th century one of the richest periods in the city's architectural history. In the 20th century, Philadelphia was one of the first to focus on problems of urban development and historic restoration. Major civic projects conceived in the early decades of the century were carried out after World War II when the city was an acknowledged leader in urban renewal, architectural design and education.

The end of the 20th century and the early years of the 21st century saw the development of the city's first tall skyscrapers, the creation of new cultural facilities and civic buildings, and a surge in downtown residential development.

The architectural heritage of over 300 years is visible in every section of the city: Philadelphia is quite literally a museum of American architecture. Its "collection" includes examples of every type of building and virtually every important style found throughout the United States. This collection includes outstanding work by such important architects as William Strickland,

Thomas U. Walter, Frank Furness, McKim Mead and White, Daniel Burnham, George Howe, Louis Kahn, Robert Venturi, Romaldo Giurgola, I. M. Pei, Helmut Jahn, Michael Graves and Robert A.M. Stern. In addition, there are thousands of distinctive buildings by outstanding local architects and builders.

This book is a catalog to that collection. It contains a limited selection of buildings intended to illustrate the city's best architecture as well as a representative sampling of building types from different historical periods.

The book is divided into two parts. The first, the catalog of buildings, contains four sections roughly corresponding to the 18th, 19th and 20th centuries and the early years of the 21st century. Each section is preceded by an essay, which describes the development of the city during that period, and by an illustrated glossary of architectural terms. Brief biographies of important Philadelphia architects are also included.

The catalog has been organized to present a variety of building types ranging from houses and apartment buildings to offices, industrial, commercial, religious and institutional buildings. The chart beginning on page 186 shows the distribution of buildings by type and general date. Entries in the catalog are listed chronologically rather than by geographic area, so that it is possible to trace the history of the city through its buildings and to follow the evolution of architectural styles. Each building is cross-referenced to tour or location maps.

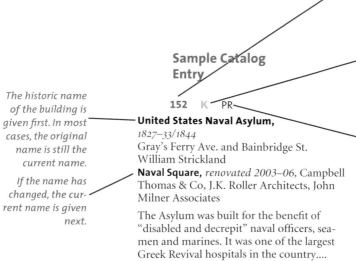

Each catalog entry has been assigned a three-digit number. The first digit corresponds to the catalog section in which the entry appears.

Sample Catalog Entry

The historic name of the building is given first. In most cases, the original name is still the current name.

If the name has changed, the current name is given next.

152 K PR

United States Naval Asylum,
1827–33/1844
Gray's Ferry Ave. and Bainbridge St.
William Strickland
Naval Square, *renovated 2003–06,* Campbell Thomas & Co, J.K. Roller Architects, John Milner Associates

The Asylum was built for the benefit of "disabled and decrepit" naval officers, seamen and marines. It was one of the largest Greek Revival hospitals in the country....

K —The map/tour(s) on which the building can be found.

OP — Open to the public.

PR — Private residence.

The second part of the book contains ten walking and driving tours as well as information about selected places of architectural interest. The tours focus on areas that have significant concentrations of buildings listed in the catalog or that represent different historical periods. Each tour entry is cross-referenced to the catalog. Other buildings of interest in the area are also noted.

The general reader or visitor will find it most useful to read the introductory essays to each section of the catalog and the introductions to the tours first. This will provide a quick overview of the development of the city and indicate areas where the most interesting buildings are located. After reviewing the catalog, tours can be selected that correspond to individual interests or time available. Persons interested in specific buildings or the work of a particular architect can use the index, catalog and maps to create an individual tour. The tours and the buildings listed in the catalog should be viewed as an introduction to the many other fascinating buildings waiting to be discovered throughout the city.

Sample Tour Entry

Catalog number.

OP — Open to the public.

PR — Private residence.

Building not in catalog but of general interest within the tour area.

107 **Christ Church**
22–26 N. 2nd St. OP

145 **Girard Warehouses**
18–30 N. Front St.

241 **Tutlemann Brothers & Faggen Building**
56–60 N. 2nd St. PR

220 **Smythe Buildings**
101–111 Arch St. PR

106 **Elfreth's Alley**
Between Front & 2nd, Arch & Race Sts. PR

a **Betsy Ross House**
239 Arch St. 1740 OP

211 **St. Charles Hotel St. Charles Court**
60–66 N. 3rd St. PR

141 **Arch Street Meeting House**
330 Arch St. OP

107
Christ Church
See pages 22–23

1

The Founding of the City

1682–1701

The Colonial Capital

1701–1835

The Founding of the City
1682–1701

William Penn

The American colonies were founded in an era of intolerance and economic unrest. Throughout most of the 17th century, English history was marked by sharp differences between kings and people. Religious persecutions sent many groups into exile on the continent and provided the initial motivation for colonial settlements in Massachusetts and Virginia. But of all the colonial settlements, none was more deliberately planned to offer a contrast to the prevailing English ideas of religious and personal freedom as was Philadelphia.

The Colony of Pennsylvania and the City of Philadelphia were created by one man, William Penn. Penn was born into a wealthy English family. His father was an admiral. Penn was a country gentleman with large land holdings, but he had lived in London and in many cities in Ireland and on the continent. As a member of the Religious Society of Friends (Quakers), Penn was persecuted for his religious beliefs and spent several periods of time in jail. While in prison he conceived the idea of a colony in the new world that would offer freedom from religious oppression.

In 1681, Penn obtained a charter for his colony from King Charles II in exchange for a debt the King owed his father. The King named the new colony Pennsylvania (Penn's Woods) and Penn chose the name Philadelphia for its principal city, from the Greek word meaning city of brotherly love.

Penn viewed his colony as a holy experiment, to be founded on principles of tolerance and justice. He offered religious and personal freedoms that were radical innovations in the 17th century. These included the freedom of worship for all people and the right to trial by jury in an open court. Penn combined his political philosophy with a liberal land policy. His concept of land development was directed toward the rural middle class, who were unable to afford sizable land holdings under prevailing conditions in England. Large tracts of land, 500 acres or more, at reasonable prices were a unique economic opportunity. This combination of political philosophy and liberal land policy attracted many colonists from England, Wales, Holland and Germany.

Penn had very specific ideas about the physical plan of his colony. This plan encompassed the entire region, not just the small city of Philadelphia. Penn expected most settlers to purchase 500 acres or more in the countryside combined with lots located in the city. He offered individuals of similar backgrounds the opportunity to purchase 5,000 acres as a group, to be subdivided as they saw fit. Through this means, he hoped to establish independent townships. The most successful of these was Germantown, settled by Daniel Pastorius and a group of Dutch and German Quakers. Similar grants to Welsh Quakers created the townships of Haverford, Mercer and Radnor. Penn also created eight manors outside the city, including his country seat at Pennsbury, each consisting of several thousand acres.

Central to Penn's plan was the establishment of a great town. Penn envisioned a town of 10,000 acres with each major landowner having 10 to 100 acres in the town in addition to his holdings in the countryside. Houses would be built in the center of the town lots, surrounded by gardens and orchards, forming what Penn referred to as a green country town.

After formulating these plans and offering land for sale in England, Penn dispatched his surveyor, Thomas Holme, to lay out the colony. When Holme arrived in 1682 he found the site selected by Penn for the great town already occupied by Swedish settlers. Holme went up the river and purchased land at the narrowest place between the Schuylkill and Delaware rivers. Here he laid out 200 of the 600,000 acres, purchased by 470 prospective colonists, in lots along the Delaware River. When Penn arrived, he was dissatisfied with the plan and extended the city westward to cover the two-mile area between the two rivers. Holme's final plan established a grid of streets broken by four public squares of 8 acres each and a central square for civic buildings at the intersection of two major streets. The overall plan is reminiscent of military outposts such as Londonderry, Ireland, which is believed to have been a precedent for the plan of Philadelphia. Holme reduced the lots in the city to one acre for each 5,000 owned in the countryside. In exchange for this reduction, 10,000 acres north of the city were set aside as "Liberty Lands"—a rural area where property owners were assigned to additional holdings. Holme laid out the initial lots on both riverfronts, in the hope that development would move inward and increase the value of the land still owned by Penn.

Thomas Holme's plan of the City of Philadelphia, 1682

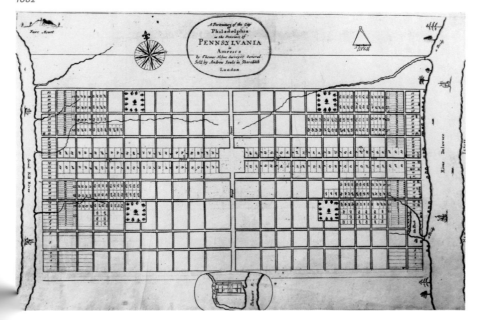

When settlers arrived, the land designated as the site of the city was covered with forest. The first homes were in caves along the Delaware River bank and then in log cabins copied from the Swedish settlers. When construction of houses began, most people remained along the Delaware River edge. No one wanted to settle inland on the Schuylkill riverfront, which was isolated from the port and other settlers by forest. At the time Philadelphia was founded, the English placed great emphasis on fireproof construction as a result of the Great Fire of London in 1666. Brick was the common building material. The ready availability of local clay in Philadelphia led to the establishment of the first brickyard in 1685. In contrast to the wood frame construction, common in New England and Virginia, colonial buildings in Philadelphia were brick almost from the start.

When Penn left the city for the last time in 1701, Philadelphia was established. There were about 2,000 people living in modest brick homes near the Delaware River. Most were Quakers of English, Dutch, Welsh and German backgrounds. But in testimony to Penn's philosophy, there were also Scots-Irish Presbyterians and Anglicans. The streets and lots of the city had been laid out according to an overall plan that would guide the city's growth for many years. The riverfront was covered with wharfs and there was sufficient activity in the port to support four shipbuilding yards. The first markets had been established on High Street (now Market Street) and the city was populated with merchants, shopkeepers and craftsmen. Though most people lived in the city, there was an established pattern of country estates and farms as well as a small independent settlement in Germantown. This expansion over a large geographic area was facilitated by the Quaker form of worship, in houses, rather than the more formal relationship to a single church building, which kept New England towns within close physical limits. Penn's plan was a social, religious and economic success; it had started the city well on its way.

Thomas Holme's plan of the Province of Pennsylvania, 1687

The Colonial Capital
1701–1835

Furnishings also reflect the changes in tastes and styles that influenced architectural design.

This silver tankard is representative of the fine craftsmanship of early Philadelphia silverwork. It was made by Johannis Nys in 1714 and was owned by James Logan, William Penn's secretary.

The slat-back chair was very popular in Philadelphia. It came in a variety of sizes, was made of maple and painted. The slats of this chair, from 1725–50, are arched and have a concave curve for greater comfort.

In the 75 years after William Penn left Philadelphia, the city grew from a modest village to the most important city in the colonies and the second largest in the English-speaking world. Throughout the 18th century, the port of Philadelphia was the primary entry point for immigrants to all the colonies. Many immigrants remained in the area because of the religious and personal freedoms established by Penn and because Philadelphia had the finest agricultural countryside of any colonial city. Land was cleared and farms created at such a rapid rate that the export of food was soon one of the major activities of the port. The growing population in the countryside increased the demand for other goods and services, which attracted craftsmen and merchants to the city.

The focus of life in the city was the port. The riverfront was covered with wharfs servicing ships that exported fur, lumber and food supplies and imported rum and sugar from the West Indies and manufactured goods from England. Shipbuilding was a major industry. The early residential sections of the city were located as close to the port as possible. Houses were built individually or in pairs on deep, narrow lots at the edge of the forest, not in complete rows as we now know them. Initially the city must have had the character of the green country town advocated by Penn, for there was ample room for barns and gardens around the houses.

The first houses were based on the country house of the English yeoman. They were modest in size and still medieval in style with steeply pitched roofs, prominent chimneys and small windows. Most were two stories high with one room per floor and a winding stair. Furnishings were simple, stressing functional requirements rather than decorative design. English building traditions were modified by the Quaker emphasis on simplicity and by the presence of craftsmen from Holland and Germany who introduced features such as glazed brick, Flemish bond brick patterns and the pent eave roof.

In the colonial city there were no large businesses or places of work. Most people were individual entrepreneurs who worked in their homes with their families or single partners often assisted by indentured servants and slaves. Even the shipyards were small, with eight or ten employees usually brought together for specific jobs. The only places set aside for purely commercial purposes were the city taverns and market sheds, and even these were of residential scale and character.

Philadelphia grew rapidly. In 1740, the city had a population of 10,000 and was second only to Boston in size and volume of trade. The developed area extended for a mile north and south along the river and as far west as 4th Street, with the greatest concentration between Market and Race streets. It was a dirty city, with unpaved streets often filled with garbage.

But by 1750, this began to change and, by 1765, the city had a population of 25,000, which substantially surpassed Boston. English and Welsh Quakers and Scots Presbyterians had been joined by Irish, Dutch, Swedish and German settlers of all religious backgrounds. The population expanded southward, necessitating the creation of a second city market and the construction of several new churches. By this time Philadelphia was the center of social and intellectual life in the colonies. It had several theaters and an active political climate centered around the many taverns. New institutions had been created, including almshouses for the poor, libraries, schools and colleges, and hospitals. Because nearly 80 percent of the housing was built as an investment to rent, the concern for property protection led to the creation of insurance and fire companies. There were several newspapers, and Benjamin Franklin had already inaugurated his postal service. Residents of the city were prominent artists; the finest doctors in the colonies; skilled craftsmen famous throughout the colonies; and prospering furniture makers, textile workers and printers. Some of the colonies' most creative individuals lived in the city, including such scientists with a worldwide reputation as John Bartram, the botanist; David Rittenhouse, an inventor; and of course Benjamin Franklin.

The transformation of the city was also reflected in its physical appearance. The low skyline of two-story houses was broken by the towers of Christ Church and the State House (now Independence Hall). New residential and civic buildings were built in the latest English architectural styles. In the early 18th century, English architecture was transformed by the rediscovery of the work of the 16th-century Italian Renaissance architect Andrea Palladio. By 1715, Palladio's adaptation of Roman classical design became the precedent for all serious English architects. The Palladian style is known as Georgian in the colonies. It was transferred through the travels of the merchants back and forth to London and through the publication of handbooks on Palladio's work.

The first Georgian building in the colonies was in Williamsburg. But after 1720, Georgian elements were applied over the basic brick shells of colonial architecture in every city. Some of the most elegant Georgian houses and public buildings were produced in Philadelphia. Exteriors often were toned down in deference to the continued dominance of Quaker attitudes, but interior rooms were large and sumptuous in paneling and details. These interiors demanded elegant furnishings usually produced by local craftsmen. The Georgian style remained popular in the city throughout the 18th century due to the conservative influence of the Carpenters' Company. The company, founded in 1724, was modeled after the builders' guilds in London. It disseminated information about building techniques, established construction prices

Dresses from the first half of the 18th century were as elaborate as Georgian design. This taffeta dress, from 1740–50, has a wide skirt supported by panniers, three-quarter-length sleeves and a low, laced bodice.

This 1755 compass-bottom chair may have come from the parlor of Samuel Powel's house on South 3rd Street. It has a handsome curved form, decorated with restrained ornament in the form of scrolls, leafage and shells.

and provided mutual aid among its members. Its Rule Book, produced in 1786, was based entirely on Georgian principles and reflected none of the later stylistic changes that became important in other cities. Most of Philadelphia's master builders belonged to the company, including Robert Smith, the greatest master builder of the times.

Massachusetts and Virginia were in the forefront when the colonies began to organize to express their differences with England. Pennsylvania had mixed allegiances; many conservative leaders were unwilling to make the break with English rule. Despite this, Philadelphia was the logical meeting place for the revolutionary cause. It was centrally located and was the most advanced city in the colonies. Delegates to the First and Second Continental Congresses were impressed with the city's cultural resources, fine houses and abundance of civic institutions. Because of its urban character, Philadelphia was the logical choice as the nation's first capital.

During the Revolutionary War, the city prospered economically. It was a chief supplier of military arms, blankets and uniforms and a major port of trade. But the city was attacked and occupied by the British for a time. Many civic buildings were converted to stables, barracks and hospitals. By the end of 1783, the city was in serious disrepair. The development of the city after the war was complicated when the Pennsylvania Assembly took over the ownership of all of Penn's holdings. The Assembly sold land rapidly to repay war debts, with little regard for Penn's plan. Lots were subdivided by numerous alleys and significant portions of the northern liberty lands were sold for housing.

By the time of the first U.S. Census in 1790, the population of the area had grown to 53,000. It was still concentrated north and south along the river but had expanded as far as 7th Street. The forest finally had been cleared to the Schuylkill River. Independent townships were established in Southwark and Frankford. The city was still dirty from the war and had no system to handle garbage. Yellow fever epidemics in 1793 and 1796 hampered the city's return to normality and forced virtu-

Growth of the city, 1776–1825

1776   1800   1825

Windsor chairs were produced in Philadelphia from 1748 into the early 1800s. They were used in houses and public buildings. This chair, produced between 1785 and 1807, was made of hardwood and was painted. Its simple lines and square back reflect the influence of the Hepplewhite and Sheraton styles.

This ensemble of sideboard, knife boxes and cellerate, made in 1825, is a rich example of the Philadelphia Empire style. It is mahogany with brass and ebony panels. Some of the details are similar to designs of Robert Adam.

ally all inhabitants to flee. Most went to Germantown, including George Washington, because it was on higher ground and thought to be safer. From then on, Germantown became a popular location for the summer homes of wealthy families.

As the city began to rebuild after the war, new construction was once again influenced by English architectural tastes. English architects interested in classical design based their work on Roman domestic architecture. One of the principal advocates of Roman design was Robert Adam. Adam's work was more graceful and delicate than the heavier and more robust Georgian style. In this country, it became known as the Federal style because it was most popular at the time of the formation of the federal government. The Federal style was not as important in Philadelphia as it was in other cities primarily because it was barely recognized by the Carpenters' Company. But many townhouses, country estates and civic buildings were designed in this refined manner and furnished with elegant furniture by Sheraton and Hepplewhite.

By the end of the 18th century, Philadelphia was once again an impressive city. Sumptuous Georgian and Federal houses lined paved streets. Country mansions had developed along the Delaware and Schuylkill rivers and in Germantown. Impressive civic and religious buildings had been built as well as many new houses, all of a uniform character, made of brick with stone or wood trim, which gave the city a strikingly modern appearance. Philadelphia was still a major port, the center of shipbuilding, and the financial center of the new nation.

In 1800, Philadelphia had a population of 80,000 in the city and surrounding countryside. It was the largest city in the country, but New York was growing at a faster pace and would surpass it by 1810. The city was concentrated in the area between 7th Street and the river, stretching north and south into Frankford and Southwark. Most of the residents still were merchants and craftsmen, working in their homes; the rich and poor, indentured servants, slaves, free blacks and their employers were mixed together in no particular pattern. But the economic conditions of the city had already begun to change in a manner that would greatly influence future patterns of development. Although the city still had an active port, Philadelphia had begun to look inland for its economic growth. Coal and iron were brought to the city by newly created canals to be exported around the world. Local businesses prospered when embargoes on the importation of European goods encouraged factories to replace them with local products. Papermaking, printmaking, books, shoes and foundries were among the more prominent businesses.

This growth of manufacturing was facilitated by the presence of many inventors in the city and by the general availability of skilled labor. Philadelphia's craftsmen were recognized as the best in the colonies.

Much of the new manufacturing located along streams outside the city. This further encouraged construction of new houses in such areas as Kensington, Spring Garden and Moyamensing. This dispersed growth presented many problems, such as an inadequate water supply and police and fire protection outside the city proper. Within the city, the population growth led to the speculative development of complete blocks of row houses. Once again, changing English architectural tastes provided the inspiration for new building design.

By the end of the 18th century, architects began to draw directly on Greek and Roman forms. Classical Greek orders became available in England through architectural handbooks. They were introduced in America as early as 1798 by Benjamin Latrobe, an English architect who emigrated to Philadelphia. But the Greek Revival did not really flourish until after 1820; not only did Greek Revival architecture sweep the country, but cities and towns were named after Athens, Sparta and other Greek cities.

In Philadelphia the prominence of Greek Revival design was due to the influence of Nicholas Biddle, president of the Second Bank of the U.S., and to the appearance of the first professional architects. William Strickland, John Haviland and Thomas U. Walter designed prominent Greek Revival buildings in the city. The use of classical orders and temple forms made buildings much more impressive than their Georgian and Federal predecessors. But beyond decoration and detail, Greek Revival buildings in gleaming white marble stood in sharp contrast to the uniform red brick of previous periods.

By 1830, the Philadelphia area had a population of 188,000. The city had expanded to 10th Street. In the countryside around the city there were mills, manufacturing centers and semi-independent townships. Each township had its own name, businesses, shops, fire companies and taverns, all loosely connected to the city. The development of new methods of manufacturing had already begun to change the way people worked and where they lived. Philadelphia was a handsome and sophisticated city on the verge of becoming an industrial metropolis.

Quaker dress, like building design, was plain and simple but usually made of fine material. The 1766 silk wedding dress with simple silhouettte has no adornment, not even buttons.

Glossary of Architectural Terms

1 ashlar
stone that has been cut and squared, generally used on a building's facade

2 balustrade
a low wall formed by a series of short posts, shaped like a vase, with a rail on top; often found along the roof-line of Georgian buildings

3 cornice
any molding or ornamentation that projects from the top of the building

4 cupola
a small, domed structure rising from the roof

5 dormer
a window in a small structure on the roof, allowing light to enter the attic

6 entablature
the horizontal member, above the column capitals, consisting of the architrave, frieze and cornice

7 fanlight
a semicircular window located above a door

8 Flemish bond
a brick pattern laid by alternating long and short ends; believed to have been acquired by exiled English

builders living in Holland during the reign of Oliver Cromwell

9 gable
the triangular section of wall on the side of a building with a double-pitched roof; the roof is often called a gable roof

10 Germantown stone
local stone, known as Wissahickon schist, found near the surface of the earth; used in its rough condition as rubble, with heavy mortor joints, or cut and dressed for use on the main facade

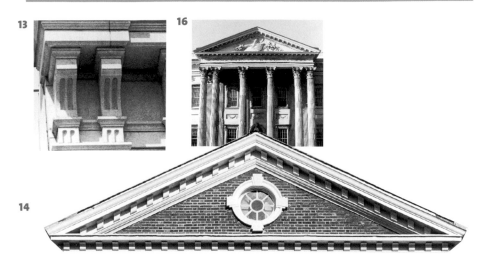

11 glazed header
the short end of a brick, with a darker glazing; used in a Flemish bond to produce a checkerboard pattern on the facade

12 Greek orders
the three forms of columns and entablatures from classical Greek architecture: Doric, with plain capitals; Ionic, with scroll capitals; Corinthian, with capitals decorated with acanthus leaves

13 modillion
an ornamental bracket used to support the cornice

14 pediment
the triangular surface formed by a gable roof and a cornice, generally used on a portico or over a doorway

15 pent eave
a small, wooden roof located between the first and second floors; originally used to protect wood and plaster facades from rain

16 portico
a roofed porch, supported by columns, found over the doorway

17 quoins
stones or bricks used to form the outside corner of a building

18 water table and belt course
elements of Georgian design in which the brick is projected slightly beyond the facade to deflect rain; the water table being the widened portion of the wall at the base, and the belt course being the projected lines of brick between the upper floors

▼
1682
Philadelphia founded
by William Penn

▼
1683
Germantown settled
by Daniel Pastorius

▼
1685
Bradford prints first
book in middle colo-
nies

102

103

101 L PR
Wynnestay, *1689/1700/1904*
5115 Woodbine Ave.
Thomas Wynne, builder

In 1681, Thomas Wynne, a Welsh physician, bought 5,000 acres of land from William Penn, on which he later built a one-room farmhouse, probably as a gift to his son. Wynne's house is typical of many Welsh farmhouses throughout the Philadelphia area. It is built of local stone found on or near the surface of the earth. The stone is set in wide mortar joints; the walls are two feet thick, with low and wide windows. Between the first and second floor of the original house is a pent eave, a common feature of early Philadelphia architecture. The pent eave was originally designed to protect plaster and wood outer walls from rain. It was incorporated into colonial designs even though the houses were built principally of stone or brick. The house was enlarged in 1904 by the addition of a rear wing in a compatible style.

102 L
Gloria Dei, *1698–1700*
929 South Water St.

While the early Welsh and German settlers were building stone farmhouses, the Swedes, who had been in the Delaware Valley since the 1630s, were building their first permanent church. Gloria Dei is the oldest church in the city and the only remaining building by Swedish settlers. The Swedes brought log construction to the new world. But for their first church, they chose brick and hired English carpenters and masons to build it.

These craftsmen built in the tradition of English vernacular architecture, a mixture of medieval and gothic influences. These may be seen in the decorative shapes created with glazed brick headers next to the tower door and in the steep slope of the roof, the narrow tower windows and steep pedimented gable.

Three years after completion, the side walls began to bow under the stress of an inadequate roof truss. A vestry and entranceway were added to buttress these walls.

103 H OP
Rittenhouse Homestead, *1707*
207 Lincoln Drive, at Wissahickon Ave.
Restored 2006, Fairmount Park Historic Preservation Trust

In 1690, William and Nicholas Rittenhouse leased 20 acres of land along the Wissahickon Creek and established the first paper mill in British North America. Paper produced at the mill was sold to printers in Philadelphia and New York for bibles and newspapers.

Rittenhouse family members continued to live on the site for 200 years, establishing an early industrial village that contained over 40 buildings on 125 acres by the mid-19th century. The site was purchased by the City in 1890-91 and became a part of Fairmount Park.

The 1707 Rittenhouse Homestead is of traditional German construction. It was built of rubble stone with flush pointing. Paired casement windows flank either side of the doorway, which is covered by a gabled roof. The roof of the house was cedar shingles covered with moss. A 1713 addition to the west is of similar construction, with a pent eave added to connect both structures. Other buildings include the 1720 Abraham Rittenhouse house, the 1730 bake house and the 1810 home of Jacob Rittenhouse.

David Rittenhouse (1732-96), renowned inventor and astronomer, was born here.

▼
1688
*First North American
protest against slav-
ery, in Germantown*

▼
1689
*Penn Charter opens;
first public school in
colonies*

▼
1690
*Rittenhouse estab-
lishes first American
paper mill*

105

106

104   E
Letitia House, *1713–15*
Lansdowne Dr. near West Girard Ave.
Attributed to James Smart, house carpenter

William Penn expected early settlers to build modest houses in the center of garden lots. He described such a house in his pamphlet, *Information and Direction To Such People As Are Inclined to America.* Letitia, one of the earliest documented houses in Philadelphia, is similar to the house Penn suggested.

Like most early row houses, Letitia is made of brick laid in Flemish bond with gray glazed headers alternating with stretchers, giving the surface an intimately scaled checkerboard pattern. The paneled shutters and the small window sash also help create an orderly, tidy appearance. The center placement of the door is unusual for a town house, as is the hood supported by carved brackets over the entrance.

The house is two rooms deep; fireplaces placed back to back in one corner share a common chimney. A space-saving set of winding stairs, in a tight vertical box, rises from the cellar to the attic.

The house was originally located near Front Street. It was moved to Fairmount Park in 1883.

105   L
Bel Air, *between 1714 and 1729*
Southwest Corner 20th and Pattison Ave.

Ambitious colonial settlers followed the English pattern of creating country homes as well as maintaining a city house. Bel Air is one of the earliest surviving country seats. It was probably built for Samuel Preston, one of the city's first mayors.

Although an early Georgian home, Bel Air shows traces of the English medieval style as seen in the steep pitch of the roof, the narrow window proportions and the angular gables set over the dormers. The wide, symmetrical facade, the horizontal axis of the belt course and the water table that thickens the wall on the first floor reflect the classical influences of the Georgian tradition. The second floor balcony, with protective hood built into the cornice, is an unusual feature in colonial architecture.

Bel Air's interior has fine Queen Anne paneling and decoration. A large Tudor arch with a heart-shaped medieval pendant decorates the hallway and staircase.

106   A,K   PR
Elfreth's Alley, *Houses from 1720*
Front and 2nd, Arch and Race Sts.

Elfreth's Alley, the oldest continuously inhabited street in the country, was created in 1703 when two property owners on Front Street made a cartway to the rear of their lots to subdivide their land. By the end of the 18th century, Elfreth's Alley had assumed its present character as a street of modest row homes. The oldest homes are simple two-and-a-half-story structures with parlors entered directly from the street. Some have pent eaves. Exterior woodwork is simple, as are doorways and transom lights. Most of the houses were built for rent and lived in by craftsmen. The Museum House at 126 is typical of these early homes. It was occupied by a dressmaker who had her shop on the first floor and living quarters above.

The three-and-a-half-story houses were built after the Revolutionary War and show the influence of the Federal style in the classically framed doorways with pilasters and pediments.

107 A,K OP

Christ Church, *1727–44*
2nd and Market Sts.
Dr. John Kearsley, supervisor
Restored 2006–08, Frens and Frens LLC

Although Penn founded Philadelphia to provide a refuge for Quakers, he extended freedom of worship to all religions. One of the first groups to exercise this right was the Anglicans of the Church of England, whose interests had also been protected by Charles II in his charter to Penn.

When the Anglicans outgrew the wooden church built in 1697, they modeled their new church on the work of Sir Christopher Wren, the English architect who rebuilt fifty-two churches in London after the Great Fire. Construction was supervised by John Kearsley, a physician, who probably was responsible for the design. He was the first of many gentlemen-architects who designed important civic buildings.

Christ Church is symmetrical in plan and elevation. The decoration on the facade is classical. Two-story brick pilasters alternate rhythmically with round arch windows. The cornice is decorated with modillions,

and a balustrade hides the vertical slope of the roof. On the east end, a large Palladian window provides light for the chancel. The classical forms are made more dramatic by the strong curving lines of fat scrolls on the east pediment and by the robust curves of the roof urns, capped by carved flames.

Christ Church was the most sumptuous building in the colonies. It was the most sophisticated example of Georgian design in spite of a few awkward details. One of the most noticeable is the failure of the cornice on the side to match the cornice line of the projecting pavilion on the east end.

Robert Smith, the most prominent master carpenter of the time, worked on the steeple, which was added in 1751–54. It also was designed with classical details: round arch windows, pilasters and pediments over circular windows. The brick tower was finished quickly, but it took three lotteries, sponsored by Benjamin Franklin, to raise enough money to add the wooden part. The 196-foot steeple, probably the tallest in the colonies, was a prominent landmark on the early Philadelphia skyline and the tallest building in the city for 100 years.

▼
1697
America's first
stone bridge at the
"Penepacka" Creek

▼
1709
First private mental
institution founded
by Quakers

108

THE GEORGIAN STYLE

*The rebuilding of London after the Great
Fire of 1666 provided a unique opportunity
to introduce new architectural ideas. Many
of the new buildings were influenced by the
recently discovered classical architecture of
the 16th-century Italian Renaissance. The
work of the Italian architect Andrea Palladio
was the dominant influence in London after
1715. Publications such as Campbell's Vitruvius
Britannicus and Gibb's Book of Architecture
made Palladio's work available throughout
England and the colonies.*

*The Palladian style incorporates classical
columns, pilasters, cornices and other decorative elements over the traditional brick
building shell. These elements may be seen in
elaborate doorways, heavy cornice lines, window treatment and brick detailing. The most
prominent exterior feature is the Palladian
window, a large, three-part window with an
arched central bay.*

*The Palladian style is known as Georgian
in the colonies. It was the dominant style for
homes of the well to do, churches and civic
buildings prior to the Revolutionary War.*

108   L   OP
Stenton, *1728*
Courtland and 18th Sts.

Stenton was built on a 500-acre estate by
James Logan, William Penn's personal rep-
resentative in the early years of the colony.
Logan was a fur trader and iron merchant.
He served as mayor of Philadelphia and
chief justice of Pennsylvania.

Stenton is a magnificent example of an
early Georgian country house. The facade is
formal and symmetrically balanced. Simple
brick pilasters mark the principal divisions
and provide a strong accent at the corners.
Modillions along the cornice provide ornament under the eaves of the hipped roof.

Logan was a Quaker, and his manor house
reflects the influence of Quaker plainness
on the Georgian style, particularly in the
restrained use of ornament.

Inside, a generous staircase and fireplace
fill the center hall, which was used as another room in the house. It is believed that
the large front room on the second floor
was Logan's library, which was the most
distinguished in the colonies.

109   A,B,K   OP
**State House
Independence Hall,** *1732–48*
See pages 26–27.

110   L
Glen Fern, *1733–39*
Livezey Lane, Fairmount Park

While Georgian houses were being built
with classical ornament, the Shoemaker
family of Germantown built a simple
farmhouse with doors and windows spaced
irregularly on a plain rubble facade. The
house was later purchased by Thomas
Livezey, who added a second story to the
original one-and-a-half-story structure.
In the 1850s, the kitchen and dining room
were added laterally to the main block, resulting in a long, rambling structure typical
of many country houses.

At its prime, the Livezey estate was self-
sufficient. It included a grist mill, a forge,
a shop for making barrels, a bridge across
the Wissahickon Creek and a smokehouse.
By the middle of the 19th century, steam-
powered machines made water-powered
mills obsolete. The mill was abandoned,
and all that remains is the farmhouse and a
dam with its mill race.

▼
1712
*First ocean-going
vessel launched on
Delaware*

▼
1713
*William Penn dies in
England*

▼
1717
*First life insurance
company: the Presby-
terian Minister's Fund*

▼
1719
*City's first newspaper
established*

111

114

111   H   OP
Wyck, *1736/ 1771–73/ 1824*
6026 Germantown Ave.
William Strickland
Restored 1974–76, John M. Dickey

Hans Milan, a Dutch Quaker, built a small stone house on this site in 1690. In 1736, his son-in-law built a second stone house in front of Milan's and in 1771-73, a later descendant tore down the original house and replaced it with a third stone house separated from the other by a carriageway. By 1799, both houses had been joined at the second floor and the exterior stuccoed.

In 1824, the Greek Revival architect William Strickland was hired to modernize the houses. In the carriageway between the houses, Strickland built a new room, which extends the depth of the house and looks out over the gardens at either end. In this new room he installed the novel feature of sliding glass doors.

112   L   PR
109–25 Kenilworth St., *1740–1800*

Kenilworth Street, like Elfreth's Alley, is an example of the modest row house developments that predominated in the 18th century. The earliest houses were crowded close to the Delaware River in the city and adjacent townships, such as Southwark. Kenilworth Street, or Almond Street as it was then known, was created when Edward Shippen sold part of his Southwark estate. The new lots were long and narrow, measuring 18 or 20 feet by 60 feet. Simple, utilitarian houses were built on the lots over a period of 60 years as the influx of immigrants steadily increased. They were occupied by shipwrights, mast and sail makers, pilots, mariners and others whose work was tied to the port and the sea.

113   L   OP
Grumblethorpe, *1744*
5267 Germantown Ave.
John Wister, builder

John Wister emigrated from Germany in 1727. He became a successful wine merchant and built an unsophisticated summer home in Germantown, six miles from Philadelphia. During the next 50 years other well-to-do families followed Wister's example and built summer homes in Germantown to escape the heat, noise and smell of the city.

Wister's house was built of local stone, known as Wissahickon schist, as were other houses in the area. The Wissahickon schist, with flecks of mica, is dressed and coursed on the front but left as rubble on the side and rear. The pent eave has a balcony in the center, and a heavy, projecting cornice surrounds the gable end. Round windows, instead of the traditional dormers, provide light and ventilation to the attic.

114   A,K
Head House and Market Shed, *1745/1804*
2nd St., Pine to Lombard Sts.

The original markets of the city were open sheds in the center of High Street (now Market Street). As the residential area expanded south, a second market was created at Lombard Street by Joseph Wharton, a wealthy merchant, and the then mayor, Edward Shippen. The market shed, with sixteen stalls, was constructed of paired brick piers supporting a gable roof over a vaulted plaster ceiling. Farmers set up their carts beneath and around the shed. By 1797, the market extended to South Street and was terminated by a firehouse, later demolished.

The market was also extended north to Pine Street, and the present Head House was built in 1804. It housed fire apparatus and served as a meeting place for volunteer

109 A,B,K   OP

State House
(Independence Hall), *1732–48*
Chestnut St. between 5th and 6th Sts.
Andrew Hamilton with Edmund Wooley

In 1729, Philadelphia lawmakers decided
to move the government from the cramped
quarters of the Town Hall at Second and
Market streets. Andrew Hamilton, a well-
known lawyer, proposed the block of Chestnut Street between Fifth and Sixth streets
as the site of the new building, and the Provincial Assembly voted to buy the land even
though it was on the outskirts of town.

Although not all scholars agree, it seems
likely that Hamilton also drew the plans.
He had traveled to England, had seen the
recent work of English designers and also
owned the requisite books on architecture.
He worked on the State House complex
until his death, in close collaboration with
Edmund Wooley, a member of the Carpenters' Company and master carpenter.

The State House was conceived as a five-
part plan based on the Palladian principle
of two secondary buildings linked to a main
block by arcades. The State House is an
outstanding example of Georgian design.
Although it was an important civic building, it is not as elaborate as Christ Church.
In fact, except for its length, it is domestic
in scale and detail. The main building is a
self-contained rectangular block, visually
framed by quoins or cornerstones. The
cornice, balustrade, belt courses and water
table emphasize the horizontal. The soap-
stone panels between the second and first
floors, the marble keystones and the acan-
thus-carved modillions provide restrained
decoration for the facade.

In 1750, the Assembly voted to commemorate the fifty years of Penn's Charter
of Liberties by adding a tower to the rear
of the State House. Wooley was in charge,
and he made some awkward mistakes. For
example, he placed the Palladian window
almost directly on top of the door frame,
omitting the proper classical spacing. At the
same time, a large clock was built against
the west end of the building. The long case,
made of rusticated stone, hid the weights
and lines necessary for an eight-day clock.

The high point in the history of the State
House was the turbulent years before the
Revolutionary War. The Assembly Room,
the setting for the dramatic debates on
independence, was the room in which the
Declaration of Independence was signed.
For ten years (1790–1800), the State House
was the capitol of the new nation before the
government moved to Washington.

In 1830, John Haviland, the Greek revival
architect, was hired by the city to restore
the building to attract new tenants. His restoration marked the first of many. In 1950,
the National Park Service undertook an archeological study of State House buildings,
which provided the information necessary
to restore it to its 1776 appearance.

▼
1723
Benjamin Franklin,
age 17, arrives from
Boston

▼
1724
Carpenters' Company
founded

▼
1728
John Bartram estab-
lishes first botanical
garden

115

117

fire companies. The building is late Georgian, with Federal-style fanlights flanking
the arched passageway. It is topped by a
cupola, which once contained a firebell. The
Head House and sheds, restored in 1960,
are the oldest of their kind in the country.

115   H
Green Tree Tavern, *1748*
6023 Germantown Ave.

Green Tree Tavern is one of the best examples of Georgian architecture in Germantown. It was built by Daniel Pastorius,
grandson of the founder of Germantown.
The tavern is made of Wissahickon schist.
The pent eave and heavy cornice across
the front are typical of most Germantown
buildings. Because the land rises uphill,
the southern sides of buildings along Germantown Avenue were visible to people
coming from Philadelphia. Consequently,
the south walls usually were treated just like
the fronts. On the tavern this wall also has a
pent eave and gable cornice and is dressed
with ashlar stonework. The remaining two
sides are rubble.

In 1930, the tavern was moved to accommodate an addition to the First United
Methodist Church of Germantown, which
uses the tavern for its parish offices.

116   L   PR
Workman Place, *1748/1812*
742–46 South Front St.
George Mifflin, John Workman, builders

As more immigrants came into the city,
many property owners built small houses
or tenements for rent on the rear of their
lots. Workman Place is typical and is one of
the earliest rental housing complexes still in
similar use. The first small tenements were
built by George Mifflin, as evidenced by his
initials and the date 1748 worked in brick.
These houses originally had one room to a

floor and two apartments in each building.
He sold these houses and a large lot to John
Workman. Workman added three elaborate
houses on Front Street, which created the
courtyard.

The Workman family owned these properties until 1906. By that time the houses
had become slums as immigrants crowded
the older housing near the Delaware River.
The houses were bought by Lydia S. Clark,
an early advocate of housing reform, and
subsequently taken over by the Octavia Hill
Association, which continues to operate
them as rental properties.

117   A,K   OP
St. Peter's Church, *1758–61*
3rd and Pine Sts.
Robert Smith, carpenter-architect

By 1750, Christ Church could no longer
accommodate the number of people who
wanted to have seats there. It also was in-
convenient for parishioners living south of
Walnut Street. The Penn family donated
land for a second Anglican church, which
was operated jointly with Christ Church
until 1832. Robert Smith designed and built
the church. Dr. John Kearsley, who had
directed work on Christ Church, was the
supervisor.

St. Peter's is a subdued version of a Palladian church. It contains a grand Palladian
window on the chancel wall, and the sides
of the church are pierced by round arch
windows, but there is an absence of elaborate detail. St. Peter's still retains its original
high-backed pews, raised off the floor to
keep out drafts. In an unusual arrangement,
the altar and pulpit are at opposite ends of
the main aisle.

The steeple was added in 1842 by William Strickland. The simple tower, six
stories high, is in keeping with the church's
restrained exterior.

▼
1731
*Library Company
formed*

▼
1732
*Stage coach line to
New York inaugu-
rated*

▼
1736
*Franklin organizes
world's first volunteer
fire company*

119

120

---

118   B   PR

Abercrombie House, *1759*
268–70 South 2nd St.

Early 18th-century houses had small rooms and were only two or three stories high. Georgian houses were much larger, often with large libraries and ballrooms on the upper floors. This Georgian townhouse was built for a Scottish sea captain who settled in Philadelphia. The house is situated on high ground that must have once commanded a fine view of the port, possibly explaining the decked gable roof with balustrade, a feature not found in any other remaining house in the area. In spite of its height the house retains a horizontal emphasis, typical of Georgian design, through the use of belt courses, water table and a heavy cornice. The house, used as a warehouse early in this century, was restored in the 1960s and occupied by a toy museum for many years before returning to residential use.

---

119   B

Man Full of Trouble Tavern, *1760*
127 Spruce St.

In colonial days, inns were places for socializing. Over a meal and drink people would exchange business and political information as well as gossip. Man Full of Trouble Tavern is one of the many taverns that served the colonial city. The tavern had rooms for travelers on the second floor and in the attic, whose gambrel roof gave more head room than the more common pitched roof.

In the colonial period, there was very little difference in the design of residential or commercial buildings. Only the sign in front that graphically depicted the Man Full of Trouble indicated that the structure was more than a home.

---

120   E   OP

Mount Pleasant, *1761*
Mount Pleasant Dr.
Restored 2006, John Milner Architects

Of all the country estates around Philadelphia, Mount Pleasant was the most elegant. It was built by Captain John MacPherson, a Scottish privateer. He drew on Palladian principles of design, building a main house symmetrically flanked by two small buildings. The distinguishing feature of Mount Pleasant is the projecting pavilion with its pediment. Both the east and west sides of the building have Palladian windows. MacPherson contrasted the texture and color of brick in the belt courses and quoins with a warm-colored stucco ruled to look like stone. This provides a pleasing variation on the usual solid brick or stone houses. The interior is equally handsome, with finely carved paneling.

MacPherson could not afford to live in his expensive mansion. In 1779 he sold it to Benedict Arnold, who planned to give it to his wife as a wedding present. Before the couple could move in, Arnold was charged with treason.

---

121   H   OP

Cliveden, *1763–67*
6401 Germantown Ave.
Benjamin Chew with Jacob Knor, master carpenter

Cliveden was one of the most elegant Georgian estates in the colonies. Benjamin Chew, an important lawyer, designed the house himself, probably working closely with Jacob Knor, a local master carpenter. The house represents a compromise between Palladian fashion and the local Germantown building tradition.

The exterior is distinguished by a projecting pavilion, capped by a pediment, and an entrance framed with classical details. The facade is dressed with ashlar of Wissahickon

▼
1740
*University of Penn-
sylvania founded as
"charity school"*

▼
1741
*America's first maga-
zine published*

▼
1747
*American Philosophi-
cal Society founded*

▼
1748
*First exclusive danc-
ing society, the
Assembly, founded*

121

123

schist, while the rear wall is plain rubble. On the sides, stucco over rubble is scored to imitate stone.

The center hall, the largest room in the house, was the most elaborate of its type in the colonies. It is separated from the stairhall by a screen of four finely carved, fluted Doric columns.

The Chew family lived in the house until 1972, when they gave it to the National Trust for Historic Preservation.

---

122   B

Shippen-Wistar House, *1765*
238 South 4th St.

William Shippen, a leading colonial physician, built this house and gave it to his son, probably as a wedding present. From Fourth Street it looks like most other townhouses in the area except that there is no front door. Shippen took advantage of the corner lot to place the door on the long side of the house, allowing for a more interesting interior plan. The first floor has two rooms on each side of a central hall. The rooms are more easily accessible and of better size than in a typical plan, where the rooms are lined up behind one another.

---

123   B,K   OP

Powel House, *1765*
244 South 3rd St.

The Powel House is the finest Georgian row house in the city. It was built by Charles Stedman. Before he could live in it, he sold it to Samuel Powel, the first mayor of Philadelphia after the Revolution.

Powel was a Quaker who later turned Anglican. This change can be seen in his house. The restrained exterior reflects the Quaker concern for simplicity. The brick facade is Flemish bond, with cheaper common bond on the side. The only decoration is the Doric frame surrounding the door. Inside, restraint gives way to luxurious

rooms decorated with fine paneling, elaborate carving and delicate plaster work.

The plan of the house is quite sophisticated compared to the typical town house. The front door enters into a generous hall. The parlor and dining rooms are to one side, and at the rear, framed by a large arch, is an open mahogany staircase. A ballroom with elaborate woodwork and plaster ceiling is on the second floor.

Robert Smith, the prominent carpenter-architect, worked on this interior.

---

124   B

Old Pine Street Presbyterian Church,
1766-1768
4th and Pine Streets
Robert Smith; *1857*, John Fraser
Restored 1951, 1980s; stencils, Emily Lapham

Old Pine Street Church is the only colonial Presbyterian church building still standing in Philadelphia. The original building, a simple Georgian-style brick structure, was badly damaged by British troops during the Revolutionary War; it served first as a hospital, and later as a stable.

In the mid-19th century, the church was remodeled. The interior was divided into two levels with the worship space on the second floor. A Greek Revival-style portico with Corinthian columns was added, as well as new windows and the entire building finished in stucco. From 1868 to the 1880s, the ceiling and walls of the sanctuary were decoratively painted with stencils and stained glass windows were added. The interior was restored in the1980s and the stencils recreated in beautiful cream, rose and blue colors. In addition to many Christian symbols, the thistle and wave motifs incorporated into the interior decoration are reminders of mergers in 1953 and 1959 with the Holland-Scots and the Mariners Presbyterian churches.

▼
1751
Pennsylvania Hospital, first in America, founded

▼
1752
First American fire insurance company: The Contributionship

▼
1753
The Argo leaves Philadelphia; First Arctic expedition

▼
1754
First American stock exchange opens

124

127

125   L
St. George's Methodist Church, *1769*
4th and New Sts.

St. George's was the center of Methodism in the colonies and is the oldest Methodist church in continuous use in the United States.

Originally, Philadelphia Methodists met in private homes. But, in 1768, they purchased the shell of this church from a German congregation that had fallen on hard times. The church exterior is almost as plain as a Quaker meetinghouse. The only ornamentation on the facade is the barely noticeable corner pilasters, whose caps blend into the cornice line. Even the classical frame found around the door of most churches is absent. This plain exterior masks a delicately scaled, attractive interior, which was finished by the Methodists.

In 1921 the church was almost torn down to make way for the Benjamin Franklin Bridge. It was saved by moving the bridge 14 feet south and lowering Fourth Street. A flight of steps was added to reach the ground floor of the church.

126   L   OP
Bartram Hall, *1730/1770*

See page 32.

127   A,B,K   OP
Carpenters' Hall, *1770–74*
320 Chestnut St.
Robert Smith

In the 18th century, building trades in the city were dominated by members of the Carpenters' Company. The company was founded in 1724 and modeled after English builders' guilds. In addition to building design and construction, members assisted contractors and clients in determining the fair value of completed work. The company's Rule Book, published in 1786, contained principles for measuring and fixing prices. Only members were allowed to see it.

Robert Smith, a member, was chosen to design the company's meeting place. He created a cruciform plan based on one of Palladio's Italian villas and the town halls of his native Scotland. The building's details are Georgian, such as the pediments over the north and south doors and the cupola on the roof. The first floor was a large meeting hall; the second was divided into smaller meeting rooms. The members used the hall for their meetings, but also rented space to other organizations. The most famous group to use the hall was the Continental Congress in 1774.

128   H   OP
Deshler-Morris House, *1750–72*
5442 Germantown Ave.

David Deshler, a well-to-do merchant, built a summer home in Germantown, following the example of his uncle, John Wister. He finished the house in 1772 by adding a large front section facing the street. To dress up the facade Deshler covered the building with stucco ruled to look like stone. He added a classical frame around the doorway with Tuscan columns topped by a pediment, which was the fashionable custom in the city. On the first floor the rooms are divided by a center hall, an advanced plan for colonial houses in Germantown, where most rooms on the first floor had separate doors to the outside.

In the summer and fall of 1793, yellow fever devastated the city. President Washington moved his family to Deshler's elegant home and, having enjoyed his stay, returned the next summer.

126 L OP

Bartram Hall, *1730/1770*
54th St. between Elmwood and Gibson Aves.
John Bartram, builder
Renovated 1990, Dagit / Saylor Architects; *2002,* Frens and Frens LLC

John Bartram was an eccentric Quaker farmer and a respected, self-taught botanist. He traveled extensively along the unexplored east coast in search of new botanical specimens, which he collected for his nursery and sold to English farmers.

Bartram enlarged a small stone Swedish farm house in two stages. By the second stage, his taste was more sophisticated. He dressed the stone and laid it in roughly equal courses with thick mortar joints. This more formal ashlar work is paired with a two-story Ionic portico that looks out over the Schuylkill River. The rather novel columns are built up in horizontal courses of the same dressed stone. The windows are framed with carved volute surrounds in a rough imitation of Baroque curves. In true Georgian fashion, the facade is for show; around the corner, the walls are rubble and stucco.

The seed house, also on the grounds, is another delightful example of Bartram's handiwork. It is rubble with stone chips set decoratively in thick joints.

▼
1757
First streetlights installed; designed by Franklin

▼
1759
Southwark, America's first theater, opens

▼
1765
First medical school in colonies established

▼
1767
First American play, "Prince of Parthia," produced

129

THE FEDERAL STYLE

By 1770, Robert Adam and his brother were the most prominent architects in England. Adam continued the tradition of classical investigation by publishing a book on Roman architecture. Adam used new information about details and decoration and the variety with which classical orders were used in Roman domestic architecture to form his own style.

The Adam style is known as the Federal style in the colonies because it reached its popularity in the period after the Revolution, when the new government was being formed. The Federal style is light and delicate compared with the robust richness of Georgian design. Columns, pilasters and other moldings are narrow and flat. Windows are narrow, with slender mullions. Exterior decoration is limited and usually confined to doorways. Interior ornamentation is equally delicate, with an increased used of curved and oval forms in the plans of rooms, in bay windows or fanlight windows over the main door. The overall effect is one of refinement and grace.

129   B   OP
Hill-Physick-Keith House, *1786*
321 South 4th St.

This house is the only remaining example of the many freestanding mansions that once existed within the row-house fabric of the colonial city. It is also one of the finest examples of Federal-style architecture. Colonel Henry Hill, a prosperous wine merchant, built the house, which was later owned by Dr. Philip Syng Physick, the father of American surgery.

Federal-style ornamentation is more delicate than its Georgian predecessor. On the Hill-Physick-Keith House, ornament is limited to projecting keystones and cornice modillions. Brick courses, separating the floors and outlining the main door, are

nearly flush with the wall surface. The finely crafted double door, surrounded by intricate carving and topped by an impressive fanlight, imparts a grace and monumentality more often found on country mansions. The spacious interior contains thirty-two rooms, including a ballroom on the first floor finished with elaborate woodwork.

130   L
Reynolds-Morris House, *1786–87*
225 South 8th St.
The Morris Hotel, *2006*

The Reynolds-Morris House was built by William Reynolds, a doctor, and his brother John, a gentleman bricklayer. It was later purchased by Luke Wistar Morris, a merchant, whose family owned the house for 120 years.

The house was built on a double city lot, allowing an elegant center hall plan. Although the Federal style was more popular at the time, the Reynolds-Morris House was designed in a Georgian manner, as seen by the Flemish bond brickwork, articulated with string courses between floors. The heavy lintels with keystones, the cornice modillions and louvered shutters all hark back to the Georgian era.

131, 133   A,B   OP
Congress Hall, *1787–89*
6th and Chestnut Sts.
U.S. Supreme Court, *1790–91*
5th and Chestnut Sts.

As early as 1736, plans for the State House complex included two buildings for county and city government. The buildings were not started until after the Revolutionary War, when the Federal style was more popular than the Georgian style of the State House. The difference is especially visible in the window treatments. The State House windows are held by a heavy wooden frame.

▼
1768
*Regular street clean-
ing and garbage
collection begins*

▼
1770
*Separate school for
black children opens*

▼
1774
*First Continental
Congress meets*

▼
1775
*First U.S. carpet
woven
First U.S. piano made*

132

134

The windows on the new buildings have thinner mullions, due to the use of a lighter frame known as a reveal, which was re-cessed into the wall. The first-floor windows are particularly graceful. Another difference between the two styles is the detailing of the cornice. The heavy modillions of the State House are replaced by delicate fretwork and a tapering keystone shape.

While the federal government was in Philadelphia, the buildings were used for meetings of Congress and the Supreme Court. Later, the buildings reverted to city and county use until the new City Hall was completed in 1894.

132   L   OP
Woodlands, *1742/1788–89*
Woodland Ave. and 40th St.

Woodlands is situated on the former estate of Andrew Hamilton, a lawyer and designer of the State House. The original mansion, built by his son, was expanded by Hamil-ton's grandson, William. It was one of the finest mansions of the period and an early example of the Federal style.

William added the east and west wings, which terminate in bowed walls enclosing oval rooms. The informal interior has an oval dining room and oval parlor open-ing off a circular entrance hall. William's addition to the south front was one of the first American domestic examples of a free-standing projecting portico. Other Federal-style details are the giant Ionic pilasters on the north front, the blind arches with Pal-ladian windows and the elliptical fanlight over the central door. The slender propor-tions, delicate scale and stuccoed facade distinguished Woodlands from neighboring country mansions.

William also designed the grounds, one of the earliest American examples of the English romantic garden. The property was sold to Woodlands Cemetery in 1843.

134   L
Pennsylvania Hospital, *1755/94–1805*
8th and Pine Sts.
Samuel Rhoads / David Evans, Jr.
Center Pavilion *restored 1977,*
Bartley Long Mirenda Architects; *2008,* S. Harris & Co

Pennsylvania Hospital, the first hospital in the colonies, was founded by Dr. Thomas Bond. Benjamin Franklin helped raise funds for the first building, which was built on a site far from the noises and smells of the city. It was designed by Samuel Rhoads us-ing the same materials and proportions as domestic architecture.

The center pavilion and west wing speci-fied in Rhoads's plan were not built until after 1794. The center section, designed by Evans, is one of the finest examples of the Federal style in the country. The facade shows a new sophistication in public ar-chitecture. Monochromatic brick replaces the checkerboard pattern of Flemish bond and glazed headers. The first floor is faced with marble, and giant Corinthian marble pilasters stretch from the second floor to the cornice. The center pavilion projects slightly and has a fashionable oval window in its pediment. Evans designed a circular amphitheater on the top floor, marked by an exterior balustrade. It was here that modern surgery was first performed in the United States.

135   B,K   OP
First Bank of the United States,
1795–97/1901
120 South 3rd St.
Samuel Blodgett / James Windrim

After the Revolutionary War, the new fed-eral government established a single form of currency and an institution to handle

▼
1776
*Declaration of
Independence signed*

▼
1777
*Battle of
Germantown*

▼
1780
*Pennsylvania first
state to abolish
slavery*

▼
1781
*First U.S. corporate
bank authorized*

138

its extensive war debts. The First Bank was created by Alexander Hamilton, who was responsible for the country's initial monetary policies.

As the first national bank building in the country, the founders wanted to convey the qualities of strength, dignity and security. Blodgett, a businessman and amateur architect, modeled his design on Thomas Colley's Exchange in Dublin. The bank was the most imposing structure of its day. The design incorporates typical Palladian motifs: a two-story Corinthian portico, hipped roof with balustrade, corner quoins and marble facing.

In 1901, James Windrim replaced the barrel vault over the banking hall with a skylit rotunda on Corinthian columns. The building was sold to Stephen Girard in 1812 and used as a bank until 1926; it was restored in 1957 by the National Park Service.

---

136 L OP
Loudoun, *1796–1801/1829 /1850*
4650 Germantown Ave.

Thomas Armatt first settled in Loudoun County, Virginia, before coming to Philadelphia. He was one of the many city dwellers who moved to Germantown following the yellow fever epidemics in the 1790s. He built a Federal-style house for his son, Thomas Armatt, Jr., who became a successful Philadelphia merchant and trader.

Loudoun stands on the summit of Naglee's Hill at the gateway to Germantown. From this prominent point one could see ships arriving on the Delaware. The outstanding feature of the house is the freestanding Corinthian portico on the south facade. This Greek temple front was added to the original mansion in 1850 by Armatt's son-in-law, James Skerrit.

137 H
Upsala, *1755/1797–1801*
6430 Germantown Ave.
John Johnson 3rd, builder

Dirck Jansen, one of the early settlers of Germantown, built a house on land he later sold to John Johnson Sr., who bequeathed this property to his family. The front portion of the house was added by his grandson and is one of the finest examples of Federal architecture in Germantown.

By contrast with the Georgian style of Cliveden, directly across the street, Upsala is simpler and more delicate in scale and details. The facade is made of ashlar Wissahickon schist with marble trim. The windows are smaller than Cliveden's, and the doorway is marked by a refined Doric portico and pediment. On the interior, the house has four rooms to a floor, entered from a central hall. The rooms have fine woodwork, and there is a graceful stair leading to the second floor.

In the 19th century the house was named Upsala, after the Swedish university city. It remained in the Johnson family until 1941.

---

138 L OP
Fort Mifflin, *1798–1800/1870s*
Fort Mifflin Road
Thomas Mifflin and Pierre Charles L'Enfant

Philadelphia had no military fortifications because William Penn had determined to live in peace with the Indians. In 1772, however, the British began to build a fort to protect the Delaware River. After the Revolutionary War began, the fort was completed by the colonial army, directed by Major General Thomas Mifflin. The British marched into Philadelphia to attack Washington's troops in 1777. A line of defense between Fort Mifflin and Fort Mercer, across the river, held off the British fleet long enough for Washington's troops to

▼
1784
First U.S. daily
newspaper published

▼
1786
Fitch demonstrates
steamboat on the
Delaware River

▼
1787
Constitutional
convention held

▼
1789
City incorporated

140

reach Valley Forge. In the process, the fort was nearly demolished.

Reconstruction of the fort was carried out in several phases. The major portions were planned by the French architect Pierre Charles L'Enfant, who designed the plan for Washington, D.C. He also designed the commandant's house. Other notable structures include the officers' quarters, the artillery shed and the bombproof underground shelters. Fourteen structures have been authentically restored ranging in date from 1778 to 1875.

The fort remained in active military use until 1954.

---

139   L   PR

Sansom's Row, *1799*
700 Blocks of Walnut and Sansom Sts.
Benjamin Latrobe / Thomas Carstairs

Early Philadelphia row houses were usually built one or two at a time. As more and more immigrants poured into the city, however, the need for rental housing generated the first speculative developments.

William Sansom's project was the first complete row of houses built at the same time. Latrobe designed 22 houses for Walnut Street, followed a few years later by 20 houses on Sansom Street by Carstairs. Because the site was on the outskirts of the city, Sansom paved the street at his own expense to help attract tenants. The simple plan of the row house and the repetition of identical units were the principal design determinants. The design implications of a unified block-long facade were suggested by paired doorways, contiguous beltcourses and battlements at the end of each pair. Except for 707 Walnut, the remaining houses have been substantially altered.

---

140   E   OP

Lemon Hill, *1799*
Lemon Hill Dr.

By 1774, Robert Morris, a prominent financier, had assembled 300 acres along the Schuylkill River. He established a country estate complete with a splendid mansion, farm and greenhouses filled with lemon trees. When his fortunes declined, Morris sold 140 acres to Henry Pratt, who built the present house, which he named Lemon Hill. It is a lyrical example of the Federal style.

The house is rubble covered with stucco and granite trim. It has a curved central bay on the garden facade created by an oval room projecting through the rectangular plan. There also is an oval parlor and bedroom. The Palladian window was carried over from the Georgian era, but is more restrained, flush with the wall surface and squeezed between the doorway and cornice. Lemon Hill also had elaborate gardens that attracted many visitors.

In 1844, Lemon Hill was purchased by the city to protect the municipal water supply. It became the initial part of Fairmount Park in 1855.

---

141   A   OP

Arch Street Meeting House,
1803–5/1810–11
330 Arch St.
Owen Biddle
Renovated 1968, Cope and Lippincott

William Penn and many of the original settlers of Philadelphia were members of the Society of Friends, commonly known as Quakers. The Friends worshiped in gatherings without a minister and shared their spiritual thoughts. The meetinghouses built for their services usually contained two rooms: a large entrance and gathering room and the meeting room itself.

The Arch Street Meeting House is the

▼
1790
*Franklin's funeral
attended by 20,000*

▼
1790
First U.S. census

▼
1792
*First U.S. mint begins
operation*

▼
1793
*First circus held;
First American
balloon flight*

141

largest in the city and second oldest. It was built on land given to the Friends by Penn in 1693 and initially used as a burial ground. There are two rooms in the central structure and two flanking wings used for annual meetings, when men and women met separately.

The building is a plain brick structure with flat exterior surfaces, marble steps, wood shutters and simple columned porticos over the doors. The center structure and east wing were designed by Owen Biddle, author of the influential trade book, Young Carpenter's Assistant (1805).

---

142   L   PR

York Row, *1807*
712–16 Walnut St.
Joseph Randall, carpenter

York Row was another speculative housing development started by William Sansom. The plan of the houses and the simple repetition of units are similar to his previous project across the street. Certain details, such as the splayed lintels with projecting keystones above the windows, are typical of Georgian design. But the absence of belt-courses and cornice modillions, combined with the profusion of detail around the entrances and the delicate details and scale, indicate that the overall design is based on the Federal style. The houses were altered significantly in 2003 for the construction of the St. James Apartments.

---

143   L

Spark's Shot Tower, *1808*
29–31 Carpenter St.
Thomas Sparks and John Bishop

Spark's Tower was the first shot tower in the United States and is one of the last remaining examples. It was built by one of the city's first "plumbers," makers of leaden vessels, to manufacture shot for sport. Shot

was made by pouring molten lead through perforated pans at the top of the 142-foot tower. As the lead descended it spun into droplets, which hardened when they hit cold water at the bottom. The tower became a munitions factory during the War of 1812, and continued to produce shot up to 1907. Since 1913, the structure has been part of a recreation center.

---

144   L   PR

Franklin Row, *1809–10*
236 South 8th St.
Robert Mills

Robert Mills was an active builder and the first native-born American architect. His designs were influenced by the neoclassical ideas of Thomas Jefferson and Benjamin Latrobe, but Mills interpreted these ideas in an innovative manner.

Mills constructed a speculative row of houses in the tradition of Sansom and York rows, but only one structure remains. The tripartite window and recessed arch on the facade convey a monumentality that must have been impressive when repeated across a row of houses. The three remaining buildings of the Carolina Row, 929, 931 and 933 Spruce Street, also attributed to Mills, have a similar treatment.

---

145   A   PR

Girard Warehouses, *1810*
18–30 North Front St.
Renovated 2009, Bower Lewis Thrower

Early warehouses in Philadelphia were simple, four-story brick structures, built on long, narrow lots, with one large room to a floor. The west side of Front Street contains some of the oldest and most beautiful warehouses in the city. Numbers 18–30 were owned by Stephen Girard, who at his death was the wealthiest man in the United States. They are typical of early 19th-century

▼
1801
*Public waterworks
opens; Chamber of
Commerce established*

▼
1804
*Market Street bridge
spans Schuylkill River*

▼
1805
*Pennsylvania Acad-
emy of Fine Arts
founded*

▼
1811
*First medical textbook
in U.S. published*

146

warehouses. The ground floor had a store in front and a counting room in back. The facade is brick on the upper floors, but the first floor is granite, a popular material for storefronts at that time. The Trotter warehouses at numbers 36–44 are equally handsome and were occupied by the same company from the 1830s to 1985.

---

146   E   OP

Fairmount Waterworks, *1812–15*
Fairmount, at Schuylkill River near 25th St.
Frederick Graff
Restored 2001–03, Mark B. Thompson Associates

The first city waterworks, designed by Benjamin Latrobe, were located on Center Square. When a new system was required, Graff, a draftsman on the original project, became the architect and chief engineer. The new facility was one of the most notable engineering accomplishments of its day. The original steam pumping station carried nearly four million gallons of water every day from the Schuylkill River to reservoirs at the top of "Faire Mount" (now the Art Museum), where it was gravity-fed to homes and hydrants.

The complex, added to throughout the 19th century, was modeled after Roman temples and arranged around paved courts and walkways. Galleries inside the pump rooms allowed visitors to view the machinery. The grounds were extensively landscaped, creating a very picturesque setting that became one of the first parts of Fairmount Park. The waterworks, abandoned in 1911, were used for an aquarium until 1962 and then as an indoor swimming pool until 1973.

A lengthy restoration of the entire site began in the 1980s supported by the Junior League. In 2003, an interpretive center on the history of the site and the Schuylkill River watershed opened in the lower level of the Engine House. It contains a working model of the original water works. In 2006, the first floor became a restaurant and the south garden and cliff walk were restored.

THE GREEK REVIVAL STYLE

By the early 19th century, Roman architectural models had been replaced by classical Greek orders, available in England and the colonies through such handbooks as Stewart and Revett's Antiquities of Athens. The use of Greek orders flourished in the United States during the 1830s and 1840s because of the new nation's identification with the democratic ideals of ancient Greece.

The first Greek Revival building in the country was designed by Benjamin Latrobe in Philadelphia in 1798. But it was not a popular style until after 1820. The first book to include Greek orders was John Haviland's The Builders Assistant, published in Philadelphia in 1818.

Greek Revival buildings are easily recognizable through their use of the temple form, complete with pediments; heavy cornices; Doric, Ionic or Corinthian columns; and their use of white marble as the primary building material.

---

147   A,B,K   OP

Second Bank of the United States,
1818–24
420 Chestnut St.
William Strickland

The Second Bank was founded in 1816. Nicholas Biddle, its most influential president, was a tireless champion of Greek architecture. When the bank held a competition for the design of its new building, Biddle required all architects to use the Greek style.

Strickland's design is one of the first Greek Revival public buildings in the country. Modeled on the Parthenon, it features plain Doric columns and little decoration

▼
1812
Philadelphia Academy
of Natural Sciences
established

▼
1817
First public building,
the State House, lit
by gas

▼
1818
Public school system
organized

▼
1820
Maine admitted to
union as free state;
Missouri as slave.

147

148

except for the triglyphs and metopes on the entablature. The structure appears to be of solid marble, but really is brick faced with marble. In contrast to the Greek exterior, the interior is Roman. A barrel-vaulted ceiling covers the banking hall.

President Jackson's veto of the bank's charter in 1832 led to its demise. Strickland altered the building in 1844 for use as the U.S. Customs House, which it remained until 1935. Now part of Independence National Historical Park, the Second Bank houses a portrait gallery with 185 paintings of colonial and federal leaders by such artsts as Charles Wilson Peale and Gilbert Stuart.

148   L
St. Stephen's Protestant Episcopal Church, *1822–23/1878–79/1888*
19 South 10th Street
William Strickland / Frank Furness / George C. Mason

Many new churches were constructed in the early 19th century to serve the changing population of the city. St. Stephen's, built on the site where Franklin flew his famous kite, was the first designed in the Gothic Revival style.

Strickland's Gothic designs, of which this is the only survivor, were neoclassical buildings with applied Gothic details. St. Stephen's is Gothic by virtue of the crenelations over the screen on the facade, the lancet windows in the twin towers and the pointed, arched windows on the screen. Originally, the octagonal towers were crenelated as well.

The church contains outstanding examples of religious works of art. These include two marble effigies and a baptismal font by Steinhauser and a richly carved marble reredos. Over the altar is a mosaic of the Last Supper, inlaid with 180,000 pieces of Venetian glass. Three Tiffany windows adorn the south wall.

The north transept and vestry room were added in 1878–79 by Frank Furness. In 1888, George C. Mason designed the parish house, west of the vestry room.

149   K   OP
Eastern State Penitentiary, *1823–36*
See pages 40–41.

150   C,K
Pennsylvania Institution for the Deaf and Dumb, *1824–26*
320 South Broad St.
John Haviland
University of the Arts, Hamilton Hall
Renovated 1983, F. Daniel Cathers and Associates

In 1820, Broad Street was a rural pastureland on the edge of town. Social and cultural institutions moved here to escape the noise of the city. One of the first, the Pennsylvania Institution for the Deaf and Dumb, was designed by John Haviland, then at the peak of his career as the most prolific Greek Revival architect in the city. Haviland adapted the Greek Revival style to the individual project, rather than imposing archaeological correctness like his contemporary, Strickland. The Doric portico and pediment on the granite facade are Greek Revival, as is the simple massing of forms, typical of Haviland's style. The exposed basement, however, resulting from the raised entrance, is a Roman feature, while the shallow inset arches on the wings, added in 1838 by Strickland, derive from the Federal style. The building was renovated in 1983 by the Philadelphia College of Art, now the University of the Arts, which has occupied it since 1893.

149 K OP

Eastern State Penitentiary, *1823–36*
Fairmount Ave. at 21st St.
John Haviland

"The exterior of a solitary prison should exhibit . . . great strength and convey to the mind a cheerless blank indicative of the misery that awaits the unhappy being who enters within its walls." These were the directions to architects in the competition for the design of the Eastern State Penitentiary. Haviland's winning entry was a fortress with an austere granite facade and a forbidding iron portcullis.

The interior was based on Sir Samuel Bentham's 1787 radial plan, used for jails and insane asylums in England. The plan consists of seven long cell blocks radiating from a central surveillance rotunda. The cell blocks contained dark passageways lined with individual cells.

The prison features such early Gothic details as lancet windows, square towers flanking the entrance and battlemented turrets at the corners. But the simple, massive forms are typical of Haviland's Greek Revival style. The design was enormously influential; it was copied in more than 500 prisons around the world. Eastern State was opened to the public as an historic site in 1944. It is deliberately maintained as a "preserved ruin." Among its most famous inmates were Willie Sutton and Al Capone, whose cell is pictured above.

▼
1825
*Five Center City
squares given current
names*

▼
1825
*Thomas Jefferson Uni-
versity opens*

▼
1827
*Hicksite-Othrodox
Separation 1827
Society of Friends
(Quakers)*

152

---

151 A OP

Franklin Institute, *1825*
15 South 7th St.
John Haviland
Atwater Kent Museum

The Franklin Institute was founded by
Samuel Merrick, a businessman and manufacturer who wanted to promote research,
education and communication among
scientists and inventors. The institute was
involved in many important 19th-century
scientific activities, including the first
weather bureau, plans for the first coal gasi-
fication plant, standardization of machine
parts and the promotion of the incandescent light bulb. It gave the first architectural
courses in America, with such teachers as
Thomas Walter and William Strickland.
Haviland based the design of the building
on the Greek Monument of Thrasyllus.
Because of the restricted site, however,
he compressed the elements into simple
masses, austere surfaces and bold proportions.

The Franklin Institute vacated the building in 1933, and it was almost demolished.
In 1938, A. Atwater Kent, an inventor, radio
magnate and manufacturer, established a
museum of the history of the city, which
continues to occupy the building.

152 L PR

United States Naval Asylum,
1827–33/1844
Gray's Ferry Ave. and Bainbridge St.
William Strickland
Naval Square
Renovated 2003–06, Campbell Thomas &
Co, J.K. Roller Architects, John Milner As-
sociates

The Asylum was built for the benefit of
"disabled and decrepit" naval officers, seamen and marines. It was one of the largest
Greek Revival hospitals in the country.
The main building, Biddle Hall, contained
public rooms, a domed auditorium, dining
rooms and officers' quarters. Men's dormitories were located in the wings.

Strickland imposed an Ionic portico,
based on Stuart and Revett's illustrations
of an Athenian temple, onto a utilitarian
building. The cast-iron columns on the
balconies were an early use of this new
economical and fire-resistant material.
Their delicate scale, continuing the graceful
rhythms of the portico columns, helps to
lighten the massive structure.

In 1844, Strickland added the governor's
and surgeon's residences. Each is brick
faced with stucco and features a verandah
with cast-iron supports. The ornamental
ironwork contains naval motifs of dolphins,
anchors and ropes.

The asylum was the first home of the
U.S. Naval Academy, and later a home for
retired naval personnel, until it was closed
in 1976. It was closed in 1976 and remained
vacant for 30 years.

▼
1830
First history of Phila-
delphia published by
John Fanning Watson

▼
1831
Stephen Girard dies,
leaves estate to found
Girard College

▼
1833
Reading Railroad
begins operations

154

155

153   L
Walnut Street Theatre, *1808–9/1827–28*
829–33 Walnut St.
John Haviland

The first theater company in the United
States opened in Philadelphia in 1749.
Quaker opposition hindered the early development of a permanent theater, but by
1820, Philadelphia was the theatrical center
of the country.

When the Walnut Theatre was built,
it was at the western edge of the city. The
theater was renovated in 1816 and again
in 1828, when John Haviland added a
Greek Revival facade for Joseph Randall,
the developer of York Row. Haviland's facade was decorated with painted cast-iron
details. The facade was obscured by later
renovations by J. C. Hoxie and Willis Hale,
which were removed when the building
was restored in 1970–72. The theater had
a national reputation and attracted great
performers of the period, including Forrest, Booth, Bernhardt and Barrymore. It is
the oldest continuously used theater in the
country.

154   B   PR
Girard Row, *1831–33*
326–34 Spruce St.
William Struthers

Row houses were a favorite investment for
Stephen Girard, millionaire banker and
merchant, who considered them a way of
beautifying his adopted city. He died before this row was completed, but they were
finished by his estate.

In contrast to the uniform red brick of
earlier row houses, the ground floors of
the Girard houses are surfaced in marble, a
fashionable Greek Revival building material. The first residents of these townhouses
were goldsmiths, shoemakers, house carpenters, bricklayers and merchants.

155   L   PR
Portico Row, *1831–32*
900–930 Spruce St.
Thomas U. Walter

Portico Row is an outstanding block of
early 19th-century row houses. It was
built by real estate speculator John Savage,
who hired the young architect Thomas U.
Walter to design sixteen houses for sale to
upper-middle-class lawyers, doctors and
merchants. The houses were elaborately
designed on both the exterior and interior.
The brick facades, with marble lintels, are
distinguished by a series of projecting porticos supported by marble Ionic columns.
Each portico provides entrance to two
houses. The interior rooms were spacious
and richly finished. Highly polished marble
was used for all fireplaces, walnut or mahogany for doors and trim. Even the water
closets were built of walnut, and the bath-
room floors were marble.

Sarah Hale, editor of the fashionable
Godey's Lady's Book and one of the best-
known arbiters of 19th-century taste, lived
on Portico Row for several years.

156   B,K
Merchants' Exchange, *1832–33*
143 South 3rd St.
William Strickland

When Philadelphia businesses became
too numerous to meet in coffee houses
and taverns, merchants formed the Philadelphia Exchange Company. Strickland
designed their building, now the oldest
stock exchange in the country, which was
considered to be one of the most beautiful
structures of its kind.

The building consists of a rectangular
main structure with a semicircular portico;
Strickland used the Corinthian order on
the colonnade, reflecting the evolution of
a more elaborate Greek Revival style. He

▼
1833
*American Anti-Slavery
Society Founded*

▼
1834
*Free School law cre-
ates tax supported
public schools*

156

crowned the building with a lantern meticulously copied from the Choragic Monument of Lysicrates, one of the most copied
monuments of the period.

The Exchange Room, in the curved portion of the building, was sumptuous. It had
a mosaic floor, a domed ceiling supported
on marble columns and frescoes on the
walls. Real estate dealings, auctions and
business transactions of all kinds took place
in this room, where shipping news and
newspapers from all over the world were
posted.

The Exchange dissolved during the Civil
War. When wholesale food markets took
over the area, sheds were erected around the
east end of the building. These remained
until 1952, when the Exchange was purchased by the National Park Service.

---

157 L

Frankford Arsenal, *1833–1950*
Bridge and Tacony Streets
Arsenal Business Center

Although the Frankford Arsenal was
founded in 1816, the first significant building construction occurred in the mid-19th
century. The arsenal was established by
the U.S. Army on a 20-acre site along the
Delaware River and Frankford Creek. Philadelphia was selected as the site because it
had an active gunpowder industry, a sizable
community of skilled German gunsmiths
and good access by water to iron and
timber. Until 1850 the arsenal was an ammunition depot and repair shop. The early
buildings consisted of officers' quarters,
storehouses, kitchens and the commandant's house. These are clustered around a
quadrangle, known as the Parade Ground.
Most of the buildings completed by the
1830s are designed in the Federal style, with
fanlights, elliptical windows, stringcourses
and restrained decoration. The cast-iron ve-

randa of the commandant's house, added in
the 1850s, was a common feature of other
buildings of that time.

In the decade prior to the Civil War,
the arsenal began its transformation from
a depot to a munitions fabricator. New
buildings were designed in a utilitarian version of the Greek Revival style, with arched
bays on the facades, classical pediments
and decorative details. The most significant
building of this period, and perhaps the
most significant building at the arsenal, is
the Rolling Mill, designed by John Fraser
in 1865. The mill is constructed of iron
trusses supported by wrought-iron columns strengthened with iron plates. These
are known as Phoenix columns and Fink
trusses. On the exterior the mill introduced
an Italianate style, which predominated at
the arsenal for the next 80 years.

Other buildings added before the two
world wars followed the industrial Italianate style of the Rolling Mill. One exception
is the Ammunition Proof House, from
1917–18, which has Gothic battlements,
oriels and hood moldings. Buildings constructed after 1940 adopted simple functional forms consistent with the modern
movement in architecture. When the arsenal finally closed in 1977, it contained 246
buildings on its 110-acre site.

The northern portion of the site now
provides public boat ramp access to the
Delaware River. The southern portion has
been converted to a light-industrial and
office park.

158 K

Founder's Hall, Girard College, *1833–47*
Girard and Corinthian Aves.
Thomas U. Walter
Roof restoration 2007–08, Vitetta

In his will, Stephen Girard, the first American multimillionaire, bequeathed $2 million for a school for "poor white male orphans."

The architectural competition held to select designs for the College was won by Walter, who had been practicing architecture for only three years. His design soon changed, however, under pressure from Nicholas Biddle, president of the board of trustees. Biddle believed that the two great truths in the world were the Bible and Greek architecture. He seized this opportunity to build the most correct Greek temple in America.

In response to this direction, Walter wrapped marble Corinthian columns around the entire building and raised the temple on a flight of steps that circled the peristyle. The roof and walls are covered with local Chester County marble. Inside, the four rooms to a floor, required by the will, are vaulted. Under the roof, pendentive domes with skylights make use of the space behind the entablature.

Founder's Hall, one of the most expensive buildings of its time, took fourteen years to build. It was the climax of the Greek Revival style in America. The building worked poorly and was abandoned as a schoolhouse in 1916. It remains a tribute to Stephen Girard, whose tomb is on the first floor.

Girard College was integrated in 1968, following years of significant civil rights litigation.

2

The Industrial Metropolis

1835–1902

The Industrial Metropolis
1835–1902

William Penn's concept of a central city surrounded by rural countryside remained substantially intact through the end of the 18th century. But in the 19th century, the Industrial Revolution brought about a dramatic transformation. It changed the way people worked and where they lived; it created big cities with socially diverse populations spread over large geographic areas.

Philadelphia was in the forefront of the Industrial Revolution in the United States. Many of the forces that transformed the city were initiated before 1840. The invention of the steam engine in 1803 allowed factories to locate anywhere and become larger than water-powered mills. Railroads brought coal and iron to the city but also enabled wealthy and middle-class residents to move out. By 1840, the majority of the 250,000 residents lived outside the city; by 1860, the population of 565,000 was distributed in 40 independent villages and townships scattered throughout the once rural countryside.

While the most extensive changes occurred in Philadelphia county, the city, laid out by Penn between Vine Street, South Street and the two rivers, was altered substantially. The port, second in size only to New York, continued to be an important center of economic activity, exporting iron, coal, steel, sugar, textiles and other manufactured products. But manufacturing businesses increased steadily, although most people still were employed in small establishments. Printing and publishing, textiles, and the manufacture of paint, chemicals and drugs were important businesses. In the 18th century, most people were individual entrepreneurs of similar economic status. Industrialization separated places of business and work, and created clear class distinctions among business owners, managers and employees.

By 1850, the fashionable neighborhood in the city was between Seventh and Broad streets, south of Walnut Street. The older areas east of Seventh Street deteriorated as a result of overcrowding by the poor and recent immigrants. New brick row houses, larger and more spacious than their predecessors, were heated by coal furnaces and had indoor plumbing. Most were built speculatively, but not in a continuous pattern. Open space existed east of Broad Street, and in 1850, the area west from Broad Street to the wharfs along the Schuylkill River was largely undeveloped.

Although housing expanded, the residential population of the city started to decline. Commercial development predominated and followed the westward growth of housing. Chestnut Street was the main street for fashionable shops and elegant hotels, while Market Street became a new manufacturing and commercial district. The market sheds at Second Street were removed in 1859 and a farmers' market created at 12th Street. Museums, an opera house, and theaters provided cul-

Furniture influenced by the Gothic Revival had strong vertical lines and ornate detail. This cathedral chair from 1845–55 was made in New York and owned by a family on Spruce Street. It is black walnut with ash trim.

By the mid-19th century, French design influenced dress as well as architecture. This silk taffeta wedding dress of 1854 followed Paris fashions with a three-tiered skirt supported by a stiff crineline hoop undergarment and bell-shaped sleeves trimmed with matching bands.

tural activities. In 1855, Fairmount Park was founded on the edge of the city to provide a place of recreation and to protect the city's water supply.

The steady increase in construction encouraged the introduction of new architectural ideas, usually derived from English sources. London townhouses and clubs, modeled after urban palaces of the Italian Renaissance, became the predecent for similar buildings in the city. New churches were constructed in most new neighborhoods. Their design reflected the return to the Gothic style in England, resulting from a resurgence of interest in medieval liturgy and construction.

Commercial buildings also presented an opportunity for new architectural ideas. Loft buildings were designed in the Italian Renaissance style, but after 1850, businessmen who wanted to express their success adopted the more ornate Italianate style then popular for suburban houses. Commercial Italianate design flourished with the introduction of cast iron, which permitted the mass production of ornamentation at low cost. As a structural system, cast iron made it possible to use big windows to light large floor areas of commercial structures.

While these transformations were occurring in the city, even more dramatic changes were taking place in the county. Steam-powered plants, belching smoke, were widely dispersed throughout the county. Because transportation was predominantly by foot or horse, people of all economic classes lived close to their jobs. New residential areas surrounded centers of employment. Each area was an independent village or township with its own ethnic character, which made it easy to assimilate the different immigrants coming to the city.

While these settlements were a major factor contributing to the growth in the county, railroad lines and horse-drawn trolleys in the 1850s enabled middle-class residents to commute easily from Germantown,

Growth of the City

1850   1875   1900

J. E. Caldwell and Co. made this silver pitcher in 1857 as a presentation piece. The pitcher is decorated with a water-lily motif and is similar to designs exhibited in England and Europe in the 1850s.

This chair was owned by James Dobson, co-owner of Dobson Mills. It is made of ebonized cherry and was originally upholstered in damask woven at the mills. The delicate scale, rococo shape and carved rose and leaf motifs are indicative of the fine craftsmanship of its manufacturer, Gottlieb Vollmer.

Chestnut Hill and West Philadelphia, east of 42nd Street. These areas, characterized by tree-lined streets, freestanding and twin houses with small yards, were a sharp contrast to the dense brick row houses of the city. The exodus to the countryside was part of the Romantic movement then prevalent in England and the United States. English architects responded by reviving the Gothic style, which seemed more appropriate for country houses because of its asymmetry and ornamentation. The Gothic villa started the picturesque movement; its popularity encouraged English architects to explore other sources of picturesque design, particularly the vernacular architecture of the Italian countryside. The Italianate style offered the same opportunities for informality and asymmetry. It was popular with wealthy families because of its elaborate detailing and ornamentation.

The development of the city during this period did not proceed without some difficulty. The abundance of cheap labor, at a time when industries were becoming increasingly mechanized, created competition for jobs between native-born residents and the new immigrants, particularly the large influx of unskilled Irish Catholics. Riots were common in the 1840s. Some were expressive of anti-Catholic sentiments; others directed against blacks and others caused by volunteer fire companies. The riots were difficult to control because of the absence of common police services outside the city. This difficulty, as well as the inability to provide uniform fire protection and water supply, led to the political consolidation of the city and county in 1854.

At the time of the Civil War, Philadelphia was a prosperous city. The war had a limited social impact on the city, since slavery had been eliminated by 1820. But it did have a substantial economic impact. As a major manufacturing center, the site of the U.S. Navy Yard and Frankford Arsenal and the first large city north of the Mason-Dixon line, Philadelphia was a major supplier of military goods. The war strengthened the city's economy and consolidated its position as a leader in industrial manufacturing. After the war, Philadelphia considered itself the "workshop of the world." It led the nation in the production of steam engines, locomotives, street cars, textiles, and steel ships. It was also a major producer of rugs, hats, sugar, cigars and the site of many breweries. Because of its industrial prominence, Philadelphia was selected to host the 1876 Centennial Exposition, which celebrated the new technology.

In 1870, the population of the city was 675,000; by 1876, it was 820,000. In the following decades immigrants poured into the city; by the end of the century more than 1,300,000 people lived in Philadelphia. The first wave of immigrants came primarily from Germany and Ireland, but there were also many blacks from the South. Toward the end of the century, the influx of Irish was matched by a sixfold increase in the Italian population. Other immigrants, many from Russia and Eastern Europe, contributed to the diversity of the city's population.

Building in the city boomed. More than 100,000 houses were constructed in the 1870s and 1880s. Most were built by speculative developers. The availability of cheap land, the dispersion of manufacturing plants, the extension of the street grid in 1858 and the introduction of street railway lines in the same year contributed to this rapid expansion. Newly created building and loan associations provided financial assistance, so that even working-class families could own their own homes. Houses in South Philadelphia, built for the poor and new immigrants, were small and crowded together. North Philadelphia was the focus of middle-class expansion. Mansions of wealthy individuals along North Broad Street encouraged the creation of large and distinctive row houses west of Broad Street. These thousands of row houses, in contrast to the tenements of New York, gave Philadelphia the reputation as a city of homes.

By 1890, 25 of the city's 125 square miles were urbanized, extending north to Erie Avenue, west to 49th Street, and south to Snyder Avenue. Chestnut Hill and Germantown also grew but remained separated from the rest of the city by undeveloped land. The

Frank Furness designed this desk and chair in 1875 for his brother's house. Both pieces have an architectural character and contain elements also found in Furness's buildings. The desk has a Moorish arch and ornamental details worked into the walnut similar to those found in the brickwork or terra-cotta panels of his buildings. The chair has a simple, rectangular form typical of English furniture of the 1870s.

Daniel Pabst made this night table for his daughter in 1875. It is decorated with floral motifs cut through the maple veneer to expose the walnut underneath. Pabst executed some of Furness's furniture and also drew upon English designs of the 1870s for the details and ornamentation of his own work.

physical pattern of separate villages disappeared, but neighborhoods were still segregated by ethnicity and race. The introduction of the electric street railways, in 1892, increased mobility and began to modify these patterns.

Within the central area of the city, fashionable residential areas moved further westward, focusing around Rittenhouse Square. Houses were even more spacious than earlier in the century, reflecting the common practice of live-in servants. Older residential areas east of Broad Street deteriorated as the downtown became an increasingly commercial district. The second half of the 19th century saw a substantial increase in the production of consumer goods. The mass production of clothing and other household goods created totally new types of stores, such as Lit Brothers and John Wanamaker's department store.

The westward growth of downtown influenced the decision to build a new City Hall on Center Square, set aside by Penn for civic buildings. The grandiose City Hall epitomized the self-confidence of the period. Its construction immediately shifted the financial and governmental center away from Independence Square. In response, the railroads created new terminals east and west of City Hall. These were followed by a new scale of commercial and office building, made possible by the invention of the elevator and the use of fireproof steel construction.

After the Civil War, American architects no longer felt confined to a single historical style. Many different styles were used and often mixed with one another. This eclectic attitude was the basis of Victorian design. The principal historical influence was Gothic, but the Gothic of Venice rather than England. John Ruskin, the English art critic, drew attention to the use of color in Venetian buildings. The High Victorian Gothic style followed Ruskin's suggestions, creating color and texture through the use of different materials or variations in the use of brick. The application of this style to speculative row houses, particularly in North and West Philadelphia, produced some of the most inventive and distinctive houses ever built in the city. Many outstanding commercial and civic buildings were designed in this style, which reached its apex in Philadelphia in the work of Frank Furness.

Architects who were tired of the heavy, somber Victorian style adopted the lighter and more informal Queen Anne style, which was based on houses built in England in the transitional period between medieval and Georgian design. Many houses were also built in the Second Empire style, derived from civic buildings. Row houses with mansard roofs, arched doorways and decorative arched lintels over windows were fashionable in many sections of the city.

This beautiful cream and dark-green silk dress of 1885 is typical of the late 19th century. It is draped in front and has a prominent bustle in the back to create the "receding silhouette" considered fashionable at the time.

This Renaissance Revival clock from 1865–75 was sold by J. E. Caldwell and Co. It is made of marble with gilded bronze and contains architectural motifs found on Second Empire–style buildings.

Civic and commercial architecture, in the last decades of the century, sought a monumental expression consistent with the economic prosperity of the period. To achieve this effect, the great railroad stations, collegiate buildings and churches drew on a variety of styles ranging from the High Victorian Gothic to the Renaissance Revival, Gothic Revival and Romanesque Revival. The most impressive building of the period, City Hall, was designed in the Second Empire style derived from the monumental buildings created in Paris by Napoleon III. This return to classical forms reflected the dominance of the École des Beaux-Arts in Paris in architectural education. Virtually every important American architect of the late 19th century attended the École or worked for someone who did. The popular impact of neoclassical designs at the 1893 Columbian Exposition in Chicago gave impetus to a classical revival just at the time that modern architecture had its first beginnings in Chicago.

The end of the 19th century was one of Philadelphia's best periods. The city was a prosperous manufacturing center. Large portions of the city had been developed, but there was still ample land for future growth. The city was no longer the financial capital of the nation, nor the leading cultural center. But its place as an industrial center, and one of the major urban areas in the country, seemed secure. Philadelphians entered the 20th century content and optimistic.

Glossary of Architectural Terms

1 bargeboard
a decorative, often ornately carved board attached to the edge of a gable roof

2 battlement
a low wall, at the edge of a roof, which is broken by vertical slots

3 bracket
a small support of stone or wood under the eave of a roof or other overhang; more decorative than functional and usually quite elaborate on Italianate houses

4 brownstone
dark brown or reddish sandstone used on the facades of late 19th-century houses

5 cast iron
iron that has been smelted and shaped in a mold; used for interior columns and the facades of commercial buildings from 1860 to 1900

6 corbel
a projecting stone block or bricks supporting an arch, beam, roof or other feature on the exterior of a building

7 crocket
a carved projection in the shape of leaves; used on Gothic buildings to decorate the edges of spires or gables

8 lancet window
a narrow window with pointed arch

9 lantern
a small structure on a roof, with windows on all sides providing light to the interior of a building; commonly found on Italianate houses

10 mansard roof
an attic roof with two planes, the lower one being steeper; named after its French inventor, François Mansart; a distinguishing characteristic of the Second Empire style

11 oriel
a projecting bay window on an upper floor

12 pilaster
a flat representation of a column, attached to a wall

13 terra-cotta
fine-grained, red-brown fired clay used for roof tiles and facac ornamentation; somet glazed to look like cera tile for decorative facac

▼
1835
Liberty Bell cracks;
First rowing regatta
on Schuylkill

▼
1836
Philadelphia Gas
Works established

▼
1837
Edgar Allan Poe
moves to city

202

---

201 B

Philadelphia Contributionship for the Insuring of Houses from Loss by Fire,
1835–36
212 South 4th St.
Thomas U. Walter

The Contributionship, the oldest mutual fire insurance company in the country, was organized by Benjamin Franklin in 1752. The company originally met in coffee houses or taverns and later in the home of the treasurer. The directors wanted their permanent office to look like an elegant house and to provide a residence for the treasurer. Walter drew upon his Greek Revival design for Portico Row. The building is a simple brick structure with an elegant portico supported by fluted marble Corinthian columns. Offices were on the ground floor, the kitchen in the basement and the living quarters on the top two floors.

In 1866 the portico had to be replaced. Collins and Autenreith followed Walter's design, but expanded the living quarters with the addition of a stylish mansard roof. A marble cornice also was added between the third and fourth floors. The Contributionship's seal of four hands clasped in the fireman's carry is located on both ends of the building.

---

202 E,K OP

Laurel Hill Cemetery, *1836*
3822 Ridge Ave.
John Notman

John Jay Smith, head of the Library Company, wanted to establish a nonsectarian cemetery outside the city. He acquired 50 acres overlooking the Schuylkill River and created a corporation to attract affluent customers.

Laurel Hill is designed in the picturesque English garden tradition. Notman based his plan, selected through a design competition, on the Kensal Green Cemetery, in London. Roads and paths radiate from a central

circular drive. Gazebos and lookout points provide lovely views throughout the site, which was planted with exotic trees and shrubs. The gatehouse, also by Notman, is modeled on the classical Palladian plan of a central building flanked by colonnades. It still retains the original wood paneling painted to imitate stone.

The cemetery was the burial ground for wealthy families, who built large mausoleums in various architectural styles. Many were designed by such prominent architects as Notman, Strickland and Walter. Originally, Laurel Hill was an important recreation area and tourist attraction, with up to 30,000 visitors a year.

---

203 B OP

Old St. Joseph's Roman Catholic Church,
1838–9
Willings Alley, near 4th and Locust streets
John Darragh, master builder *1886*, John Deery; *1905*, Walter Ballinger & Emile Perrot; *1986*, H. Mather Lippincott and Gail Winkler; *2001*, DPK&A

Old St. Joseph's was the first Roman Catholic congregation in the city. English Jesuit missionaries erected a small chapel on the site in 1733 and a larger church in 1757, which was replaced again in 1839. From 1733 until the Revolution, this was the only place in the British Empire where the Catholic mass could legally be offered in public. In the 18th century, Old St. Joseph's cared for victims of the yellow fever epidemics. In the 19th century, it became an exemplary urban immigrant parish, responding to the needs of thousands of immigrants and African Americans.

The gated courtyard off Willings Alley has been a defining characteristic of the site since the 18th century. Surrounding the courtyard are the 1839 church and the original St. Joseph's College building of 1851, created by expanding the 1789 clergy house to Willings Alley.

▼
1838
Central High School founded;
First U.S. Naval Academy opens

▼
1839
Saxon takes first U.S. photograph

▼
1840
First lager beer manufactured in U.S.

▼
1842
Philadelphia and Reading Railroad begins operation

203

205

The church retains the original 1839 Corrie tracker organ and the altar ensemble of Ionic columns surmounted by a carved entablature. The stained glass windows by Alfred Godwin & Co. and ceiling painting by Filippo Costaggini date to an 1886 renovation, which cut back the balconies and altered much of the interior. Recent renovations have restored the interior to its 1886-1904 colors and character.

---

204   B

Philadelphia Saving Fund Society,
1839–40
306 Walnut St.
Thomas U. Walter

PSFS, founded in 1816, was the first savings bank in the United States. For its first headquarters the bank wanted a building that would recall the treasury buildings of antiquity. Walter's design is a modest Greek Revival structure, made of brick faced with hand-rubbed Chester County marble. The two-story Ionic portico gives the small building a monumental quality. Within the building special fireproof precautions were taken: the cellar was vaulted in stone and brick and windows were covered with iron shutters.

The pediment was added to the facade in 1881, when PSFS sold the building.

---

205   B   OP

The Athenaeum, *1845*
219 South 6th St.
John Notman

A group of young men formed a social and literary club in 1814 named the Athenaeum, after Athena, the Greek goddess of wisdom and learning. When they could afford to build a library, they chose John Notman. Notman's design reflected the work of the English architect Charles Barry, who had been influenced by the urban palaces of

Italian princes. It was the first Renaissance Revival building in America.

The building is simple and symmetrical, with corner quoins and a large overhanging cornice. The floor-to-ceiling windows on the second story are treated decoratively, with entablatures supported by scroll brackets. The building was to be covered in marble, but brownstone, a new building material, was used to save money. Notman's design and the use of brownstone influenced a number of later residences and clubs, including the Union League.

THE EARLY GOTHIC REVIVAL STYLE

The Gothic Revival began in England and paralleled the development of the Greek Revival style. It was advocated by those who found the Greek orders too rigid and uniform. The Gothic style was considered more appropriate for country houses: its asymmetry and ornate details were in keeping with the forms of nature. The Gothic style also was a significant influence on church design. The English Cambridge Camden Society, founded in 1836, advocated proper Gothic design and construction as the only appropriate ecclesiastical form.

Although the first American residence incorporating Gothic details was designed by Benjamin Latrobe as early as 1799, the style did not become popular until the 1840s, when the romantic movement was at its height in England and the United States.

The Gothic Revival style is distinguished by the pointed arch and the vertical emphasis on most elements. Towers, steep gable roofs, asymmetrical plans, window tracery and ornamentation in the form of foliage are common features of residential and religious buildings.

▼
1842
*First minstrel show
in U.S. at Walnut
Street Theatre*

▼
1843
*First steamship with
screw propeller
launched*

▼
1844
*Moore College begun:
oldest women's art
school in U.S.*

206

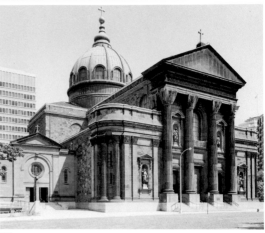

207

---

206   L
Church of St. James the Less, *1846–49*
Clearfield St. and Hunting Park Ave.
Robert Ralston, from the drawings of
G. G. Place

Robert Ralston, a prominent Philadelphia
merchant and owner of a summer estate in
Falls of Schuylkill, decided to establish an
Episcopal church for the growing community of mill families and summer residents.
He obtained measured drawings of a 13th-
century English parish church from the
Cambridge Camden Society. These plans
were carried out faithfully by John E. Carver,
superintendent of construction, whose only
revision was the addition of one bay to the
nave.

The church has a steeply sloping roof,
a small attached chancel, a crowning bell-
gable on the west wall, buttresses and
rubble-textured granite walls. Many of the
interior details were made in England.

St. James the Less became the source
for subsequent Gothic Revival churches
in America. It remains unsurpassed for the
authenticity and completeness with which
it interpreted the English model.

---

207   D,K   OP
Cathedral Basilica of SS. Peter and Paul,
1846–64
18th and Race Sts.
Napoleon LeBrun / John Notman
Renovated 1914–15, Henry Dagit; *1956–67,*
Eggers and Higgins

Although Catholics had always been present
in the city, their numbers were not significant until after the Irish immigration in
the 1830s. By 1844, the Irish population
was large enough to support the building
of a cathedral. The cathedral is the oldest
building on Logan Circle, one of the original
five squares in Penn's plan. It was one of the
most sumptuous churches in the country

when completed, and remains the center
of Catholic life in Philadelphia.

The original plans of the grand Italian
Renaissance-style structure were drawn by
Reverends Mariano Maller and John B. Tor-
natore and reworked by LeBrun. Notman
and Reverend John T. Mahoney added the
copper-covered dome and the elegant Palladian facade. The facade is brownstone, which
Notman had introduced at the Athenaeum.

The sumptuous interior has been modified
a number of times. The nave, covered by a
huge coffered barrel vault, was extended in
1957 to provide a semicircular apse behind a
new altar, which is covered by a domed bal-
dachino (canopy). Giant Corinthian pilasters
encircle the nave and transept. Decorative
features include murals by Constantino Bru-
midi, stained glass windows and mosaics.

---

208   L
St. Augustine's Church, *1847–48*
4th and New Sts.
Napoleon LeBrun
Restored 1995–96, Brawer & Hauptman
Architects

St. Augustine's is the fourth oldest Catholic
church in Philadelphia. The original church
was burned in 1844, when anti-Catholic
sentiment was at its peak. The new building
incorporated elements of the original plan.
It is a strong Palladian form, with tall blind
arches, a cornice with modillions and a
staged tower, which was completed by
Edward Durang in 1867.

The sanctuary is a Palladian design
modified by renovations in 1895 and
1923. The ceiling frescoes, some of which
were added by the Italian painters Nicola
Monachesi and Philip Costaggini, give a
neo-Baroque flavor. Especially notable are
the arched, white marble altar, composed of
a skylit dome resting on splendid Corinthian
columns, and the organ facade painted in
gold, bronze and ivory. Above the galleries
are tribune boxes, a rare feature in church

▼
1846
New York–Philadel-
phia telegraph line
opened

▼
1847
American Medical
Association formed

▼
1848
Women's rights
conference at Seneca
Falls

▼
1848
First regular comic
paper published

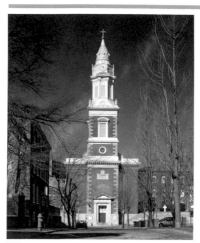

208

209

design. The tower's octagonal spire and domed top, dismantled in 1992 after suffering damage in a hurricane-force storm, were recreated in 1995.

The entrance was lowered during the 1920s to accommodate the construction of the Benjamin Franklin Bridge.

---

209 L
St. Mark's Church, *1848–51*
1625 Locust St.
John Notman

The founders of St. Mark's were influenced by the Anglican reform movement, which advocated correct medieval Gothic design as a way of returning spiritual ardor to the church. Notman's plans were sent to the Cambridge Camden Society in England for review, to ensure correct Gothic construction.

The exterior of the church is in keeping with the 19th-century interest in picturesque design. Each of the elements is given separate expression, in contrast to the simple rectangular form of 18th-century churches. The tower and entrance door are set off from the nave, the center aisle and side aisles are expressed by different rooflines, and the chancel is a separate mass with a lower roofline.

As was typical of medieval churches, construction materials are left in their natural condition on the interior. This gives the church an unusually impressive character. The walls and ceiling are of hammer-dressed stone, and the exposed trusses are of oak. Gothic details are present in the pointed arch windows with tracery, the quatrefoil shapes of the piers and on the capitals of the piers, some of which were left uncarved to symbolize that the work of the church is never finished.

The church has been enriched by gifts of the faithful, of which the most impressive are the Lady Chapel, designed by Cope

and Stewardson from 1899–1902, and the richly sculpted silver altar, both donated by Rodman Wanamaker.

---

210 L PR
1600 Block of Locust St., *1848–1908*

In the 19th century, many of Philadelphia's finest families lived in elegant mansions around Rittenhouse Square or in fine townhouses nearby. This block of Locust Street is unique because of the number of houses designed by prominent architects.

Italian Renaissance Revival brownstones predominate on the south side of the block. Numbers 1604, 1620, and 1622 have been attributed to Notman. The brownstone at 1618 was altered at the turn of the century by Wilson Eyre. The frame of the first-floor window is carved in rich floral motifs with a human face emerging from the swirling leaves.

The two houses at 1631–33, by Cope and Stewardson, reflect the late 19th-century taste for Georgian Revival. The white limestone Beaux-Arts style house at 1629 Locust was designed by Horace Trumbauer. Frank Miles Day designed the house around the corner at 235 South 17th Street in a medieval style with gables, bay windows and dark brick offset by limestone trim.

---

211 A PR
St. Charles Hotel, *1851*
60–66 North 3rd St.
Charles Rubican, builder
St. Charles Court
Renovated 1980, Adaptive Design

American hotels of the 19th century were small and designed for middle-class patrons. They were often modeled after Italian Renaissance palaces. The St. Charles was designed in this style using cast iron, a new building material, rather than stone. The iron was cast in a foundry into smooth panels, which were then painted a stone color

▼
1849
*Wooden water pipes
replaced with iron*

▼
1850
*Oldest continuous
female medical
college founded*

▼
1852
*Uncle Tom's Cabin
published*

212

214

with sand added to the paint to create a granular texture.

Local newspapers covered the construction of the hotel, describing the innovative plan, which included a bar and reading room on the first floor, a second-floor parlor for women and three floors for the more than 50 hotel rooms. Later, the same newspapers commented on the crowds who came to see the cast-iron front that imitated stone. The building was converted to apartments and office space in 1980.

212   L   PR
1800 Block of Delancey Place, *1853–80*

After 1850, Philadelphia's elite families moved west of Broad Street, a section of the city that was still largely undeveloped. Speculative developers followed, building blocks of large row houses between Walnut and South streets for the affluent middle class. The size of the houses was indicative of rising economic conditions and the presence of live-in servants.

Delancey Place, one of the earliest of the new developments, was opened as a street in 1853 on a parcel of land granted by Christ Church. Most of the houses on the north side were completed by 1860, with the remainder finished by 1880. The Biddle family was the principal property owner. The houses were designed in the Italianate style, but later additions to several houses by Wilson Eyre and Cope and Stewardson have given the block a more Victorian appearance.

213   L
Gaul-Forrest Mansion, *1853–54*
1346 North Broad St.
Stephen Button
Freedom Theatre
Renovated 2000

For half a century, North Broad Street was one of the best addresses in Philadelphia, rivaling Rittenhouse Square. Many houses were built by wealthy, self-made men. This house was designed for William Gaul, a successful brewer. It is a fine example of an Italianate townhouse in brownstone, the popular building material of midcentury. The second owner was Edwin Forrest, a famous Shakespearean actor. Forrest added a new wing to house an art gallery and installed a private theater below.

In 1880 the house was purchased by the Philadelphia School of Design for Women, the first industrial arts school for women, and now the Moore College of Art. James Windrim was hired to enlarge the building. Along the Master Street facade, he used galvanized iron trim, pressed into ornate shapes and painted to look like brownstone.

Freedom Theatre, the oldest African American theatrical company in Pennsylvania, has occupied the building since 1966. It renovated the interior to create a 300-seat, state-of-the-art theater named for its founder, John Allen.

214   D
Arch Street Presbyterian Church,
1853–55
1724 Arch St.
Joseph C. Hoxie

The Presbyterians were active church builders in the 19th century. As the population of the city moved westward, Presbyterian churches followed. The design of the Arch Street Church is a blending of several styles, a common practice at the time, and one at which Hoxie was particularly adept. Here, Baroque, Roman and Gothic forms are unified by the use of the Corinthian order. The exterior of the church is especially impressive, with a copper dome influenced by the design for St. Paul's Cathedral in London. The original building included a cupola, two bell towers and a balustrade with urns, all of which have been removed.

▼
1853
High Street renamed
Market Street,
market sheds
removed

▼
1854
City consolidation
act passed

215

216

The sanctuary is a masterpiece of the Classical Revival style and one of the most beautiful interiors in the city. The Corinthian columns and pilasters are exquisitely scaled and detailed. The dome and ceiling over the altar and transepts are treated with coffers, some of which are faced with glass, allowing natural light to bathe the altar.

---

215   L   OP

Tenth Presbyterian Church, *1854*
17th and Spruce Sts.
John McArthur, Jr.

The Tenth Presbyterian Church is another example of the many churches built by the Presbyterians to serve the developing neighborhoods in the western section of the city. It was designed by John McArthur, one of its members. McArthur was the architect of City Hall and is chiefly remembered as a leading exponent of the Second Empire style. But he was firmly established in the eclectic tradition and designed competently in many styles. For this church he drew on three principal influences. The spire and recessed porches are reminiscent of French Gothic; the base of the tower and the walls of the church are paneled in colonial fashion; and the round-headed windows, pilaster strips and corbel tables are suggestive of the Romanesque style.

THE ITALIANATE STYLE

The Italianate style grew out of the continuing English search for the picturesque, which began with the Gothic Revival. Based on the rural Italian villa, it allowed flexible planning and elaborate exterior forms. In the United States, Andrew Jackson Downing popularized the Italianate style as an appropriate style for country homes. It became nationally influential in the decade before the Civil War. The application of the Italianate style to commercial buildings led to the mass production of certain decorative elements in cast iron and pressed metal.

The first house in the Italianate style was designed by John Notman in Burlington, New Jersey. Residential buildings in this style usually have a square tower placed off-center within an asymmetrical grouping of other rectilinear shapes. Roofs are low pitched, with heavy overhangs supported by brackets. Houses usually have round-headed windows with elaborate frames, bay windows, porches or verandas. Most are wood-frame buildings covered with light-colored stucco. Commercial buildings are very ornate, with many of the details executed in marble, granite or cast iron.

---

216   J   PR

Piper-Price House, *1854*
129 Bethlehem Pike
Samuel Sloan

Chestnut Hill began its slow transformation from farmland to suburb with the extension of rail service to the community in 1854.

The Piper-Price House is believed to be the design of Samuel Sloan, based on its similarity to a villa published in Sloan's book, *The Model Architect* (1852).

Sloan's pattern books helped popularize the Italian villa, a style valued for its picturesque qualities as well as its generally affordable cost. The Piper-Price House was typical of the style. It was symmetrical in plan, with a simple square form and center tower from which to view the countryside.

The simple massing is relieved by round-arched windows with dark trim set off against the light-colored stucco and a generous porch. Later additions enlarged the house while maintaining its simple, block-like character.

218

220

---

217 A

Elliot and Leland Buildings, *1854–56*
235–37 Chestnut St.
Joseph C. Hoxie
Independence Park Hotel

By midcentury, commercial buildings
and warehouses were being designed by
architects. The basic plan of the buildings
remained the same as earlier warehouses on
Front Street. The first floor was a store or
office, and each upper floor was one large
room used for storage or manufacture. In
contrast to its shallow four-story predecessors, however, the 19th-century commercial
building was taller and deeper.

The Elliott and Leland buildings are fine
examples of the Italianate commercial style.
Each has a granite facade and is five stories
high. The depth of the buildings made it
essential to open up the facade to gain as
much light as possible. Hoxie achieved this
by organizing the facade in response to the
structural system rather than as a wall with
windows placed in it. The window spandrels
are recessed and the columns and capitals
emphasized, producing a simple and direct
form.

---

218 A

Farmers' and Mechanics' Bank, *1854–55*
427 Chestnut St.
John M. Gries
American Philosophical Society, Franklin Hall
Renovated 1984, 1993, Bower Lewis Thrower

Commercial banks increased in the 19th
century, locating near the center of government at Independence Square. So great was
their concentration that the blocks between
3rd and 5th streets on Chestnut were
referred to as Bank Row. The Farmers' and
Mechanics' Bank illustrates the prevailing
notion that banks had to look like Italian
Renaissance palaces to convey an image
of wealth and substance. The symmetrical
marble facade has arched windows on each

floor and ornate cornices and belt courses
decorated with sculptural heads of sheep and
other animals. The main banking room in
the rear of the building was three stories high
and covered with a skylight. It was reached
by a grand hall decorated with Corinthian
columns.

The bank was technologically advanced
for its time. Iron was used for the entrance
doors, bank counters and skylight shutters. A
wrought- and cast-iron truss supported
the roof of the banking room. The bank had
the most up-to-date sanitary facilities and
a complex heating and ventilation system,
which changed the air in the building once
an hour.

---

219 A

Leland Building, *1855*
37–39 South 3rd St.
Stephen Button

The Leland Building is one of the best
remaining examples of the 19th-century
utilitarian commercial building. It was
designed for Charles Leland, a prosperous
merchant. The building was very unusual
for its time. The plan was imaginatively
organized around an inner court to provide
light and increase the size of usable interior
space. The building also contained the latest
in plumbing, heating and lighting systems.

On the exterior, Button emphasized the
height of the building by an unorthodox
arrangement in which the horizontal spandrels are recessed behind plain pilasters,
which rise uninterrupted to the top floor.
Button eliminated most of the typical Italianate ornament, giving the facade a simple
appearance. This approach found immediate
favor and influenced commercial building
throughout the decade.

▼
1856
First Republican
National Convention
held

▼
1857
Academy of Music
opens

221

222

---

220   A   PR
Smythe Buildings, *1855–57*
101–11 Arch St.
Renovated 1984, Hans P. Stein Architects

The introduction of cast-iron facades made it possible to achieve the architectural effects of the popular Italianate style on commercial buildings in an economical manner.

The facade of the Smythe Buildings is the best example of cast-iron design remaining in the city. The facade was produced by the Tiffany and Bottom Foundry in Trenton, New Jersey, and probably designed by a company draftsman. The building originally extended half a block, with a continuous facade composed of the delicate cast-iron columns and arched windows. In addition to its rich appearance at relatively low cost, cast iron appealed to the commercial developer because of the ease of construction and the large amount of window area relative to the structural support required for the facade. The middle section of the facade was demolished in 1913 to make room for a trolley turn-around. When the buildings were converted to apartments in 1984 this section was reconstructed in fiberglass using old section molds.

---

221   C,K
Academy of Music, *1855–57*
232–46 South Broad St.
Napoleon LeBrun and Gustave Runge
Renovated 1994–2007, Vitetta, Keast & Hood Co.

Philadelphia's musical development was slow compared with other cities, partly because of the dominant Quaker conservatism. Musical entertainment was provided in small theaters and concert halls, but by the 1850s the public was eager for opera on a grand scale. A site for a concert hall was acquired on Broad Street, a largely undeveloped, quiet location.

The plan, selected by a competition, was modeled after La Scala, in Milan. LeBrun and Runge fashioned the interior like a huge barrel, excavating a well beneath the parquet, ballooning out the ceiling in a dome, placing a sounding board in the orchestra pit and curving the rear walls of the auditorium. To allow the walls to settle, the building stood for a year without a roof. When finished, the Academy was acoustically unsurpassed.

The neo-Baroque interior is one of the most lavish in the city. Huge Corinthian columns mark the proscenium, and an immense Victorian chandelier hangs from a ceiling decorated with murals by Karl Heinrich Schmolze. The Academy is the oldest musical auditorium in the country still serving its original purpose.

---

222   L
Pennsylvania Hospital for Mental and Nervous Diseases, *1856*
111 North 49th St.
Samuel Sloan, with Thomas Story Kirkbride
The Kirkbride Center

In 1841, Pennsylvania Hospital moved its psychiatric patients to a rural 37-acre site in West Philadelphia, two miles beyond the city limits. The new facility was supervised by Dr. Thomas Kirkbride. Isaac Holden won the competition for the first building with a design based on the echelon plan, which used extended wings to isolate the separate wards of the hospital. It was the first example of the echelon plan in the country and was so successful that it became the model for many other facilities.

Sloan's design for a second building, to be used exclusively for male patients, duplicated Holden's plan. The large structure has a central pavilion flanked by two L-shaped wings with pedimented pavilions at the ends. The small dome over the central pavilion held iron tanks, which supplied water to the entire building. The east facade has a broad pediment and is faced with cutstone. A

▼
1858
Street grid extended
to entire city

▼
1859
First U.S.
zoological society
formed

223

225

granite Doric portico is the only decoration. The west facade is similar but is stucco and has a smaller portico.

Sloan was the most prominent hospital architect of the period. At his death he was credited with designing 32 hospitals for the insane and three general hospitals.

223   J   PR
Watson House, *1856*
100 Summit St.

George Watson, a carriage maker, built one of the first suburban houses in Chestnut Hill following the introduction of rail service to the area. During the next 20 years, others followed his example, constructing similar homes along Summit Street. Watson's house is an imposing Italianate villa with a tower, or campanile. The house is set back from the street and built on high ground. It is stuccoed, as were many houses in the Italianate style. One of its distinguishing features is the bracketing under the eaves, which looks like icicles and recalls the brackets on Swiss chalets.

224   H   PR
Mitchell House, *1856*
200 West Walnut Lane

Joseph G. Mitchell, a bank president, is said to have built four houses in Germantown. He lived in this one for two years, then sold it for a quick profit. The house has been considered the work of Samuel Sloan, but no documentary evidence supports this claim.

The Mitchell house is an example of the Gothic villa, a house type popularized by A. J. Downing. Gothic villas were designed to blend into their natural settings by harmonizing with the shapes of nature, where few things are ever symmetrical.

The house is built of Wissahickon schist. It has a projecting tower entrance that gives the facade a picturesque asymmetry. The gable roof is steeply pitched with decorated

barge boards; the crenelated tower projecting above the roofline was usually reserved for grander Gothic villas. Typical Gothic hood or drip moldings of stone surround the window openings.

225   L
St. Clement's Episcopal Church, *1855–59*
20th and Cherry Sts.
John Notman

Real-estate developer William S. Wilson provided the land and some money for St. Clement's, hoping it would attract buyers to the speculative houses he was building nearby. Notman was both architect and contractor. He used brownstone and the medieval Romanesque style, characterized by round arched openings. This style was less expensive to construct and more flexible than the Gothic style. Notman maintained the eastern orientation of the chancel by placing the doorway in the middle of the block and the chancel on the street facade. He emphasized the round shape of the chancel by rounded, individual stones and the sloped wall.

After 1870, a Lady Chapel was added, with wrought-iron gates by Samuel Yellin. Later, the floor and ceiling of the chancel were raised and small Gothic lancet windows added on the second story. In 1929 the church was moved forty feet west to allow for the widening of 20th Street. Over three days, the 5,500-ton stone structure was moved an inch at a time with no damage to the building.

226   L
Church of the Holy Trinity, *1856–59*
Walnut St. on Rittenhouse Sq.
John Notman

The Church of the Holy Trinity was built at the same time as St. Clement's by the same architect, in a similar style and with the same brownstone building material. Holy Trinity,

228

229

however, has a more dramatic facade, made possible by placing the chancel at the west, rather than in the traditional eastern location.

The church was one of the first accurate renditions of the Romanesque style in the country. The three doorways are deeply recessed and carved with geometric and foliate designs in typical Romanesque fashion. A rose window dominates the third story, and a massive tower adds picturesque asymmetry. The interior is relatively simple, in keeping with the simple service of the Low Church, but it has beautiful stencil work on the vaulted ceiling. In the 19th century, Holy Trinity had a fashionable following from the well-to-do families who lived around Rittenhouse Square.

227 A PR
Bank of Pennsylvania, *1857–59*
421 Chestnut St.
John M. Gries
The Bank Building
Renovated 2005–07, Tackett and Co., DPK&A

When the Bank of Pennsylvania was formed, it selected a site on Chestnut Street near the city's other major financial institutions. Gries recently had completed the adjacent Farmers' and Mechanics' Bank and designed this building in a similar Italianate style. The bank is based upon Renaissance palaces of Venice, a highly ornate version of Italianate design that prefigured the Victorian love for richness of detail. Like the Farmers' and Mechanics' Bank, this bank also had a rear banking hall that was originally covered by a cast-iron dome, which was demolished from 1892–93.

The bank failed during the financial panic of 1857, when the building was only half completed. It was finished by the subsequent owner, the Philadelphia Bank.

228 L OP
Burholme, *1859*
Burholme Park, Cottman and Central Aves.
Restored 1983, Vitetta Group

Burholme is one of the finest Italianate villas in Philadelphia. Joseph W. Ryerss, a railroad entrepreneur, built the mansion and matching carriage house on an 85-acre estate, which he named after his ancestral estate in England. The name means "house in a woodland setting."

Burholme is an extravagant example of the Italianate villa. The building is stone covered with stucco and is surrounded on three sides by a veranda. Its richness of detail is exemplified by the crowning belvedere, with stained-glass windows, added after 1888. During the Civil War, Burholme served as a station on the underground railroad, aiding runaway slaves. Later, Ryerss's sympathy for stray animals led to the founding of the Ryerss Infirmary for Dumb Animals. Some of his adopted pets are still buried on the grounds.

229 H OP
Ebenezer Maxwell House, *1859*
200 West Tulpehocken St.

The extension of the railroad to Germantown in 1832 initiated one of the first suburban developments in the country. Tulpehocken Street was opened in 1850 and soon filled with pretentious houses. One of the most striking was the Ebenezer Maxwell House, built for a prominent dry-goods merchant. The design has been variously attributed to J. C. Hoxie, Samuel Sloan and an unknown carpenter-builder. The mansion is an early masterpiece of the eclectic tradition, skillfully blending elements of the French Renaissance, Gothic, and Italianate styles. Maxwell was a speculative developer, who built this house and three others on the street to be sold for profit. Much of the exterior woodwork is painted to look like stone. On the interior, inex-

230

231

pensive wood is grained to look like oak or mahogany, and the slate mantelpieces look like marble.

The house, in danger of demolition in the 1960s, was saved by Maxwell Mansion, Inc. It has converted the mansion into a museum, and the grounds have been replanted according to the principles of A. J. Downing, America's leading landscape architect in the 1850s.

230   K

Lit Brothers, *1859–1907*
Market St., 7th to 8th Sts.
Collins and Autenreith
Mellon Bank Center
Renovated 1989, Burt Hill Kosar Rittlemann and John Milner Associates

By 1859, commercial development along Market Street had extended to the 800 block. Among the businesses were the J. M. Maris Co., a dry-goods company located in a modern five-story structure, and the J. B. Lippincott publishing company.

In 1891, the Lit family opened a small shop specializing in women's clothes at the corner of 8th and Market streets. Their advertising techniques were so successful that within a few years they established one of the city's largest retail stores. Between 1895 and 1907 they purchased the entire block and added the two large buildings at either end, designed to blend with the Renaissance style of the Maris, Lippincott and Bailey buildings.

The Lit Brothers store is the only complete block of Victorian commercial architecture in the city. The use of a common window unit with a classical arch and a single painted color creates the appearance of a single building with a cast-iron facade. There are several buildings, however, of which only the facade at 719–21 is cast iron. The others are brick with marble or granite sheathing on the front. The two end buildings with octagonal towers are brick with terra-cotta and galvanized iron trim.

After the store closed in 1977, the buildings were in danger of demolition for many years. A vigorous public campaign for preservation and the efforts of a local developer, Growth Properties, led to the renovation of the buildings for offices and stores.

231   L   PR

1500–2300 Blocks of Green St., *1860–90*

Green Street's principal growth occurred after the extension of the street railway system, when wealthy industrialists were building mansions along North Broad Street. This encouraged speculative builders to create high-quality row houses nearby for the rising managerial middle class.

By the end of the century, the row houses were joined by more elaborate houses of well-to-do industrialists. The grandest of these is the Kemble-Bergdoll Mansion. Other notable examples are 2223, designed by Willis Hale, with an unusual facade of brick enlivened by multicolored ceramic tile; 2220, a Romanesque revival house with a corner tower; and 2301, also designed by Hale. All were owned by the Fleisher family, wealthy textile manufacturers, who have lived in the area for three generations. The handsome brownstones at 2144–46 Green, with the ribbon carved in stone over the doorway, are attributed to Wilson Eyre. The generous brownstone at 190–3 has been attributed to The Wilson Brothers. The house at 1708–10 is thought to be the work of Hale, and the distinctive, exuberant Queen Anne–style house at 1533 Green has been attributed to John Fraser.

There are also two notable churches on the street: the Romanesque Revival Lutheran church in the 1500 block, designed by Stephen Button, and St. Francis of Xavier Catholic Church in the 2300 block, a later and richer example of the Romanesque style, designed by the prominent church architect E. F. Durang.

▼
1863
Abolition of slavery

▼
1864
Octavius Catto protests white-only streetcars

▼
1865
Lincoln's body lies in state at Independence Hall

232

---

232   K   PR

Woodland Terrace, *1861*
Samuel Sloan
500–520 Woodland Ter.

West Philadelphia also developed after the extension of the street railway system. Speculative builders created housing for the affluent middle class, who sought to escape the dense urban environment of the city.

The houses on Woodland Terrace were designed as Italianate villas. Because they were built as twins on narrow lots, they were more vertical in their massing than individual houses. A special feature of these houses is the terrace, or garden plot, separating the house from the street. Woodland Terrace is probably the best preserved example of this type of housing in the city. The most expensive and picturesque houses were placed at either end of the block, where they were most visible. They are built of stone, and each is graced with a curving Corinthian-columned porch and prominent tower. The houses on the interior of the block are built of stucco or brownstone and have a simpler appearance.

---

233   L

St. Timothy's Protestant Episcopal Church,
1862–66
5720 Ridge Ave.
Emlen T. Littell / Charles Burns

St. Timothy's is a handsome, country parish church set within a walled churchyard. It was designed in the High Victorian Gothic style and built in stages over 23 years. The gable-roofed sanctuary was designed by Littell, a New York church architect. The corner tower, added in 1871, has terra-cotta battlements similar to those on the Penn Library, suggesting it may have been designed by Furness. The 1874 nave and parish house were extended in 1885 by Burns, architect of the Church of the Advocate.

In spite of the many additions, the church appears to be a single design. Common

materials unify the composition. Uncoursed ashlar, interlaced with rose-colored mortar, and brick string courses are the dominant materials. Particularly noteworthy are the hipped roof of red and gray slate shingles, the terra-cotta battlements on the clerestory tower and the bell tower, which is decorated with brick corbels and scalloped louvers.

The intimately scaled interior has a hammer-beam ceiling, delicate stenciled designs on the nave walls and an imposing pre-Raphaelite mosaic behind the altar.

---

234   L   PR

William Montelius House, *1863–65*
223 South 42nd St.
John D. Jones, builder

The Montelius House was built by John D. Jones, a speculative real-estate developer and builder. He constructed a group of houses on the east side of 42nd Street, which was the western edge of development until the end of the 19th century.

The Montelius House, named for the coal-shipping merchant who first owned it, is an Italianate villa similar to other suburban houses of the period in West Philadelphia and Chestnut Hill. It is made of brownstone rather than stucco, has a columned porch topped by a balustrade and a handsome corner tower.

THE SECOND EMPIRE STYLE

The Second Empire style was based on the monumental buildings constructed in Paris during the reign of Napoleon III. The style of these buildings was copied throughout Europe and introduced into the United States in the 1860s. In this country, the Second Empire style was closely associated with large public buildings, such as federal office buildings, post offices, courthouses and city halls.

The chief characteristic of the style is the mansard roof with dormer windows of all shapes and sizes, which permitted the attic to become a usable floor. Larger buildings have

---

▼
1865
John Stetson begins hat business

▼
1866
Hires invents root beer

▼
1867
First merry-go-round operated in U.S.

▼
1868
Navy Yard moves to League Island

235

238

projecting pavilions in the center or at the corners and such heavily embellished classical elements as pediments, balustrades or windows flanked by paired columns. Residences are less decorative but always retain the mansard roof.

235   C,K

Union League of Philadelphia, *1864–65*
140 South Broad St.
John Fraser
Restored 2006, DPK&A

The Union League was one of many political clubs organized during the Civil War years. It was an outgrowth of the Union Club, organized by a group of aristocrats to raise funds and recruit troops for the Union cause. By 1865, the League had a membership of several thousand.

The brick and brownstone building was one of the few buildings erected in Philadelphia during the Civil War. It is an early example of the Second Empire style. The design includes a mansard roof—the distinguishing characteristic of the Second Empire style—dormer windows, projecting pavilions and a monumental stairway. The original ornamental iron roof trim and asymmetrical tower, removed during the 1920s, were replaced as part of a complete restoration of the exterior in 2006.

The large annex to the rear was added by Horace Trumbauer from 1909–11. Its formal Renaissance design is a startling contrast to the main building.

236   L

Philadelphia Saving Fund Society,
1868–69 /1897–98
700–710 Walnut St.
Addison Hutton / Furness Evans and Company

For their second headquarters, PSFS sponsored a design competition, which was won by the firm of Sloan and Hutton. The building established the career of Hutton, who completed the design after his partnership with Sloan dissolved. It is a fine example of an Italianate bank, constructed of brick with granite ashlar facing. The flat roof is surrounded by a balustrade, and there are two round arched entrances on the facade.

The building was expanded by Hutton from 1885–86 and again by Furness from 1897–98. Subsequent interior alterations included work by Howe and Lescaze from 1929–31. The historic interiors were covered over when the building was converted to a restaurant in 2006.

237   D   OP

Masonic Temple, *1868–73 /1890s*
1 North Broad St.

See page 70.

238   L   PR

2000–2100 Blocks of Spruce St., *1868–80*

Brownstone became a popular building material because it was cheap, attractive and easily carved. Many brownstone houses were built prior to 1880, when it was discovered that the stone fell apart over time. The brownstones on these two blocks are fine examples of the many found in the Rittenhouse Square area. They show the influence of the Second Empire style in the use of mansard roofs and round-headed windows with keystones and framing pilasters.

In addition to brownstones, the 2100 block has several houses by prominent architects. The house at 2111–13 was designed by Furness. Wilson Eyre designed 2123–25, an elegant Colonial Revival house. The unusual double house at 2132–34, attributed to Furness, is notable for its giant brownstone arch and pressed metal ornament. A colorful note is added to the block by the facade of 2129, which was resurfaced with Mercer tile in 1913.

▼

1869
*Fairmount Park ex-
panded to 3,000 acres*

▼

1870
*First women's
suffrage
demonstrations*

239

240

At the corner of 21st and Spruce streets are four of the finest Victorian row houses in the city. The three brick houses were designed by George Hewitt, of which 2100 Spruce, built in 1883 for Lucien Moss, is the most interesting.

THE HIGH VICTORIAN GOTHIC STYLE

High Victorian Gothic reached its peak of popularity in England in the 1860s. The development of this style was influenced by the writings of John Ruskin, a prominent art historian and architectural critic. Ruskin advocated the use of color on buildings, emanating from the natural color of building materials. He directed attention to the buildings of Venice, in contrast to the exclusively English medieval base of the early Gothic Revival. Architects designing in this style were not so much concerned with beauty as with forceful character.

The High Victorian Gothic style was popular in the United States after the Civil War. The buildings of Philadelphia architect Frank Furness are among the finest examples of this style in the country.

High Victorian Gothic is very colorful in its use and combinations of materials. Two kinds of stone are often used in the same wall: brickwork is banded with stone, usually pink or gray granite or limestone, and combined with terracotta panels. Brick is laid in many patterns and textures, with heavy ornamentation. Rooflines are broken by a profusion of dormer windows, often giving buildings a top-heavy appearance.

239   L

Second Presbyterian Church,
1869–72 / 1900
2036 Walnut St.
Henry Sims / Frank Furness
First Presbyterian Church
Renovated 1953, Harold Wagoner

The Presbyterians kept pace with the westward development of the city, erecting new churches as fashionable neighborhoods expanded. They were always designed in the latest style, making it possible to trace the history of 19th-century church architecture through a chronology of Presbyterian churches.

Second Presbyterian was the most socially prominent. It was a major landmark in a neighborhood of fashionable homes designed by Chandler, Trumbauer and Cope and Stewardson. Sims, a founder of the Philadelphia AIA chapter, designed the church in the High Victorian Gothic style. This differs from the early Gothic Revival in its grander scale, bulkier details and proportions, flamboyant decoration and mixed use of materials—brownstone, with granite trim. The tower was added by Furness in 1900. After separating in 1743, the First and Second Presbyterian churches reunited in 1949, taking the name First Presbyterian Church while occupying Second Presbyterian's building.

240   F

University of Pennsylvania, College Hall,
1871–72
Locust Walk, between 34th and 35th Sts.
Thomas W. Richards
Exterior restoration 1988 on, Marianna Thomas Architect

In 1870 the university decided to move from Ninth and Market streets to the Hamilton estate in West Philadelphia. A competition was held to select a design for the first building to house the Collegiate and Scientific departments. It was won by Richards, an instructor in mechanical drawing, who had worked for Samuel Sloan and placed second in the Academy of Fine Arts competition. The trustees were so pleased by College Hall that they promoted him to professor and asked him to design three more buildings.

College Hall set the standard for Collegiate Gothic design on campus. The exterior is characterized by a picturesque massing of

237 D OP

Masonic Temple, *1868–73 /1890s*
1 North Broad St.
James Windrim / George Herzog

Freemasonry prospered in Philadelphia from colonial times, despite the rise of anti-Masonic sentiment during the early 19th century. Several temples were built, culminating in this magnificent structure, one of the world's greatest Masonic temples.

The Masons held a competition and selected Brother James Windrim, a 27-year-old freemason, as the winner. Windrim's design was modeled on a medieval style known as Norman. This is reflected in the massive carved doorway that projects from the wall; the ashlar stone work; the fortresslike towers; and the corbel tables,

a round-arch decorated cornice under the roofline. Many of the granite blocks for the temple weighed as much as six tons.

The temple took five years to build. The interior design was begun 14 years later and took 15 more years to complete. George Herzog, who had trained in the royal workshops of Ludwig I of Munich, was the primary designer. The spectacular interior spaces include seven lodge halls, each lavishly decorated in a specific style. The most renowned is the Egyptian Hall, replete with accurate hieroglyphics. The temple was one of the first buildings in the city to be lighted by electricity.

▼
1871
Independence Hall
restored as national
memorial

▼
1872
City Hall cornerstone
laid

245

volumes, which once included towers and pinnacles. In typical late Gothic fashion, a variety of contrasting surface materials is used, including a brownstone base, cornices and gables of Ohio stone, polished red granite columns and walls of green serpentine ashlar stone.

---

241   A

Pennsylvania Company for Insurances on Lives and Granting Annuities, *1871–73*
431 Chestnut St.
Addison Hutton
American Philosophical Society, Richardson Hall
Renovated 2007–08, Always By Design

This building is the last remainin post–Civil War banking structure on Bank Row. It was built at the same time as Frank Furness's two flamboyant banks on the same block, both of which have been demolished. The squat columns at the third-floor windows are reminiscent of Furness's style and may have been influenced by his neighboring buildings. In contrast to early banks, Hutton placed the main banking room in the front, with light entering through a vaulted ceiling from skylights above.

---

242   D,K   OP

Pennsylvania Academy of the Fine Arts, *1872–76*
See pages 72–73.

---

243   C,D,K   OP

City Hall, *1871–1901*
See page 74–75.

---

244   L

Dobson Carpet Mills, *1872–73*
4041 Ridge Ave.
Renovated 1991, Cassaway Albert and Associates.

From 1870 to 1900, Philadelphia was one

of the country's largest industrial centers. Factories and mills were developed throughout the city. Many located in Falls of the Schuylkill, of which Dobson's Mill is the only one still standing.

James Dobson and his brother emigrated from England in 1854. They established their first mill at Ridge Avenue and Wissahickon Creek, where they made woolen blankets for the Union army. When it was demolished to extend Fairmount Park, a new mill complex was built on Scott's Lane.

Dobson's mill was one of the largest textile complexes in the city. The main building is patterned after English factories of the same period. It is made of closely laid stone blocks, with brick jack-arches above the windows. Spinning, weaving, combing, carding and spooling took place in the main building, while adjacent buildings were used for a printing yarn room, coloring and dyeing. Dobson's complex closed in 1927.

---

245   K

Victory Building, *1873–75*
1001 Chestnut St.
Henry Fernback
The Victory
Renovated 2003, J.K. Roller Architects

The Victory Building, a branch office of the New York Life Insurance Company, was the first commercial building in the city designed in the Second Empire style. Originally the building was three stories high with a mansard roof. When it was enlarged, the mansard roof was removed and then set back in place after three floors were added. A balustrade on the facade marks the division between the old and the new. The lower three stories are richly textured with classical pilasters and columns; the upper floors are more restrained.

The building was designed to be fireproof. The exterior is faced in granite, and the interior has iron posts and girders and iron

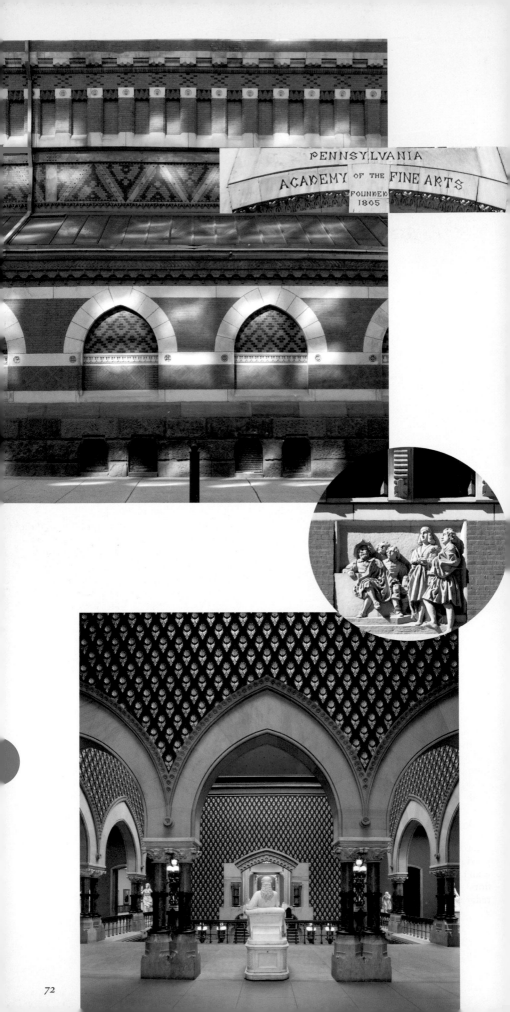

Pennsylvania Academy of the Fine Arts,
1872–76
Broad and Cherry Sts.
Furness and Hewitt
Restored 1976, Day and Zimmermann
Associates

The academy, founded in 1805, was the first
art school and museum in the country. Its
most famous student was Thomas Eakins,
who became a dominating presence as a
teacher from 1876–86. Originally located
at 10th and Chestnut streets, the academy
moved to Broad Street after the start of the
new City Hall. The new building was planned
as part of the 1876 Centennial. The building
committee wanted a two-story, fireproof
building with two entrances: one for students
and one for the public. Students' rooms
were to be on the first floor, with skylighted
galleries on the second floor, accessible by a
main stairway.

The academy is the most outstanding
example of Furness's work and one of the
most magnificent Victorian buildings in the
country. In contrast to the somber tones of
previous Victorian architecture, the interior
is an explosion of color: the walls have gilt
floral patterns incised on a field of Venetian
red; the cerulean blue ceiling is sprinkled
with silver stars; the gallery walls are plum,
ochre, sand and olive green. Furness's work
is characterized by overscaled and unusually proportioned structural details and the

extensive use of carved floral patterns. These
can be seen throughout the interior in the
form of cast-bronze foliation along the stair
rail, compressed iron columns in the galleries
and the use of dwarf columns supporting
massive arches. In answer to the building
committee's fireproofing specifications, Furness laced the building together with brick,
stone and iron. Some of the I-beams and columns were left exposed, making this an early
example of expressed iron construction.

The facade is an amalgam of historical
styles, fused in an aggressively personal
manner. The pointed arches, floral ornament
and use of color are derived from English
Gothic design, while the mansard roof,
projecting central pavilion and panels of
incised tryglyphs come from French sources.
This riot of forms is executed in rusticated
brownstone, dressed sandstone, polished
pink granite, red pressed brick and purplish
terra-cotta.

For many decades the academy was considered to be an unattractive building, and
its ornamental brilliance was obscured. A
comprehensive restoration in 1976 returned
the building to its original appearance.

243   C,D,K   OP

City Hall, *1871–1901*
Broad and Market Sts.
John McArthur, Jr., with Thomas U. Walter;
Alexander Milne Calder, sculptor
Restorations: Conversation Hall, *1982,* Day
and Zimmerman Associates; City Councel
Chamber, *2003,* DPK&A; Exterior, *2001–09*
Vitetta, Kelly/Maiello Inc., Marianna
Thomas Architects, Norton Art Conserva-
tion, Keast & Hood Co.

Penn set aside Center Square as a site for
public buildings, but it was not used as such
until the city expanded westward, justifying
the relocation of the city hall from Independence Square. City Hall is the largest
municipal building in the country and the
finest example of the Second Empire style.
It contains 14½ acres of floor space, occupied
by city and county offices, courtrooms and
several ornately detailed public spaces.

The building is organized around a central
public courtyard, which is reached through
monumental arched portals on all four sides.
Second Empire motifs are combined with
an abundance of sculpture to give the exterior a rich yet intimately scaled appearance.
Among the most prominent features are
the projecting corner pavilions; the towered
pavilions over the entrance portals; the mansard roof with dormers, connected to one
another by curved frames; and the large-scale
paired columns, which help to make the
building's eight stories look like three. Solid
granite, 22 feet thick in some portions, forms
the first floor and supports a brick structure
faced with white marble.

Calder created all the sculpture on the
building. There are groups of figures representing the seasons, continents, arts and

science, as well as allegorical figures, heads
and masks. Calder also designed the 27-ton
cast-iron statue of Penn atop the tower,
which is the largest single piece of sculpture
on any building in the world. The 548-foot
tower is the world's tallest masonry structure
without a steel frame. It is granite up to the
clock, then cast iron painted to look like
stone.

Public spaces within the building are
among the most lavish in the city. The City
Council chamber is larger than the House of
Lords in London; it is ornately detailed and
uses such expensive materials as alabaster
on the walls. The Mayor's Reception Room
is extremely handsome; it has a blue and
gold ceiling, beautiful woodwork and red
Egyptian marble columns. Conversation

Hall, restored to its original elegance in 1982, is dominated by a magnificent chandelier. John Ord, chief architect from 1890–94, is thought to have been responsible for much of the interior detailing. Other notable features are the octagonal cut-stone staircases in each of the four corners and the Supreme Court Room, which was designed by George Herzog.

The tower is open to the public and affords a wonderful view of the city.

▼
1876
*Centennial Exposition
opens;
First telephone
demonstrated*

▼
1877
*John Wanamaker
opens new-style de-
partment store*

250

252

249   C,K
**Pennsylvania Institution for the Deaf and
Dumb,** *1875*
320 South Broad St.
Furness and Hewitt
University of the Arts

Fifty years after the completion of Haviland's
building for the Pennsylvania Institute for
the Deaf and Dumb, Furness designed
an addition on the 15th Street side that more
than doubled its size. It is a fine example
of Furness's mature work in the Victorian
Gothic style. Patterns in the brickwork
produce contrasts of texture and shadow,
while the placement of chimneys, gables and
dormers results in a rich clustering of forms.
The Philadelphia College of Art, originally
the Pennsylvania Museum School and now
the University of the Arts, has occupied the
building since 1893.

250   L   PR
Thomas Hockley House, *1875/1894*
235 South 21st St.
Frank Furness

Thomas Hockley, an influential lawyer,
was an early supporter of Frank Furness.
He assisted Furness in obtaining commissions for a number of his later buildings.
Furness designed this house when he was just
emerging as a leading architect.
    The house has the standard Victorian
forms, such as the mansard roof, pointed
dormers and projecting bay window. But the
ornament and the variety of brick patterns
are distinctively Furness. There are variations
of cut, pressed, diapered and diagonally laid
brick; string-courses and stepped corbels;
and a blunt-headed chimney, which seems
to grow out of the wall from corbeled stems.
The oversized, formalized flower designs in
the porch tympanums resemble Furness's use
of similar motifs on the facade of the Pennsylvania Academy.

The use of brickwork to create rich textures and patterns was copied in many other
houses of the period.

251   G,K
Centennial Bank, *1876*
32nd and Market Sts.
Frank Furness
Paul Peck Alumni Center, Drexel University
Renovated 2000, Voith Mactavish Architects

The Centennial Exposition sparked a
building boom in West Philadelphia. The site
of the Pennsylvania Railroad's main depot, at
32nd and Market streets, was a key intersection. Of the many commercial buildings in
that area, only the Centennial Bank remains.
    The bank is characteristic of Furness's
style. The symmetry of the facade is emphasized by a projecting bay with hip roof that
is penetrated by a window stack, which
terminates in a crocketed gable. The facade
includes all the typical Furness devices: squat
columns, pointed windows, oversized ornamentation and decorative patterns of cut
and pressed red brick. Although less colorful
than some of his other designs, the exterior
uses the unusual glass tiles also found at the
Pennsylvania Academy. Furness devised the
glass tile to give permanent, vivid color to
the facade. Light penetrates the painted tile
to a backing of gold and silver foil, whose
reflective properties intensify the color. The
interior of the bank was brilliantly colored
and lit by skylights.

252   L
Kensington National Bank, *1877*
Frankford and Girard Aves.
Frank Furness

Furness designed many banks throughout
the city, most of which have been demolished. This is the only remaining one still in
use as a bank. The stonework and projecting
central bay, which corbels out over the
entrance, are similar to his other buildings

▼
1878
*First telephone
book published*

▼
1879
*First Salvation
Army corps in
U.S. organized*

▼
1880
*Abner Doubleday
invents baseball*

254

255

but more subdued. Also typical of his style are the incised geometric floral patterns, the ironwork and variety of textures in the materials. The design is unusual because of its incorporation of classical details based on an ornamental style developed in France in the 1840s, which Furness may have acquired from his teacher, Richard Morris Hunt. The original interior, of which nothing remains, was brilliantly colored and lit through a coved iron ceiling.

---

253 K

Church of the Gesu, *1879–88*
See page 80.

---

254 L

William H. Rhawn House, *1879–81*
8001 Verree Rd.
Frank Furness
Knowlton Mansion
Renovated 1996–98

Furness designed this unusual rural retreat for Rhawn, a banker, who was one of his early patrons. The house was built on a 12-acre hilltop site purchased from the estate of Isaac Livezey. It is one of Furness's few remaining suburban designs.

Furness based the complex design on the domestic Queen Anne style, which was compatible with his interest in irregular forms and eccentric detail. Sheds, jerkin-head dormers, arched gables, verandas, carved chimneys and bracketed balconies are standard Queen Anne features. The walls are faced with frame clapboards and fieldstone, which was quarried on the grounds. The roof is slate.

The original stained glass, light fixtures and elegant woodwork have all been preserved. The woodwork in the stairhall shows the influence of Charles Lock Eastlake and the geometric designs of Japanese woodcuts, which Furness might have seen at the Centennial Exposition.

The interior was carefully restored when the house was converted to a banquet facility. Wall and ceiling stencils were recreated and rooms refurnished to replicate the mansion's original appearance.

---

255 C PR

A. J. Holman Factory, *1881*
1222–26 Arch St.
The Wilson Brothers

Bibles have been published continuously in Philadelphia since 1743, when Christopher Saur of Germantown printed a German bible, the second bible published in America. Andrew J. Holman formed his bible publishing company in 1872 with two members of the renowned William J. Harding Company, with which he had trained. Within a decade Holman's company had outgrown its headquarters.

The new building is one of the few commercial loft buildings of the period that has been well preserved in its original form. The facade is faced with brick. It is more embellished than the Leland Building, but is still restrained compared with the ornamental treatment of The Wilson Brothers' other projects, such as the nearby Reading Terminal.

---

256 K PR

Disston Mansion, *1881–83*
1500 N. 16th Street
Edwin F. Durang
Addition 1906, Hale and Kilburn

In the late 1880s, North Broad Street was the location of mansions of wealthy industrialists including P.A.B. Widener and Henry Disston, founder of the largest saw manufacturing plant in the world. Henry's son Albert and his wife constructed a mansion nearby, which is one of the few surviving mansions in North Philadelphia from this period.

Durang was primarily a church architect and this is one of the few residences he

253 K

Church of the Gesu, *1879–88*
18th and Stiles Sts.
Edwin F. Durang;
Exterior restored 1991, John Blatteau
Associates

When St. Joseph's College outgrew its original quarters, the Jesuit fathers decided to create a grand church and ecclesiastical college in North Philadelphia. Father Burchard Villeger directed the move. A chapel and rectory were built in 1868, but as the surrounding area developed, a new church was required. Villeger decided to model the church after the Gesu in Rome, and hired Durang, who had designed the chapel and was the foremost architect of Catholic churches of the time.

The church has a breathtaking scale and magnificent sanctuary, reminiscent of Baroque churches of Europe. The most notable aspect of the church is the interior space. The enormous nave, once the widest unobstructed nave in the country, is covered by a barrel vault, which spans 76 feet and rises to a height of 72 feet over the altar. It is then topped by an aspidial dome. The rich interior decoration includes gilded plaster in the nave coffers and monumental sculptured figures in the nave and galleries.

The exterior reflects the Second Empire style through the use of superimposed classical orders and heavy sculptural ornament.

▼
1881
Electric street
lighting introduced

▼
1882
Walt Whitman's
Leaves of Grass
published in Phila-
delphia

▼
1883
Phillies baseball
team founded

257

designed. It is three-and-one-half stories with a marble front and brick sides with marble trim. The symmetrical Italianate facade is ornamented with belt courses, round-headed windows framed by stone surrounds and is topped by a shallow, pedimented cornice. A second-story balcony supported by deep brackets projects over the door. However, the main entrance was via a porte-cochere on the south side that enters onto a cylindrical entrance hall. The sumptuous interiors, attributed to designer George Herzog, have been immaculately preserved.

The house was purchased by the Unity Mission Church Home and Training School in 1946, an affiliate of Father Divine's Peace Mission movement, which maintains the house as a mission and residence for visiting colleagues.

Other outstanding houses on the block include 1501-02, 1505-07 and 1511 designed by Thomas Lonsdale.

257   J

Gravers Lane Station, *1883*
Gravers Lane near Stenton Ave.
Frank Furness

When the Philadelphia and Reading Railroad extended commuter rail service to northwest Philadelphia in the 1870s and 1880s, Frank Furness designed many of its commuter stations. This is the only surviving example. The building has a simple rectangular plan, with waiting rooms on the first floor and the station manager's residence above. Its complicated appearance is created by a porte cochere jutting out to the rear, a shed porch extending over the platform and a conical ticket tower, which terminates in a complex grouping of shed and gable dormers. The apparently awkward proportions, contrasting materials and the heavy brackets and trusses are characteristic of Furness's work. The station was restored in 1982 and painted with its original cream and brown colors.

THE QUEEN ANNE STYLE

The Queen Anne style was developed by the English architect Richard Norman Shaw. He was inspired by older, rural structures built during the transitional period when Georgian motifs were overlaid on medieval forms. Shaw's work was published extensively in architectural journals and greatly admired in the United States.

The style was introduced in this country in two staff residences built by the British government for the 1876 Centennial. These buildings were notable for their picturesque qualities and lightness, in comparison with the heavy-handed Victorian Gothic style.

The Queen Anne style is characterized by the use of contrasting materials: brick or stone on the first floor, with stucco, shingles or horizontal paneling above. Large medieval chimneys, often made of molded brick, are common. Bay windows or projecting bays are used to break up the massing of the houses, which are topped with gables or high-gabled roofs.

258   J   PR

Anglecot, *1883 /1910*
Evergreen Ave. and Prospect St.
Wilson Eyre;
Renovated 1983, Greg Woodring and Associates

Anglecot was built for Charles Adam Potter, a manufacturer of oil cloth and linoleum, and so named because of its angle to the street. It was designed in the Queen Anne style by Eyre when he was 25. The Queen Anne style favored by American architects was based on colonial design, particularly early buildings in New England.

Anglecot was altered by Eyre a number of times. Many original details are gone, but some typical Queen Anne motifs remain, such as the corbeled chimneys, the broad gables across the front and the whimsical eyelid dormer window in the attic. Eyre's

▼
1883
Ladies Home
Journal *first*
published

▼
1884
First steel-frame
skyscraper built in
Chicago

▼
1884
First black
newspaper started

259

260

interest in seaside resort buildings is reflected
in the informal plan and the way the house
appears to ramble over the site. The interior
contains a living hall, a room that combines
the function of the hall and staircase with
that of a living room, complete with fireplace
and built-in sitting area. The house
has been subdivided and converted to
condominiums.

259   J
Wissahickon Inn, *1884*
500 West Willow Grove Ave.
G. W. and W. D. Hewitt
Chestnut Hill Academy, *1898*
Arts Center Addition *2002*, Ueland Junker
McCauley Nicholson

The Wissahickon Inn was built by Henry
Howard Houston, a shipping executive
and financier. Houston used his influence
as director of the Pennsylvania Railroad to
have service extended on the west side of
Germantown Avenue, where his real-estate
holdings were located. He built the inn as
a vacation spot for city dwellers, whom he
hoped would be encouraged to purchase
houses he was building in Chestnut Hill.

Hewitt had worked with Notman and
Furness before opening a firm with his
brother William. They were the principal
architects for all of Houston's work. The
inn was designed in the picturesque Queen
Anne style. It had 250 rooms and was completely surrounded by a generous porch. The
exterior woodwork is particularly rich, with
sunflower relief panels on the corner bay
windows and half-timbered dormers. The
windows on the upper floors are typical
of the Queen Anne style, with a large lower
pane and small upper panes.

The exterior of the inn was completely
restored at the time of the arts center
addition.

260   H
St. Vincent's Parish Hall, *1884*
109 E. Price St.
Victor Briannd de Morainville

St. Vincent's is the oldest Catholic parish in
Germantown. By the mid-19th century, the
importance and growth of the parish was
reflected in the construction of a large, Italianate church completed in 1851. The dome,
added in 1857, is a prominent landmark.

Briannd de Morainville, a member of the
parish, was a civil engineer who supervised
construction for the Reading Railroad,
including buildings by Furness. His design
for the parish hall is a distinctive example
of High Victorian Gothic design, obviously
influenced by Furness. The main facade is
divided into three bays reflecting the interior
plan, where a central stair leads to the large
auditorium. The steeply pitched pyramidal
roof over the western bay, corner turret,
pressed-metal cornice and arched windows
enrich the design, but the side facade is even
more dramatic. Three very large, wide dormers with steep gables add to the complexity
of the roofline, and the wall is broken into
several surfaces, with strong horizontal bands
of trim similar to those of the main facade.
The building is stucco, lined to look like
stone, with terra-cotta and wood trim.

261   F
Tabernacle Presbyterian Church,
1884–86
3700 Chestnut St.
Theophilus Parsons Chandler
Tabernacle United Church
Renovated 1988, Hugh Zimmers and
Associates

The Tabernacle Presbyterian Church was
once the center of a wealthy neighborhood
and had a sizable congregation. The church
was designed in the English Decorated
Gothic style, a favorite of Chandler's, which
is characterized by profuse decoration. The

▼
1885
Muybridge begins
"animal locomotive"
photographic studies

▼
1885
Metropolitan Opera
begins visits to Phila-
delphia

262

263

heavily rusticated exterior of the church is detailed in precise Gothic terms, as evidenced by the corbel tables around the cornice and above the second stage of the tower, the elaborate window tracery and the multiple pinnacles and gables. The interior contains an outstanding hammer-beamed ceiling decorated with wood-carved flying angels bearing shields.

The growth of the University of Pennsylvania and changes in adjacent neighborhoods reduced the size of the supporting congregation. The sanctuary was converted to a theater for use by the University's performing arts department without altering the interior. A nursery school area was renovated as a space for worship for the Presbyterian congregation and the United Church of Christ congregation that have shared the church since 1958.

---

262   L

First Unitarian Church, *1885–86*
2125 Chestnut St.
Furness, Evans and Company

The Reverend William Henry Furness was instrumental in having his son selected to design a new church for his growing congregation. Furness created a two-story, cruciform structure with gable-roofed nave and transept. The exterior of the church has been significantly altered. The massive carriage porch has been removed. The south porch, decorated with carved ferns, survives, but the original rough-face stonework has been smoothed.

The interior of the church has fared better. The sanctuary is covered with an elaborate hammer-beam ceiling, composed of iron rods and wood timbers. Skylights along the ridge illuminated the sanctuary, but these are now covered. Simple wood wainscoting surrounds the plaster walls, which were painted cerulean blue. The ceiling is painted a rust red and stenciled with gold-leaf daffodils,

one of the few remaining stenciled designs by Furness. The oak pews and chancel area are also notable, especially the carved altar and reading desk.

---

263   J   PR

Houston-Sauveur House, *1885*
8205 Seminole Ave.
G. W. and W. D. Hewitt

Henry Howard Houston built close to one hundred houses within a few years after the Pennsylvania Railroad opened its Chestnut Hill line. Houston wanted control over his neighborhood, so rather than make an immediate profit on cheap housing, he built fashionable, solid and substantial houses both for sale and to rent.

This house was originally rented, then sold to Louis Sauveur. It is a magnificent example of the Queen Anne suburban house. The design contains typical medieval motifs, such as the steeply pitched roof and half-timbered gables. These are enhanced by classical details, including a swan's-neck pediment over the second floor and a Palladian-style window on the front. The house is built of several materials, principally rough-textured stone and wood shingles, and is distinguished by a generous double-decked porch surrounded by delicate railings.

---

264   J   PR

Druim Moir and Brinkwood, *1885–86*
West Willow Grove Ave.
G. W. and W. D. Hewitt
Renovated 1982, DACP Associates

Henry Howard Houston was once the largest single landholder in Philadelphia. His estate, Druim Moir, which means "great crag" in Gaelic, was set on 55 acres of virgin woods.

The house was designed to look like a Scottish baronial castle. It has heavy stone walls of Wissahickon schist, projecting bays and a massive porte cochere. Druim Moir was substantially altered in the early 1940s by

264

266

Robert McGoodwin, who removed turrets, gables and some floors to make the house easier to maintain.

Houston also built a more informal house for his son. Brinkwood was executed in the shingle style. The basement is coursed in Wissahickon schist, while the two stories above are sheathed with stained cedar shingles, staggered to create a checkerboard pattern. A dentil molding along the eaves and some of the woodwork on the porches draw on 18th-century classical details.

Like many large estates, Druim Moir became too expensive to maintain as a single family residence. Its subsequent development is a model for saving large houses on large estates. The main house was converted to three attached houses without altering the exterior appearance. New houses, designed in a revival style, based on early 20th century houses in the area, are grouped together, leaving half the estate undeveloped and in common ownership.

---

265 L PR

Houses for a Moravian Community,
1885–89
1600 St. Paul St., corner Rowan St.

William F. Shaw, a devout Moravian, built these houses for the small Moravian community in the Nicetown section of Philadelphia. Shaw was a transplanted Englishman, and he wanted the development to look like a cozy English village. He chose the Queen Anne style, simplifying its normally complex shapes but retaining the picturesque tower, steep gables and front porches. As a further amenity, he turned the center of Rowan Street into garden plots. The houses were restored in the late 1960s by the existing homeowners.

266 K PR

1500 Block of North 17th St., *1886*
Willis Hale

P. A. B. Widener and William Elkins became wealthy industrialists through their monopoly over the street railway system. They used their wealth to develop significant portions of North Philadelphia for middle-class families working in the growing manufacturing centers of the city. Widener and Elkins used Hale to design a number of blocks in the area, including the 1800 and 2300 blocks of West Thompson Street. This row of houses on 17th Street is typical of Hale's exuberant style. The 29 twin houses are of brick with molded brick details, terra-cotta panels and brownstone trim. Heavy, rough-textured stone surrounds the windows and arched entrances. Particularly flamboyant are the mansard roofs with stepped gables supported by projecting corbels.

---

267 K PR

4206–18 Spruce St., *1886*
G. W. and W. D. Hewitt

William Kimball followed John D. Jones as the developer of the area around 42nd Street. He directed his efforts to middle-class homeowners and retained the Hewitt brothers to design several projects, probably including the 200 and 300 blocks of South 42nd Street.

This row on Spruce Street is the most distinguished block of late 19th-century houses in the city. It was designed as a unified composition in the Queen Anne style. The center is marked by a large gable; second-floor bay windows, projecting out at either end, visually frame the rambling structure. The Queen Anne style is exuberantly exploited for its picturesque effect through the steeply pitched gables, the wooden, stick-style porches and the variety of building materials, which include hung tiles and cut-brick details.

▼
1888
*First revolving door
invented; Temple
University founded*

▼
1889
*Raquet Club founded;
Acorn Club for women
founded*

267

---

268 G PR

Poth Mansion, *1887*
216 North 33rd St.
A. W. Dilks
Alpha Pi Lambda, Drexel University, *since
1939*

Powelton was one of the earliest settlements
in West Philadelphia. Many of the houses
were built in the 1850s in the Italianate style,
including several designed by Samuel Sloan.
After the Centennial Exposition, the area
attracted wealthy homeowners, such as Frederick A. Poth, a brewer, for whom this house
was built.

Dilks had worked for the fashionable
architect T. P. Chandler. This house was
probably his first independent commission. The design reflects the High Victorian
love of rich colors and details and the visual
prominence wealthy industrialists sought for
their homes. The walls have semicircular and
polygonal bays and towers of red brick and
brownstone trim in a variety of textures.
A large porch, with delicate wood detailing,
sweeps dramatically across two sides of the
house.

---

269 H PR

Charles Lister Townsend House, *1887*
6015 Wayne Ave.
G. W. and W. D. Hewitt

Charles Lister Townsend, a broker and
president of the Philadelphia Stock
Exchange, built this 12-bedroom castle
from which he commuted to downtown
Philadelphia. The house was modeled after
Druim Moir, the castle the Hewitt brothers
had designed the previous year for Henry
Howard Houston. Like Druim Moir, the
Townsend house has a large, round-arched
porte cochere and is built of coarse-textured
Wissahickon schist. It has stepped Flemish
gables and a corner tower topped with a
curving mansard roof.

270 C

Keystone National Bank, *1887/1890*
1326 Chestnut St.
Willis Hale

The Keystone Bank was built in an era when
self-made millionaires used architecture to
express their success. Willis Hale, according
to his obituary, was fortunate "to have as clients a number of men whose desire to spend
their easily gotten millions was not controlled by education or inherited standards
of taste; and to this fact should be attributed
some of the lack of restraint that marked his
work."

The bank is a fine example of Hale at
his flamboyant best. The design is derived
from the French Renaissance revival, based
on chateaux of the Loire Valley, which
combined both classical detail and Gothic
verticality. Classical details include the pilasters, brackets and frieze; the tower, steep
roof pitch, chimneys and decorations on
the wall and dormer are clearly Gothic. The
elaborate facade is made of sharply outlined,
rock-faced limestone. The high mansard roof
is even more elaborate, with dormers and
chimneys creating an almost chaotic jumble
of shapes.

---

271 F,K OP

**Anne and Jerome Fisher Fine Arts
Building, University of Pennsylvania,**
1888–90
34th and Walnut Sts.

See pages 86–87.

271 F,K OP

Anne and Jerome Fisher Fine Arts Building, University of Pennsylvania,
1888–90
34th and Walnut Sts.
Frank Furness
Restored 1991, Venturi Scott Brown and Associates with Clio Group and Marianna Thomas Architects

The library is one of the finest remaining examples of the work of Frank Furness. When completed it was the most innovative library building in the country. It was one of the first to separate the reading room and book stacks. Books were kept in a separate wing, which was designed so that the rear wall could be removed on jack screws and new bays added as additional space was needed. Within the book stacks, translucent glass floors allowed light to penetrate from the sloping glass roof.

The most impressive interior spaces are the catalog room and the reading room. The catalog room is dominated by a monumental fireplace. The reading room is surrounded by study alcoves and lit from windows above. Curved iron beams radiate from the center of the ceiling to delicate terra-cotta leaves on top of the brick pilasters.

Like most of Furness's buildings, the exterior was highly controversial. It contains a rich use of brick and stone with terra-cotta panels, short heavy columns and unusual details, such as the scalloped crenelations on the tower and gargoyles on the north end.

Robert Venturi was one of the first contemporary architects to recognize the importance of Furness's work. It was fitting, therefore, that Venturi Scott Brown and Associates was chosen to restore the building.

87

▼
1890
Roman Catholic
High School opens:
first free Catholic
high school in U.S.

275   276   286 *(See page 94)*

272 L PR

Bedell House, *1889*
22nd and Chestnut Sts.
Wilson Eyre

Although Victorian architects had to design row houses for the same narrow lots as Georgian houses, they wanted to break up the monotony and symmetry of traditional row house design. The Bedell House is a fine example of Eyre's eclectic style. Eyre imaginatively selected elements from colonial and medieval sources to create his own version of Queen Anne domestic design. In this house he placed the door off center, created an irregular pattern of windows and designed a very visible chimney rising the height of the building. Eyre often lavished attention on the doorway, where a building is seen most closely. Here he placed medieval sculptural figures, probably designed with his sister, at either end of a ribbon stretching over the doorway. Carved in the ribbon is the date of the house.

273 B OP

Mother Bethel African Methodist Episcopal Church, *1889–90*
419 South 6th St.
See pages 90–91.

274 L

Baptist Temple, *1889–91*
Broad and Berks Sts.
Thomas P. Lonsdale
Renovated 2007–08, RMNJ Hillier

Russell H. Conwell, a pastor of the Grace Baptist Church, was one of the greatest orators of his time. He is best known for his "Acres of Diamonds" speech, which he delivered more than 6,000 times. Conwell also provided educational programs for students of limited means and in 1888 established an urban college, which is now Temple University.

Conwell's enormous following necessitated a larger church. Lonsdale adopted the Romanesque style for the building, which was a combination church, meeting hall and community center. The exterior has the appearance of a conventional church, but the interior is a large auditorium with excellent acoustics, accommodating up to 4,200 persons.

The temple is constructed of rock-faced granite set as coarsed ashlar with wide joints. The main facade is flanked by two towers capped with large, copper-covered domes and has a prominent stained-glass half-rose window in the center. Round-headed, clerestory windows to light the interior are located below the eave of the main roof, which is also topped with two copper cupolas.

275 G OP

Drexel Institute, Main Building,
1889–91
32nd and Chestnut Sts.
The Wilson Brothers

Anthony J. Drexel, one of the nation's prominent philanthropists and bankers, founded Drexel Institute to offer courses in art, domestic science, commerce, technology and shopwork. For the site, he chose the corner where he and George W. Childs met every morning for their walk into town. Joseph Wilson was selected as manager of the institute as well as its architect.

Wilson considered this his most important commission. He chose a composite Renaissance style for the exterior, applied in the form of highly decorative, terra-cotta detailing. Especially noteworthy are the high-relief medallion portraits within the tall entrance portal.

The building focuses around a central court, which is one of the finest interior spaces in the city. It is a rococo blend of red tile, pink marble, white enameled brick and

▼
1890–91
Louis Sullivan
designs Wainwright
Building, St. Louis

▼
1891
Drexel Institute
established

277

278

once gold-tinged wrought-iron balustrades. The building is also notable for its early use of poured-in-place reinforced concrete in the first-floor slab and the supporting piers of the court.

The auditorium contains a huge Haskell organ, one of the largest pipe organs in the city, which has superbly carved wood pilasters decorated with gold.

276 C
Clarence Moore House, *1890*
1321 Locust St.
Wilson Eyre

Clarence Moore was a wealthy merchant and amateur archaeologist. Eyre's design for his house is an imaginative essay in eclectic picturesque design. The pointed arched openings are Gothic, the top floor loggia is Venetian and the tower is French, derived from the chateaux along the Loire River. The exterior is a rich study in the contrasting textures. Rusticated limestone is used for the basement, smooth limestone for the door and window trim, elongated Roman brick for the walls and slate on the roof.

Each side of the building has its own character. The facade is compact, with a sculptural chimney squeezed between the entrance and the tower. The side elevation is nearly symmetrical, bracketed by end towers with a bay of windows sheathed in limestone in the center. The elevation along the alley is treated with as much care as the facade and contains sculptured human figures and gargoyles.

277 K PR
Kemble-Bergdol House, *1890*
2201–5 Green St.
James Windrim with George Herzog

William H. Kemble, a financier, built an elaborate mansion, which he later sold to the Bergdol family, owners of one of the city's largest breweries.

The house is one of the city's finest examples of Italianate brownstone design, a style whose rich and elaborate carving appealed to late 19th-century industrialists. The symmetrical facade is very imposing and has a generous portico entrance. Porches on the rear and west elevations are constructed of copper, iron and glass. The lavish interior was principally the work of Herzog, interior designer of the Masonic Temple. It has richly carved woodwork and plaster walls, hand-stenciled with designs in gold leaf.

278 L PR
Neill and Mauran Houses, *1890*
315–17 South 22nd St.
Wilson Eyre

John Neill, a real-estate agent, commissioned Eyre to design two speculative houses a few years after he had completed the Bedell House. Once again, Eyre drew freely on the colonial and medieval sources of the Queen Anne style. These houses show Eyre's increasing predilection for simplified shapes and materials. Wall surfaces are plain brick, interrupted only by windows of different sizes and shapes. The only ornamentation is around the paired doorways, which have Gothic-arched openings and are separated by a buttress over which stands a medieval figure. Of special interest are the finely crafted doors, which are well-preserved examples of Arts and Crafts wood construction.

The huge gambrel roof, which makes the two houses look like one, is colonial in inspiration but Victorian in its exaggerated scale.

273 B OP

Mother Bethel African Methodist Episcopal Church, *1889–90*
419 South 6th St.
Hazelhurst and Huckel
Restored 2007–08, Atkin Olshin Schade
Architects

In 1787, when black members of St. George's congregation were discriminated against, Richard Allen and other black members of the church formed what eventually became the mother church of the African Methodist Church.

The church was in the center of the principal black residential area of the city. The site is the oldest piece of land continuously owned by blacks in the United States. The present building, the fourth church built on the site, was designed in the Romanesque Revival style. The stone and brick structure features a generous semicircular arched doorway with a large stained-glass window directly overhead. The rough texture of the stone and the recessed openings that reveal the thickness of the wall are typical of the High Victorian emphasis on weight and building mass. Richard Allen, the first bishop of the church, is buried in a tomb in the basement.

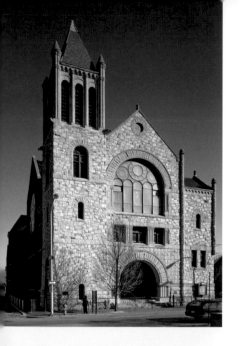

280

279   L

Germantown Cricket Club, *1890–91*
5140 Morris St.
McKim, Mead and White

The Germantown Cricket Club, founded in 1854, is the second oldest institution of its kind in the country. When the club merged with the Young America Cricket Club in 1889, the board decided to build a new clubhouse and retained Charles McKim of New York to design it.

McKim, Mead and White were the leading advocates of a return to classical models, in contrast to the complex and heavy forms of the Victorian era. The Cricket Club was one of the first examples of Georgian Revival, a style for which they became the national authorities. The building has a symmetrical facade, a quiet roofline, and uses the red brick and white trim typical of colonial design. Although the overall scale is much larger than any colonial building, the details are carried out in a similar, elegant and delicate manner. The clubhouse is named Manheim, after the street that connects it to Germantown Avenue.

280   K   OP

Reading Terminal, *1891–93*
Market St., between 11th and 12th Sts.
The Wilson Brothers
Head House *renovated 1985*, Cope Linder Associates, Bower Lewis Thrower and John Milner Associates; Train Shed *renovated 1993–94*, Thompson Ventulett Stainback Associates and Vitetta Group

The Reading Railroad was created in 1840 to bring coal and iron from western Pennsylvania. The railroad also provided passenger service to many areas north and west of the city. When steam locomotives eliminated the fear of fire from wood-burning engines, the Reading built an inner-city terminal on a site occupied by the Franklin Farmers' Market since 1860. The market was given space under the train shed, where it remains today.

281

282

The terminal is actually two buildings: the Head House, which contained waiting rooms and offices, and the shed covering the train platforms.

The Head House is constructed of wrought- and cast-iron columns, wrought-iron and steel beams and brick floors. Its Italian Renaissance exterior was applied over the structural system by a consulting architect, Frank Kimball of New York. Ornate cream-colored terra-cotta details are set off by pale pink walls and framed by a heavy copper cornice.

The shed is the only surviving single-span, arched train shed in the country. It was the largest single-span structure in the world when completed. Trains stopped using the shed after the commuter rail tunnel was completed in 1984. To preserve this important engineering landmark, the shed was incorporated into the design of the Convention Center. The Ballroom, meeting rooms and Grand Hall are located on several levels under a spectacular skylight in the shed roof.

281 E PR

Parkside Houses, *1890–1900*
4100–4400 Parkside Avenue

When the temporary hotels that lined Parkside Avenue to house visitors to the 1876 Centennial Exposition were removed, brewery founder Frederick Poth and other builders of German decent saw an opportunity for new real estate development. The large amount of available land allowed the development of elaborate houses and apartment buildings in a Flemish-revival style that is unique in Philadelphia.

Poth and other developers employed the most fashionable architects of the time. Although the buildings look as if they were built as enormous mansions, most were apartments. Frederick Newman designed 14 four-story double houses of Pompeian brick trimmed with copper and terra cotta. H.W.

Flower designed a similar row of houses west of 42nd Street. The Brentwood (1897), the masterpiece of the area, is attributed to Angus Wade. It consists of three doublewide houses with elaborate gables linked together by an ornate terra cotta porch.

One exception to the common style is the Lansdowne (4100), designed by J.C. Worthington. Its limestone facade, with minarets and pressed tin cornice, stands out against the heavy Germanic character of the area.

The Parkside houses have been lovingly restored over a period of 25 years by the Parkside Historic Preservation Corporation.

282 L

Mount Sinai Cemetery Chapel, *1891–92*
Bridge St., west of Cottage St.
Furness, Evans and Company

This chapel is one of the most successful small-scale designs of Furness's later career. Furness designed many buildings for the Jewish community, in which he demonstrated a preference for Moorish motifs. The chapel reflects this in the shapes of the window and door openings. The interior is dominated by a massive hammer-beam ceiling similar to Furness's design for the First Unitarian Church.

283 L

Church of the Advocate, *1891–97*
18th and Diamond Sts.
Charles M. Burns

The Church of the Advocate was the high point in the career of Charles Burns, principal architect for the Episcopal church at the end of the 19th century. It was built to serve the growing middle-class neighborhoods of North Philadelphia, much like the Church of the Gesu, a few blocks away. The church was made possible by gifts of the South family in honor of George W. South, a merchant and public official.

284

285

The church is a wonderful interpretation of French Gothic design. Certain features recall the Cathedral of Amiens, such as the soaring spire on the roof at the juncture of the nave and transepts, the flying buttresses and the treatment of the chancel. The interior is richly ornamented, with beautiful stained-glass windows and fine stone carvings. The nave conveys the monumental dignity of European cathedrals through the use of stone vaulting for the ceiling, a feature rarely found in American churches.

Beginning with the ministry of Rev. Paul Washington in 1962, the church became an important center of civil rights activism, serving as the site of numerous landmark events. This civil rights interest was extended to women in the priesthood when, in 1974, the Church ordained 11 women into the Episcopal Church.

The church also contains contemporary wall murals that dramatically depict key events in the civil rights movement and related Bible passages.

---

284 G

Cummings House, *1892*
240 West Tulpehocken St.
Frank Miles Day

Harry Cummings, a grain merchant and feed dealer, lived in suburban Germantown. His house was built at a time when architects comfortably combined different European styles into an eclectic composition.

Day was particularly adept at this approach. For this house he combined three different sources. The decorative details on the balcony are Italian, as are the sculptured cherubs and open loggia above the port cochere. Germanic influences are present in the steep slope of the roof, which was originally red tile, and in its generous eaves, tile-covered dormers and once tall chimneys. The semicircular portico recalls Roman designs. None of these styles predominates, however, and the result is a balanced com-

position that looks familiar but is fresh and sophisticated. Day was also creative in his use of color. The pink tint of the stucco walls is offset by buff-colored Pompeian brick that outlines the windows and forms the water table around the house and the quoins at the corners.

---

285 L

Divine Lorraine, *1892–94*
Broad St. and Fairmount Ave.
Willis Hale

In the late 19th century North Broad Street was a popular residential area lined with mansions and elaborate Victorian townhouses. It was the appropriate location for an opulent apartment building. The Lorraine offered hotel-type apartment suites with sitting rooms and private baths. Meals were prepared and delivered from a central kitchen. It continued to offer luxurious service after it became a hotel in 1900.

The Lorraine was one of the most luxurious apartment buildings of its era. The 10-story building is an early example of steel frame fireproof construction. The frame is covered with gray-tan Pompeian brick and with details in the French Renaissance Revival style. The main facade is enriched by stacked bay windows seven floors high that provided light to the apartment sitting rooms. Two monumental arches unite the north and south wings, which are divided by a central light well. Both north and south wings are capped by steep gable roofs and pedimented temple fronts. The top floors contained an auditorium and dining room.

The name was changed to the Divine Lorraine when Father Divine's Peace Mission movement purchased it in 1948. The building served as the organization's headquarters as well as a hotel, the first racially integrated first-class hotel in the city. The Peace Mission movement maintained the Divine Lorraine's historic character until it sold the building in 2003.

▼
1894
Statue of William Penn installed on City Hall tower

▼
1894
Broad Street paved with asphalt

287

288

286   C
Joseph Leidy House and Office, *1893–94*
1319 Locust St.
Wilson Eyre

See photograph on page 88.

The Leidy House was designed three years after its neighbor, the Moore House *(see page 88)*, for an antiquarian who was interested in early American history. It is an early urban example of the Georgian Revival style carried out in an imaginative, rather than historically correct, manner.

Such Georgian details as the blocks of stone that surround the arched windows and door are large and overscaled. The walls are brick with brownstone window trim of the Victorian era, rather than the colonial palette of brick and light stone. The prominent gable, with its steep pitch, and the bay windows recall medieval rather than Georgian precedents.

Eyre was a fine draftsman, and his drawings of this and the Moore house were displayed at the Columbian Exposition in Chicago in 1893.

287   L   PR
Overbrook Farms, *1893*
Overbrook Ave. and Drexel Rd., between 59th and 66th Sts.
Frank and William Price, Boyd and Boyd, Thomas Lonsdale, Horace Trumbauer, Addison Hutton, et al.

Overbrook Farms is a delightful example of a planned Victorian community. Wendell and Smith, the developers, hired a number of young architects to prepare sketches of houses according to prescribed guidelines. A few model homes were erected also. Potential residents could select the design they preferred or mix features from several samples.

The houses provide a fair sampling of turn-of-the-century eclecticism; Queen Anne, Georgian Revival, Arts and Crafts, Shingle and Italianate styles are represented. Thomas Lonsdale designed Our Lady of Lourdes Cathedral, at the center of the development, as well as 5871 Drexel Road. Charles Barton Keen and his partner, Frank Mead, designed the twin house at 6380–84 Overbrook Avenue. Addison Hutton designed the Presbyterian church at Lancaster and City Line avenues. William Price, working alone and with his brother Frank, is probably best represented. His own house, at 6323 Sherwood Avenue, served as one of the original model homes.

288   A   OP
The Bourse, *1893–95*
11 South 5th St.
G. W. and W. D. Hewitt
Renovated 1982, H2L2

The Bourse, an impressive testimony to the city's industrial and financial community, was developed by George Bartol, a local businessman. It originally accommodated a variety of financial institutions, including the Maritime Exchange and the Stock Exchange, as well as grain-trading activities. Modeled after European bourses, it was at the time the only institution of its kind.

The block-long building is steel-frame construction with bowed steel trusses spanning the trading floor. The exterior is clad with red sandstone and Pompeian brick. Giant columns and piers define the entrances on Fifth and Fourth streets. The facade is enlivened with terra-cotta decoration and topped by a large cornice.

The trading floor was a two-story skylight interior court. The court was formed by eight stories of offices.

After the stock exchange moved and the financial district relocated to the City Hall area, the Bourse declined. In 1982 it was extensively renovated to create a three-level retail shopping mall with offices above. The original skylight at the second-floor level was

▼
1895
Free Library opens;
Penn Relays begin

▼
1896
W. E. B. Du Bois writes
The Philadelphia
Negro

289

290

removed and replaced by a new structure at the top of the interior court. Ornate plasterwork, iron and brass fittings and colored floor tiles were restored. A modern glass curtain wall sheathes the offices overlooking the interior space.

289   F,K   OP

University Museum, *1893–1926 /1969–71*
3320 South St.
Wlson Eyre, Frank Miles Day and brother, Cope and Stewardson; *Addition 1969–71,* Mitchell / Giurgola Associates; Mainwaring Wing, *2003* Atkin Olshin Lawson-Bell Architects

In 1886 the city gave the University of Pennsylvania 12 acres to build a museum to house the rapidly expanding department of archaeology. Three local firms collaborated on the design, which was generally under the direction of Eyre.

The museum is a brilliant example of the 19th-century eclectic tradition: many historical styles are combined in a unified and original composition. A Japanese gate forms the entrance to an intimately scaled courtyard, created by the main building and wings of the museum. The monumental arched entrance has a stone hood supported by figures carved by Alexander Milne Calder. A prominent rotunda dominates the otherwise horizontal tile-covered roofs of the main building. Eyre's interest in Arts and Crafts design is reflected in the brickwork, laid in an unusually thick mortar bed, coarsened with pebbles to achieve a handmade character. White and colored marble, colored brick and varying brick patterns enrich the wall surface; the eaves of the main building are decorated with mosaics.

The interior of the building contains galleries for the museum's outstanding collection and includes an enormous single room in the rotunda, which is lit by arched clerestory windows. Because the museum

was never completed, interior circulation was awkward until the addition of a new wing, designed by Mitchell / Giurgola. The new wing blends with the red brick and tile-roofed exterior of the original building, but on the interior, glass and reinforced concrete are clearly expressed in a successful juxtaposition of old and new styles.

A second wing was added by Atkin Olshin Lawson-Bell for the ethnographic collections and seminar and office space. The east facade, protecting the collections, is clad in limestone with a bronze panel rain-screen. The west facade is brick and limestone similar to the original building, but has large windows providing views of the courtyard from the seminar rooms and offices.

290   F,K   PR

Men's Dormitories, *1895–1902*
Spruce St. between 36th and 38th Sts.
Cope and Stewardson
Renovated 1983–1987, Davis Brody and Associates; *1999–2002,* John Milner Architects, Ewing Cole Cherry Brott

American universities grew rapidly at the end of the 19th century. To accommodate new students, the University of Pennsylvania commissioned a new dormitory, stipulating that it be designed so that it could be built in stages and still look complete. The dormitories were inspired by the residential colleges of English universities. They are an outstanding example of the Jacobean Revival style, which was derived from English architecture in a transitional phase from medieval to classical forms.

The dormitories have a rambling, informal plan organized around a series of courtyards of different sizes, which are connected to one another by archways. The most prominent of these is the tower entrance at 39th and Spruce streets, built in 1901 in honor of the men who served in the Spanish-American War. The buildings are made of hard-burnt

▼
1897
Fairmount Park
trolleys in service

▼
1898
Delaware River mined
to keep out Spanish
navy

▼
1899
Philadelphia
Electric Co. created

293

294

brick laid in Flemish bond and offset by
Indiana limestone. Gargoyles, gables and bay
windows of a medieval style embellish the
buildings, which also contain classical balustrades, quoins and Palladian windows. Stone
sculptures in the second-floor string course
contain whimsical features, such as a monkey
with a diploma.

291 C

Crozer Building, *1896–98*
1420 Chestnut St.
Frank Miles Day

The Crozer Building was built for the
American Baptist Publication Society and
named after one of its principal benefac-
tors. It is an interesting contrast to its
neighbor, the Land Title Building. Although
the building has a modern steel structural
frame, the exterior is derived from French
and Italian sources. It is made of Pompeian
brick and terra-cotta, with heavily decorated
window frames reminiscent of Renaissance
townhouses. The top of the building, which
looks like a French chateau, was deliberately
designed to make looking up worthwhile.
Steep pitched roofs, chimneys, and giant
multistory dormer windows, with pilasters
and statues tucked into niches, are combined
to make a fascinating composition.

292 L OP

Fell-Van Rensselaer House, *1896–98*
1801–3 Walnut St.
Peabody and Stearns

Rittenhouse Square was once surrounded
by elegant mansions, many owned by the
Drexel family. Sara Drexel Fell, a widow,
built this mansion for Alexander Van Rensselaer of New York, who married her shortly
thereafter.
    The architects were Peabody and Stearns,
a Boston firm whose clients were the social
elite of Boston, Newport and Philadelphia.

The mansion, considered to be one of the
finest examples of Beaux-Arts design in the
country, is characterized by such French
motifs as paired columns, ornamental crests,
projecting bays and grand staircases. The
slightly overdone effect was both desired and
admired at the time.
    The interior was sumptuous, but all that
remains is the stained-glass skylit dome
over the central hall and the Doges Room,
in which Mrs. Van Rensselaer covered the
ceiling with portrait medallions of the popes.
The family lived in the mansion until 1942,
after which it went through a succession of
owners before being converted to a retail
store.

293 H

Nugent Home for Baptists, *1896*
221 West Johnson Street
J. Franklin Stuckert

George Nugent, a wealthy manufacturer,
lived in Mt. Airy and was dedicated to the
Baptist church in Philadelphia. At his death
he left half a million dollars for the construction of a retirement home for Baptist
ministers and elderly parishioners.
    Designed by Stuckert, a well-respected
architect of many churches, synagogues
and other religious buildings, the Nugent's
high Chateaux style and palatial size fulfilled
Nugent's desire for an architectural monument for the Baptist community. This is
one of the few examples of this style in the
Philadelphia area. The steeply pitched terra
cotta tile roof is articulated with dormers
and chimneys, and terra cotta details are set
against a brown-orange Roman brick.
    Adjacent to the Nugent Home, music
publisher Theodore Presser created another
retirement home, this one for retired music
teachers. The three-story gray brick and
limestone Renaissance Revival building was
designed by The Davis Bothers in 1913–14.

▼
1900
*Philadelphia
Orchestra founded*

▼
1901
*Mummers Parade
moved to Broad
Street*

296

297

294 L

Overbrook School for the Blind, *1897–1900*
64th St. and Malvern Ave.
Walter Cope

Philadelphia's first school for the blind was
established in 1837. When the school decided
to expand, the director wanted the buildings designed in the California Mission style.
Cope, while honeymooning in Spain the previous year, had sketched many buildings.

The Overbrook School was one of the
first successful adaptations of the Spanish
Renaissance style in the United States. It is
more informal than the Italian or French
Renaissance styles because of the use of
stucco instead of stone and the use of strong,
contrasting colors.

The entrance is dominated by a pair
of bold towers, behind which is a shallow
dome buttressed by conically shaped supports. The building was planned with two
cloisters flanking the central administration
building—one for the female dormitory,
the other for the male—to facilitate use
by the blind. The picturesque massing of
the complex is best seen from the cloister
courtyard, where the stepped, red tile roofs
descend abruptly to the serenity of the
arcaded cloister.

295 C,K

Land Title Building, *1897*

See page 98.

296 A

Corn Exchange, *1900–1901*
Second and Chestnut Sts.
Newman, Woodman and Harris

When the city's fashionable residential areas
moved westward, Dock Street became the
center of the wholesale food market. Businesses active in the food market located in
the surrounding area.

The Corn Exchange was established to
serve merchants trading in grain and gro-

ceries. The original building consisted of an
elaborate exchange room and supporting
offices. The clock tower at the corner and
second-floor offices were added later.

The exchange is a brick building based
on the Georgian style of its colonial neighborhood. It is enriched, however, with
elaborate, Baroque stone carvings. This is
particularly apparent on the round windows
above the first floor, which are surrounded
by heavy wreaths and draped with stone
swags. The exchange room has elegant classical pilasters and columns and a handsome
recessed ceiling with skylights, which can be
seen above the renovations made when the
exchange was converted to a bank.

297 A PR

**Tutlemann Brothers and Faggen
Building,** *1830–36 /1900–1901*
56–60 North 2nd St.

The Tutlemann Building, now called Little
Boys Way, may have been the last cast-iron
facade erected in this country. The original
building was a store in the early 19th century,
but over the years additions were made, and
at one point the building housed a manufacturer of buttons and trim. The side that
faces the alley is strictly factory utilitarian;
brick piers alternate with generously sized
windows to maximize light inside. But the
main facade, added in 1900, is a handsome
cast-iron grid, formed by simple but decorative piers and spandrels, similar to late
19th-century commercial architecture
in Chicago. The building was one of the
first renovated for loft apartments when the
renewal of Old City began in the 1970s.

295 C,K

Land Title Building, *1897*
Broad and Chestnut Streets
D. H. Burnham and Co.

The Land Title Building was one of the city's first major structures designed by a non-Philadelphia architect. Daniel Burnham was an early pioneer in the development of modern American architecture. His designs for tall buildings in Chicago were important landmarks in the evolution of the skyscraper and the Commercial style. Burnham also became a leading advocate of the Beaux-Arts movement and the Neoclassical Revival after his work on the 1893 Chicago Exposition.

The Land Title Building, built for the oldest title insurance company in the world, is the finest example of early skyscraper design in Philadelphia and the earliest east-coast example of this style by a major Chicago architect. It demonstrates Burnham's ability to combine classical elements with a simple expression of steel-frame construction. The sixteen-story structure, faced in buff brick, is divided into three parts. The two-story base, faced with granite, is unified by a rusticated

Ionic arcade; the central portion of the building has alternating strips of projecting and flat windows, typical of the Chicago Commercial style. The continuous vertical piers, terminating in arches at the top, express the steel frame and were standard devices used to emphasize the building's height. The top is treated as a separate unit, with a prominent overhanging roof and elaborate cornice.

Although built as a speculative office building, the interiors were finished in expensive materials, including marble and hardwood floors and marble wainscoting in the corridors. By setting the tower back from the base on the south side, Burnham created a well to ensure light and ventilation for the office floors. In 1902 a second office tower was added to the south, designed by Burnham with Horace Trumbauer. This building is taller, has a flatter facade and more overtly classical ornamentation.

▼
1902
*Horn and Hardart's
opens first automat
restaurant*

▼
1903
*First heavier than
air aircraft flight by
Wright Brothers*

298

299

---

298 H PR
Oaks Cloister, *1900*
6500 Wissahickon Avenue
Joseph Huston

Joseph Huston began his architectural career in the office of Frank Furness. However, Huston's architectural style and interest in incorporating art in his buildings were formed at Princeton University where his friends included the sculptor Alexander Sterling Calder and painter Edward Redfield.

Huston built this 20-room mansion as his home and studio, and as a place to test architectural ideas that would find their way into his most important work, the Pennsylvania State Capitol Building. Many of the artists Huston commissioned for the State Capitol also did work for his home.

Behind the modest exterior, an eclectic blend of English Tudor and Craftsman influences, are some of the most highly decorated interiors of any house in the city. The sitting room on the main floor has gilded ornament and a carved boar hunt fireplace cast by Calder. The adjacent dining room has plaster friezes and ornamental ceiling work. The stairway to the second floor contains a rare, leather-embossed gilded mural. The most elaborate room in the house is the ballroom on the lower floor reached by a curved stairway. It contains a 15th century carved caen stone fireplace with four gold leaf panels; a niche on an adjacent wall is covered with amber glass tiles gilded with silver leaf. It contained the statue *Venus in the Waves* by George Gray Barnard. The gilded and polychrome-coffered ceiling required 25,000 sheets of gold leaf when the house was restored by the current owners in 2006. A stone-arched loggia leads from the ballroom to Huston's studio.

299 L PR
St. James Apartment House, *1900–1904*
1226–32 Walnut St.
Horace Trumbauer

At the turn of the century, most Philadelphians lived in individual homes. The elegant apartment buildings built in the fashionable neighborhoods along Broad Street and surrounding Rittenhouse Square, however, attracted many wealthy families. Their style was eclectic, influenced by the Beaux-Arts movement and the neoclassical revival popular at the time. The St. James was typical. More substantial than some, it offered restaurants and other services specifically designed to draw wealthy tenants. Horace Trumbauer's ability to combine several architectural styles on a grand scale can be seen in the combination of such Second Empire motifs as the enormous mansard roof and the classical details of overscaled, voluted brackets supporting the balconies at the third and seventh floors.

This building firmly established Trumbauer's career as architect to the well-to-do families of Philadelphia.

335
Philadelphia Saving Fund Society
See pages 126–127

3

The Urban Metropolis

1902—1999

The Urban Metropolis

Philadelphia entered the 20th century a major manufacturing center and the third largest city in the country. During the early decades of the century, continued economic prosperity attracted large numbers of foreign immigrants. New mass transportation systems, automobiles and an abundance of undeveloped land allowed the city to continue the outward expansion begun in the late 19th century. But, after 1940, many of these same factors contributed to the city's problems. Manufacturing industries declined, went out of business or moved to different areas of the country as part of a national shift of economic activities away from older, northern cities to the South and West. By midcentury such large manufacturing companies as Baldwin Locomotive, Disston Tools, Stetson Hats and the Cramp Shipyard were gone. After 1960 the population of the city began to decline. More significantly, the composition of the population shifted dramatically. More and more of the city's residents were black, reaching close to 40 percent of the population by 1980, and a large portion of that population was poor.

Between 1900 and 1920 the city's population increased from approximately 1,300,000 to 1,800,000. Most of the new immigrants were poor and unskilled Poles, Eastern European Jews, and Italians, who initially located in South Philadelphia. Although many of the Italian families remained, most of the others dispersed throughout the city, usually to neighborhoods of a similar ethnic background. As foreign immigration declined after World War I, black migration from the South began to increase; between 1900 and 1920, the black population doubled.

European and black immigrants were both attracted by economic opportunities. Manufacturing industries were large and extremely diverse; the port was still one of the country's largest, and the construction of substantial civic projects required many laborers and masons. As in the past, most working people lived within walking distance of their jobs, but by the 1920s the vast majority worked in large groups, in contrast to the many small independent businesses that characterized much of 18th- and 19th-century employment.

As new immigrants moved into older neighborhoods close to their jobs, middle-class residents moved steadily outward. Beginning in 1907, subway-elevated lines, supplementing electric trolleys and the commuter railroads, opened up new sections of the city. After the completion of the Market Street subway-elevated from 69th Street to downtown, the area west of 50th Street was transformed from farmland to substantial neighborhoods, doubling the population of West Philadelphia. The Frankford elevated opened up the near northeast; the north Broad Street subway shifted the direction of growth from Ridge Avenue to neighborhoods like Olney and Logan. More than 100,000 houses were built along these transporta-

Peter Behrens was an important turn-of-the-century German architect. His buildings represent a transition between 19th-century historical styles and the unornamented style of 20th-century architecture. This oak chair was designed by Behrens in 1902. Its simple shape is in sharp contrast to 19th-century furniture; the curved lines of the back and legs suggest an Art Nouveau influence.

After 1912, the stiff formal dresses of the Victorian era were replaced by designs that had a simpler silhouette and were made of softer, looser materials. This ivory cut-and-uncut velvet dress is trimmed with beading, lace, silk and velvet flowers. The deep-cut neckline was very controversial at the time.

tion routes in the 1920s. In contrast to the older areas, these new neighborhoods were exclusively residential, with no factories in their midst; residents commuted to their jobs, many of which were located downtown.

In the 19th century, downtown Philadelphia had become increasingly commercial. By the early 20th century only the Rittenhouse Square area remained a stable residential neighborhood. Offices and banks began to cluster in the area adjacent to the new City Hall and railroad terminals. Retail shopping extended from Wanamaker's to Lit Brothers; the wholesale food markets dominated the area around Dock Street. The concentration of employment brought thousands of people into downtown each day. Trolleys and a growing number of cars and trucks caused great congestion. Between 1918 and 1930 the number of cars in the city increased from 100,000 to 250,000. So great was the congestion around City Hall that a traffic signal was installed on the tower. New roads and bridges were overlaid on the grid of narrow streets; the Roosevelt Boulevard increased access to the northeast, the Benjamin Franklin Parkway led to the northwest and the completion of the first bridge across the Delaware River, in 1926, provided access from New Jersey.

Congestion and chaos were characteristic of most major cities and led to an expression of concern at a national level. The first city planning conferences were held before 1910, and the idea of zoning controls were introduced. Most cities wanted to have the spacious character and gleaming white classical appearance of the 1893 Chicago Exposition. The resulting City Beautiful movement swept the country. In Philadelphia, this led to the creation of the Benjamin Franklin Parkway, modeled after the Champs-Élysées, and the construction of prominent neoclassical buildings to house major cultural institutions.

Growth of the City

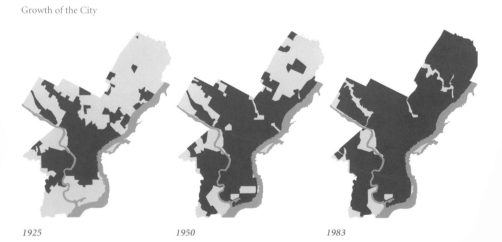

1925   1950   1983

Joseph Hoffman also was an important transitional architect, whose work in Austria influenced the development of the International style. This very simple frame chair of lacquered beech and leather, designed in 1907, anticipates the stripped-down functional style that would dominate furniture design later in the century. Hoffman's design also shows an Art Nouveau influence in its gentle curves and the decorative balls on the arms and legs.

Short skirts became the fashion in women's dress in 1925. The flapper style featured a flat, bustless design, low waistlines and skirts at knee length. This sleeveless dress from 1925 was very fashion-able; it is made of ma-nta silk georgette and amed with beads.

Architectural styles were influenced by the exposition and by American architects who studied at the École des Beaux-Arts in Paris. A revival of historical styles became very popular, ranging from Greek and Roman for civic buildings to Gothic for collegiate buildings and early skyscrapers. Residential design was modeled after picturesque English, French and Italian country houses seen by American architects traveling in Europe. New houses, particularly in Chestnut Hill, used local stone, pitched roofs and simple forms to create a handsome, pastoral residential style unique to Philadelphia.

The residential building boom of the 1920s was accompanied by a similar boom in commercial development. Tall office buildings, banks, hotels and apartment buildings transformed the city skyline. Conservative Philadelphia lagged behind New York and Chicago in the development of skyscrapers. But from 1928 to 1932, many tall buildings were constructed. They were designed in a variety of styles, indicating the transitional nature of the period. Foremost among these was the PSFS building, the first International style skyscraper in the country.

By 1930 the city's population had grown to nearly 2,000,000, where it would generally remain for the next 40 years. The Depression brought the building boom to an end. Fifty banks in the city failed, but Philadelphia fared better overall than many other places due to the diversity of its industry. The troubled times made people eager for entertainment. Lavish movie theaters were constructed and eight radio stations were established. The Depression made people more conscious of their jobs, leading to the rise of labor unions. The Depression also encouraged the city to turn attention to the housing problems of the poor. Even before federal programs began, Philadelphia organizations sponsored housing for low- and moderate-income families. When the U.S. Housing Authority was created, the city responded promptly, completing its first project in 1937. But changing administrations and conservative mayors had mixed feelings about continuing such programs.

In 1940 the city covered 90 square miles, stretching south to Oregon Avenue, west to 69th Street, north to Olney Avenue, northeast to Cottman Avenue and northwest through Manayunk, Germantown and Chestnut Hill. Two- and three-story row homes predominated, extending block after block in all directions. The decline of manufacturing during the Depression created major financial problems and high unemployment, which only came to an end with World War II. Private industries, the Navy Yard and the Frankford Arsenal operated at capacity, producing tanks, ships, arms, textiles and other products for the war effort. This revitalization of industry, combined with the large percentage of the male population in the armed forces, created a labor shortage.

Although many jobs were filled by women, immigrants were drawn to the city from rural areas of the country, contributing to an increase in the black population, which continued during the following decades.

During the war years many civic leaders expressed concern about the physical condition of the city. In spite of the new buildings of the late 1920s and early 30s, downtown Philadelphia had a Victorian appearance. The 18th-century neighborhoods east of Sixth Street were the city's worst slums. Civic leaders were also concerned about political corruption in the city government. The many reform efforts finally succeeded with the adoption of a new city charter in 1951, and with the election of new political leadership, which took the improvement of the city's physical environment as one of its major objectives.

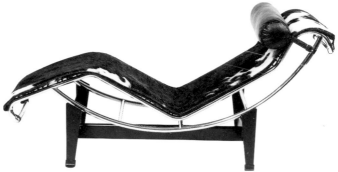

Tubular chrome furniture was a distinguishing characteristic of the International style in Europe in the 1920s. This elegant chaise longue by the French architect Le Corbusier has a lacquered steel base, curved chrome-plated steel supports and ponyskin upholstery. It is as much a piece of sculpture as it is furniture.

At this time the city began to experience a dramatic shift in its economic character. Manufacturing industries declined, went out of business or moved to other sections of the country. Factories closed in the older neighborhoods, leaving downtown as the principal center of employment. The new city government placed a strong emphasis on downtown renewal and revitalization. A major exhibit in 1947 outlined ideas that were later formalized in the 1960 Comprehensive Plan and 1963 Plan for Center City. Many buildings were demolished to provide opportunities for new construction. A very ambitious program was begun to redevelop Society Hill. In an effort to attract affluent residents back to the city, virtually all the buildings in the 18th-century area east of Fifth Street were publicly acquired. At the same time, the federal government began to restore Independence Hall and related historic structures of national importance, creating the Independence National Historical Park. The rehabilitation of these buildings and the recreation of the historic residential character of Society Hill transformed the area into an affluent neighborhood but resulted in the displacement of many black residents, who had lived there for decades. The demolition of the Broad Street Station to create the Penn Center office complex was an equally ambitious undertaking. Other renewal projects were initiated in North and West Philadelphia to remove deteriorated housing and provide new housing for low- and moderate-income families.

Olaf Skoogfors designed this silver teapot in 1956 on the principle that the design of objects should directly reflect their function. Its handsome proportions and delicate craftsmanship are typical of fine contemporary silverwork.

The Barcelona chair, designed by Ludwig Mies van der Rohe in 1929, is one of the most famous and popular pieces of contemporary furniture. It is a fine example of International style design. The chair consists of stainless-steel supports and leather cushions minimally decorated with a grid of seams.

Philadelphia was a national leader in the urban renewal movement, and its projects influenced development in many other cities.

These efforts resulted in the first major construction in the city since the 1930s. Most architecture of the 1950s was based on the principles of the International style. Buildings had little ornamentation but were simple, direct expressions of their structural system. Modern glass, curtain-wall office buildings transformed the area west of City Hall.

In 1950 the city's population was still around 2,000,000, but the population of the suburban areas was 1,500,000 and growing at a more rapid rate. By 1960 it would exceed that of the city. This rapid regional growth was fostered by government-supported mortgage financing for veterans and middle-class families, combined with an ambitious highway progam that allowed easy access to the suburbs. Middle-class families moved outward as they had done since the early 19th century. In Philadelphia this led to the rapid development of huge tracts of land in the northeast section of the city, which attracted many residents from older ethnic neighborhoods, particularly South Philadelphia. As people moved to suburban areas or the outer parts of the city, the growing black population moved into the older neighborhoods. Most of West and North Philadelphia were black by the 1960s, as well as portions of South Philadelphia and Germantown.

Although the city had established a successful downtown revitalization program that continues to the present day, it was not until the federal government created the Model Cities program in the late 1960s that serious attention was given to the deteriorating conditions in older neighborhoods of North and West Philadelphia. These areas had many vacant factories and thousands of abandoned houses. Many were demolished, leaving vast undeveloped vacant lots. Despite the fact that new rental housing was built and many rehabilitation programs were launched in the 1970s, the dilapidated character of most of these neighborhoods remained relatively unchanged.

Philadelphia's leadership in urban renewal and restoration attracted many architects to the city, including several whose work has had international impact. By the 1960s, American architects were beginning to question the simple plain forms of the Modern style. Although most buildings continued to be designed in this manner, Philadelphia was the center of new and divergent ideas, particularly through the writing and teaching of Louis I. Kahn and Robert Venturi. Kahn emphasized heavy masonry construction; Venturi gave attention to popular influences. Both reintroduced historical influences in their work. By the late 1970s the desire for a richer, more ornate form of expression had given rise to a post-Modern movement.

The total absence of ornament is as much a characteristic of modern furniture as of buildings. This waste receptacle by Paul Mayen, from the 1960s, is typical of the simple, abstract industrial quality of many objects designed for offices and public buildings.

Post-modern furniture, like architecture, incorporates references to historic styles without creating reproductions. This molded laminated plywood chair, by Robert Venturi, applies the painted image of the Sheraton style to an industrially produced object.

Throughout the last decades of the century, the population and economic trends that began in the 1960s continued to influence Philadelphia. Population in 1990 declined to 1,585,557—less than the population in 1920—and would continue to decline through the rest of the century while the suburban population increased to over 3,650,000. For the first time in its history, Philadelphia contained fewer jobs than the surrounding region. Population decline was accompanied by a demographic change as well. Although the black population remained relatively constant, from the 1980s on the city experienced an influx of Southeast Asian immigrants and growth of the Hispanic community. By the end of the century, the three "minority" groups would constitute the majority of the population of the city. A large portion of this minority population was poor and lacked the education necessary to adapt to the change from a manufacturing to a service economy. Homelessness appeared as a more dramatic urban phenomenon than it had in the past while at the same time large sections of the inner city were characterized by vacant and deteriorated houses.

Downtown Philadelphia reflected many of these trends in spite of successful urban renewal efforts that had revitalized the residential neighborhood of Society Hill and created a new retail complex along Market Street. The construction of four new office buildings between 1985 and 1991 exceeding the traditional height limit of City Hall tower changed the skyline and created a new sense of optimism. But the growth of office development projected by the City's 1988 Center City Plan didn't materialize and the city looked in other directions for economic expansion.

During the administration of Mayor Edward Rendell (1992–2000), the groundwork was laid for an increased focus on tourism and many new projects were begun that would come to fruition in the next century. The Central Philadelphia Development Corporation revived the proposal for a cultural district along South Broad Street; under Mayor Rendell's leadership $200 million was raised for its centerpiece, a new performing arts center. The completion of the Pennsylvania Convention Center led to new hotels. The National Park Service proposed the rebuilding of Independence Mall and the creation of new visitor attractions, including the National Constitution Center. These initiatives were joined by the passage of a 10-year tax abatement program for conversion of older office buildings, now substantially vacant as a result of the new high-rise towers, to residential use. On the hopes of these plans, Philadelphia, no longer a "greene country town" but a sprawling, complex social and economic environment, struggled to find its way into the 21st century.

Glossary of
Architectural Terms

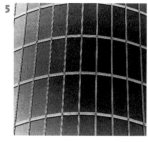

1 atrium
a large interior space, usually extending the height of a building and covered with a skylight

2 cantilever
a beam or other projection that is unsupported at its projecting end

3 chevron
an ornamental zigzag pattern of molding, found on Art Deco–style buildings

4 Chicago window
a wide window, often a projecting bay, with a fixed central glass panel and two smaller double-hung side windows

5 curtain wall
a nonstructural exterior wall, usually of glass, steel or aluminum, that is hung on the frame of a building

6 formwork
wood or metal forms into which concrete is poured for walls or columns; after the formwork is removed, the concrete is imprinted with its patterns and textures

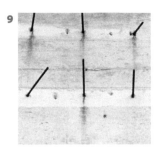

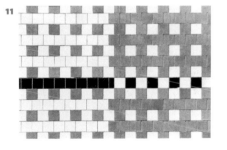

7 glass block
glass that has been poured into structural blocks

8 precast concrete
concrete columns, beams or panels that are poured and cast in molds in a factory

9 reinforced concrete
a structural system in which steel rods are placed in the formwork before the concrete is poured to add strength

10 Sculptural panels were a common feature on the facades of important buildings in the 1920s and 30s.

11 The use of color and decorative patterns is characteristic of many buildings designed in the post-Modern manner.

▼
1902
Philadelphia Athletics
win American league
penant

301

302

---

301 C,K OP
The Bellevue Stratford Hotel, *1902–13*
Broad and Walnut Sts.
G. W. and W. D. Hewitt
Remodeled 1980, 1989, Day and
Zimmermann Associates / Vitetta Group
with RTKL Architects
The Bellevue

George Boldt, the son of a German immigrant, founded the Bellevue Stratford. He began his career as a dishwasher in New York, then moved to Philadelphia to become a headwaiter at the elite Philadelphia Club. When he opened the Bellevue Stratford in 1904, it immediately became one of the leading hotels of the world. Its amenities included Turkish and Swedish baths, a library, two in-house orchestras, three ballrooms and an outdoor rose garden on the roof. Rooms were decorated in Colonial, French, Italian and Greek styles.

Although the building was constructed of steel in the most modern method, the exterior was inspired by the sophisticated architectural style of the French Renaissance. The picturesque roofline consists of a slate-covered mansard roof with large overscaled dormers and chimneys. The main portion of the hotel is sheathed in terra-cotta, and the base is of rusticated stone. The Broad Street facade is enlivened by windows that are alternately flat and projecting, similar to Burnham's treatment of the Land Title Building.

The hotel closed in 1977 after an outbreak of Legionnaires disease among guests. A 1980 renovation reduced the number of rooms from 1,000 to 545, but this proved too large for the city's needs. A second renovation reduced the hotel to 165 rooms organized around a central atrium extending from the 12th to 19th floors. The original ballroom and Rose Garden were preserved and the remainder of the building converted to offices and retail stores.

302 F
Franklin Field, *1902–4 /1913 /1922*
33rd and South Sts.
Frank Miles Day and brother

At the end of the 19th century, collegiate athletic departments began to serve all of the students and not just a few select varsity men. In response to this, the University of Pennsylvania decided to build a new gymnasium and a stadium for spectator sports. Day had worked on a number of collegiate buildings. He was supervising architect for Yale, Penn State and the University of Colorado, and designed several important buildings at Princeton.

The gymnasium closes off the open end of the horseshoe-shaped stadium, which was added in 1913 and enlarged in 1922. Both buildings are designed in the Collegiate Gothic style. Brick, laid in a Flemish bond with limestone trim, and battlements along the roofline help to unify the gymnasium and stadium into a single complex.

---

303 C,K OP
John Wanamaker's Department Store,
1902–11
1300 Market St.
D. H. Burnham and Co. with John T. Windrim
The Wanamaker Building
Renovated 1991, Ewing Cole Cherry Brott

John Wanamaker began selling ready-made clothing in 1861. By the time he moved his store to 13th and Market streets, it had become a full-fledged department store, one of the first in the country.

When Wanamaker decided to construct a new store on the same site, he also wanted the existing store to remain in operation. As a result, the building was constructed in three stages, which required considerable care to make sure that the joining of the stages was invisible. As the first phase of construction was completed, the settlement

▼
04
∘o automobiles reg-
stered in the city

▼
1905
Rev. Charles Tindley
composes "Stand By
Me"

303

305

of the building was measured and used to determine the design of the next addition.

The exterior has little ornament or detail; it is a simple block, organized in three horizontal divisions much like Burnham's design of the Land Title Building. The handsome granite and limestone facade is an adaptation of the Renaissance palace, greatly enlarged in scale. Inside, the selling floors are organized around a spectacular central court that rises five floors. It is the most impressive interior space in any commercial building in the city and contains the Wanamaker Organ, the second largest operational pipe organ in the world.

When a department store could no longer fill the entire building, the upper floors were converted to office space with the introduction of an interior atrium and generous courtyard facing the restored Crystal Tea Room. The lower floors remain a department store. With 1.5 million square feet of usable space, Wanamaker's is the largest building in the city.

---

304 G,K PR
3500 Powelton Ave., *1902–8*
Willis Hale and Milligan and Webber
The Courts
Renovated 1998

Real-estate development in West Philadelphia prospered after the introduction of the electric streetcar in the 1890s. Frederick Poth, a wealthy brewer who lived in the area, started this block as a row of speculative houses. He sold the uncompleted project to a new owner, who converted the houses to apartments. Milligan and Webber ingeniously filled in the spaces between the houses with stair towers, which are marked on the exterior by the double-story granite arches. They unified the block by placing a tower in the middle to create an appearance of planned symmetry.

The buildings are made of buff-colored brick and originally had copper sheathing on the bay windows.

---

305 C
Jacob Reed's Sons Store, *1903–4*
1424–26 Chestnut St.
Price and McLanahan

At a time when department stores were emphasizing ready-made clothing, Jacob Reed's Sons prided itself on custom services and personalized care. This attitude was reflected in its finely detailed building.

Price's later work was influenced by the Arts and Crafts movement and his interest in the use of reinforced concrete. For the Reed store, he drew on the urban palaces of northern Italy. The facade has a loggia on the top floor, a high arched entranceway and is topped with a red tile roof. But the details show his Arts and Crafts interests in the dark brown brick set in thick mortar and the handmade Mercer tiles under the eaves and soffit, which depict crafts related to the garment industry.

The store was one of the first commercial uses of reinforced concrete in the city. Concrete columns, with Mercer tile in the capitals, support a high concrete barrel vault over the central sales space, which is flanked by two side aisles. Clerestory windows between the columns were lit from behind to give the illusion of a freestanding building.

THE NEOCLASSICAL REVIVAL

The popularity of the Beaux-Arts movement, after the 1893 Columbian Exposition in Chicago, prompted a revival of classical styles that lasted into the 1920s. Unlike previous historical styles, which were derived from Englis or European movements, this was solely an American phenomenon. Most cities tried to reproduce the clear, classical images of the exposition. So many large public building

▼
1905
First radio
broadcast in city

▼
1907
Market Street Subway
opens; Henry Ford
introduces Model T

▼
1908
Breyer's Ice Cream
Co. founded

306

307

*were created that more marble was used in
the United States in 20 years than had been
used in all of ancient Rome. Many architects
designed neoclassical buildings, but McKim,
Mead and White were the acknowledged
leaders of the movement.*

*Most neoclassical buildings are based
on the Greek orders, but they are larger than
the Greek Revival buildings of the 19th century and less ornate than their Beaux-Arts
predecessors. Stone or marble buildings are
characterized by large, plain wall surfaces,
flat pilasters, pedimented porticos and the
use of single rather than coupled columns.*

---

306 C,K OP

Girard Trust Company, *1905–8*
34–36 South Broad St.
McKim, Mead and White; Furness Evans
and Co.
Ritz-Carlton Hotel
Renovated 2000, Hillier

The 1893 Columbian Exposition in Chicago introduced a revival of neoclassical
design in the United States. The Girard
Trust building is the city's best example of
this neoclassical style. Furness originally
attempted to design the bank in his heavy
Victorian manner. The bank resisted, however, and the final design is a combination
of Furness's plans with detailing by Stan-
ford White, whose firm designed much of
the work at the Chicago Exposition.

The Girard Trust building is a small jewel
surrounded by tall skyscrapers. With its
gleaming white marble walls, handsome
portico and distinctive dome, it has all the
characteristics of a classical temple. Typi-
cally, however, the building used modern
construction techniques, and behind the
marble exterior is a steel-frame structure.
The expansive dome, with skylit oculus in
the center, is constructed of marble tiles
using the technique developed by Rafael
Guastavino. The adjacent office building,

also in white marble, was added in 1923 by
McKim, Mead and White. After the bank
closed, the office building was converted
to hotel and the banking room beautifully
restored as its reception area.

---

307 L

Church of St. Francis de Sales, *1906*
4625 Springfield Ave.
Henry Dagit

As late as 1890 this section of West Philadelphia was farmland. After electric trolleys
were extended west of 42nd Street, the
neighborhood began to grow, and a Catholic church was built to serve the area.

The rock-faced limestone facade of
the church is designed in a Romanesque
manner, with round arched openings. In
contrast, the interior is one of the finest
examples of Byzantine architecture in the
country. It is richly decorated with marble
and yellow, green and white tiles, and dimly
lit by a series of windows that surround
the huge dome. The dome was constructed
in the Guastavino manner, similar to the
Girard Trust building. Layers of terra-
cotta tiles laid along the curve of the vault
allowed a large dome to be built inexpen-
sively.

---

308 J PR

100–102 West Mermaid Lane, *1909*
Wilson Eyre

Dr. George Woodward, the son-in-law
of Henry Howard Houston, continued
Houston's practice of building houses in
Chestnut Hill. He retained many creative
architects to design innovative housing
projects, primarily for rent to moderate-
income families.

Eyre's design for this pair of houses was
strongly influenced by the Arts and Crafts
movement then popular in England. These
English houses covered the entire exterior
wall surface with a smooth, even stucco

1908
Oscar Hammerstein
opens opera house on
N. Broad Street

▼
1908
Walnut Lane Bridge
opens, longest con-
crete arch bridge in
the world

▼
1909
Shibe Park opens, first
modern baseball sta-
dium in America

309

310

finish. Eyre adapted this approach to the
simple shape and fenestration of the Pennsylvania farmhouse and produced houses to
meet functional needs rather than to provide fancy show.

---

309   J   PR

Adelbert Fischer House, *1909*
6904 Wissahickon Ave.
Milton Medary

Adelbert Fischer came to Philadelphia
from Germany to establish a branch of his
father-in-law's machinery company. He
commissioned Medary, a young German
architect just beginning practice, to design
a house based on 1907 books of German
interiors.

The Fischer house is one of the few buildings in the city designed in the Art Nouveau
style. Art Nouveau was popular in Europe
at the turn of the century, but had limited impact in the United States. It was a
decorative style, featuring dynamic forms
and curving lines, and was particularly
influential on interior design and furnishings.

Art Nouveau details visible on the exterior of the Fischer house include the curved
dormer window and the door and window
frames with curved corners. The interior of
the house has a handsome tile floor in the
entry hall and ornate Art Nouveau decoration on the fireplace hoods. In recent years
the period character of the house has been
revived by Robert Venturi and Denise Scott
Brown, with wall stencils and an eclectic
combination of period and contemporary
furnishings.

---

310   L

Packard Motor Car Company, *1910*
317–21 North Broad St.
Albert Kahn
Renovated 1986, Bower Lewis Thrower and
John Milner Associates

In the early 20th century, many motorcar
companies located their offices and show-
rooms on Broad Street, which became
known as "automobile row." The Packard
Motor Car Company's building was
designed by Albert Kahn, an engineer from
Detroit who became one of the country's
foremost designers of industrial buildings.

Kahn's design was one of the earliest
uses of reinforced concrete in a commercial
structure. The concrete columns and beams
are inset with large industrial windows and
covered with decorative terra-cotta panels,
which give the facade a rich appearance.
Additional ornamentation is provided by
the handsome canopy over the entrance and
a prominent overhanging roof. The showroom, remodeled in 1927 by Philip Tyre,
was lavishly designed with a beamed ceiling
and a Spanish tile floor.

---

311   J   PR

Benezet Street Houses, *1910–16*
28–34 Benezet St. and 25–33
Springfield Ave.
Duhring, Okie and Zeigler

Dr. Woodward's residential projects for
middle- and lower-income families often
took the form of grouped houses, of which
the ones on Benezet Street are among the
most innovative.

To achieve economy each unit contains
four houses under one roof. The stucco
houses have spacious living rooms, skylit
stairways, ample front yards and trellised
"drying yards." Woodward built the houses
for rent; they were so popular he had a long
waiting list of lower-income tenants. They
are still owned by the Woodward family.

In addition to the quadruple houses,
Woodward built twin houses on Benezet
Street, which are also fine examples of high
quality and economical design. Each house
has the same plan but different exterior
materials and details.

▼
1913
Congress Hall restored
and rededicated

▼
1914
First Tastykake
packaged

312

313

20TH CENTURY REVIVALS

In the late 19th century American architects reacted against the heavy, ornate forms of the High Victorian period. Several historical styles were revived to restore order and simplicity to building design. Although the Neoclassical Revival was the most popular, the Georgian Revival, Jacobean Revival and Late Gothic Revival all carried over into the 20th century.

The Late Gothic Revival was extremely popular for collegiate buildings and churches, but was also an important influence on the design of such early commercial skyscrapers as the Woolworth Building in New York. The style, based on the English Perpendicular style, placed strong emphasis on the expression of vertical elements. Churches and collegiate buildings were usually of stone, with finely crafted Gothic details. Similar details on skyscrapers were generally executed in terra-cotta.

---

312 D

Robert Morris Hotel, *1914–15 / 1921–22*
1705 Arch St.
Ballinger and Perrot; Ballinger Company

New methods of construction did not deter architects from using historic styles for modern buildings. Gothic was a favorite for skyscrapers. For the Robert Morris Hotel, originally the Wesley Building, Gothic was also consistent with its first use as offices and a hotel for the Methodist church. The building was constructed in two stages; the top eight floors were added six years after completion of the first six. The original cornice, with Gothic tracery, is still visible above the sixth floor.

The facade is an impressive example of the use of terra-cotta as a decorative material. Because it was malleable, terra-cotta could easily duplicate rich details at low cost. The detailing of the facade reflects differences in the internal functions. Broad, basket-handle openings and rich ornament on the ground floor indicate its public use. Large pointed-arch windows on the second floor light an impressively detailed ballroom. The Gothic detailing continues inside the lobby, which has a ribbed, groined vault and a main stairway of marble with carved and gilded railings.

---

313 J PR

High Hollow, *1914*
101 West Hampton Rd.
George Howe

Howe designed High Hollow for himself, based on one of his final projects at the École des Beaux-Arts. It was the first of many beautiful country homes he would design over the next decade.

High Hollow is built of red and dark brown Chestnut Hill ledge stone, obtained from an abandoned quarry reopened especially for Howe. It is beautifully sited on a steep slope overlooking Fairmount Park, with broad terraces linking the house and landscape. The facade is enriched by red brick stringcourses and frames around doors and round-arch windows. Although not based on any specific historic style, a French influence is apparent in the steep pitch of the hipped roof and the corner turret between the main house and service wing.

The interior is organized around a spacious center hall. The principal rooms have glass doors that slide into the masonry wall and give access to balconies with dramatic views of the park.

1916	1917	1918
▼	▼	▼
Philadelphia's first golf course opens	U.S. enters World War I	Benjamin Franklin Parkway completed

316

317

314 E,K OP
Philadelphia Museum of Art, *1916–28*
See pages 116–117.

315 J PR
Lincoln Drive Development, *1917–26*
Lincoln Dr. from Springfield Ave. to
Pastorius Park
Robert McGoodwin, Herman Louis
Duhring, and Edmund B. Gilchrist

Dr. Woodward, impressed with the planned residential community around London's Hyde Park, wanted to create a similar community in Philadelphia. He acquired untilled farmland around Pastorius Park and hired his three favorite architects to draw up a general plan. The plan, designed to provide housing for both affluent and middle-class families, includes large single-family houses, court houses, twin houses and row houses.

Each architect carried out a portion of the plan. Duhring designed the Half Moon Houses at 7919–25 Lincoln Drive, a distinctive example of court houses sharing a common sunken garden. McGoodwin designed a similar court at 131–35 Willow Grove Avenue. The stucco-covered brick homes along the 8000 block of Crefeld Street and the brick rowhouses at 103–13 West Willow Grove Avenue, known as Linden Court, were designed by Gilchrist, one of the most innovative of the Chestnut Hill architects.

The house at 200 West Willow Grove Avenue is a replica of George Washington's ancestral home in England. It was built for the Sesquicentennial Exposition and subsequently moved and reconstructed here by Duhring.

Most of these houses are still owned by the Woodward family.

316 K OP
Free Library of Philadelphia, *1917–27*
Vine St. between 19th and 20th Sts.
Horace Trumbauer

In the 18th and 19th centuries, Philadelphia libraries were privately owned. The first free library, conceived by Dr. William Pepper, began operating out of City Hall in 1894.

The library's rapid growth made it a logical institution to occupy one of the sites on Logan Circle, designated for civic buildings in the parkway plan. Since the parkway was modeled after the Champs-Élysées, it was logical for the library to take its form from the twin palaces on the Place de la Concorde, which occupied a similar position on the boulevard. This choice was probably influenced by the recent trips to France of Julian Abele, a black architect who was Trumbauer's chief designer.

The library was one of the largest and most modern in the world. It was considered the ultimate in fireproof construction, with steel and aluminum furnishings and trim throughout the building. The spacious interiors are treated in neutral tones and materials, except for the use of pink Tennessee marble in the halls and Welsh quarry tile and terrazzo on the floors. Each of the principal rooms has an unpainted, decorative plaster ceiling.

317 J PR
Pepper House, *1920*
9120 Crefeld St.
Willing and Sims

Chestnut Hill houses of the 1920s and 30s were influenced by French, Italian and English country houses. Many local architects developed a distinctive form of residential design based on these sources, which became known as the Philadelphia style.

Willing and Sims was one of the prominent firms of the time. Their houses were

314 E,K OP

Philadelphia Museum of Art, *1916–28*
Benjamin Franklin Pkwy. and 26th St.
Horace Trumbauer, C. Clark Zantzinger,
Charles L. Borie, Jr.
Exterior renovations 2007–08, Vitetta

By 1893, Memorial Hall was considered
no longer suitable for the city's art museum.
After many years of discussion, a site for
a new museum was selected on the hill
known as Faire Mount, at the end of the
recently completed Benjamin Franklin
Parkway. Trumbauer's chief designer, Julian

Abele, the first black graduate of the University of Pennsylvania architecture school,
returned from Greece with the idea of
building three temples on a solid rock base.
The final design is a compromise among his
ideas and those of the other architects.

At the start of construction not enough
money had been raised to build the entire
building. Eli Kirk Price, one of the fundraisers, suggested building the two wings
first, on the correct presumption that Philadelphians would not leave the museum
unfinished.

The museum is reached from the parkway by a monumental flight of stairs flanked by cascading fountains. The stairs lead to a large terrace with a spectacular view of the city. The museum consists of three interconnected temple structures with very tall porticos, topped by finely detailed pediments. The pediment of the north temple contains a brilliantly colored terra-cotta sculpture with 13 figures, representing sacred and profane love. The warm, yellow Minnesota Mankato and Kosota ashlar on the facade and gabled blue tile roof give the building a distinctive appearance.

The most impressive interior space is the great hall at the east entrance. A grand staircase, with Augustus Saint-Gaudens' statue "Diana" on its landing *(opposite page, top)*, leads to the second floor galleries. The museum also contains rooms representing different architectural styles and periods, most of which were built as WPA projects during the 1930s. They include a medieval cloister, a Japanese teahouse, an Indian temple, a reception hall from a Chinese nobleman's palace *(opposite page, bottom)*, a French Empire room and many others.

▼
1920
*19th Amendment
ratified: women
given right to vote*

▼
1920
Prohibition begins

▼
1920
*John B. Kelly wins
Olympic gold medal
in single sculls*

▼
1922
*First radio station,
WIP*

319

320

notable for the fine use of rough stone and for the sensitive relationship of interior spaces to exterior gardens and terraces. The Pepper House, one of the most charming houses in Chestnut Hill, is an excellent example of the firm's work.

From the street the house appears quite simple. A round tower at the corner is the only distinguishing feature. The L-shaped plan, however, focuses on a small but beautifully designed formal garden with terraces overlooking Fairmount Park and High Hollow, immediately below. A living room with beamed ceiling and the dining room enter onto the garden through French doors. The house achieves its distinctive character by its simple volumes and materials. There is little ornamentation except for the decorative details on the iron balconies, the use of heavy cornices and an elaborate dormer window on the garden facade.

318 B
Public Ledger Building, *1924*
6th and Chestnut Sts.
Horace Trumbauer

The *Public Ledger* was Philadelphia's first penny journal and the city's leading newspaper until 1940. It was founded in 1836 by Cyrus H. K. Curtis, publisher of many of the country's leading magazines, including *The Saturday Evening Post.* When the Ledger moved to Independence Square, it joined several other publishing firms already in the area, including the Curtis Publishing Company, immediately adjacent. Although the new building was designed in a grandiose Georgian Revival style, its general form, height and materials were similar to the Curtis Building, designed by Edgar Seeler in 1910.

Marble and arched openings define the ground floor and the top floors of the building; the central portion is brick with

simple, rectangular windows reflecting the basic office use. A shallow Ionic portico marks the entrance. Typical of Trumbauer's elaborate style are the decorated coffers around the doorways, the lobby with its coffered barrel vault and the ornate reception room.

319 L
Reading Company Grain Elevator, *1925*
411 North 20th St.

In the 18th and 19th centuries, Philadelphia was a distribution center for grain grown in the rich farmlands of Pennsylvania. For a long time grain elevators were a common sight in the city, but only this one remains. Grain was delivered by wagon to the entrance on 20th Street, then stored in the silos until it was loaded onto trains and taken to the port.

The simple, low-cost industrial structure was designed by staff architects of the Reading Railroad. Concrete was economically poured in place in a process known as continuous pour, which required the building to have a simple shape. The windowless grain silos comprise most of the building, with machinery towers on top; lower levels terraced down to the railroad tracks.

In 1976, Kenneth Parker, an interior designer, purchased the grain elevator and converted the lower floors to offices. The silos were left untouched, but the machinery towers were transformed into a penthouse apartment with landscaped terraces, giving the appearance of a garden in the sky.

321

322

320 K
Philadelphia Divinity School, *1925–26*
42nd and Spruce Sts.
Zantzinger, Borie and Medary

The Philadelphia Divinity School was founded in 1857 to educate Episcopalian priests. In 1917 the school purchased the Clark estate to establish a theological college as an adjunct to the University of Pennsylvania.

Although never completed, the school complex was considered one of the most significant architectural undertakings of the time. The buildings, located on a dramatic, hilly site, were designed in the Gothic style then popular for collegiate buildings.

The most impressive building is the chapel, located on the highest point on the site. Its interior is a masterpiece of Gothic design and one of the most beautiful religious spaces in the city. The plan follows the Oxford tradition, with choir stalls for students and faculty, an antechapel for the laity and a rear sanctuary leading to the altar. Gothic ornamentation of superior craftsmanship embellishes the stone structure, which has a hammer-beam ceiling decorated with polychrome figures. A European atmosphere is created by the Gothic detailing of the choir stalls, the ornamental iron screens by Samuel Yellin and the stained-glass windows by Nicholas D'Ascenzo.

321 C
Drexel and Company Building, *1925–27*
135–43 South 15th St.
Day and Klauder

Francis M. Drexel was a portrait painter turned banker. The company he founded in 1837 quickly became the city's most important financial institution. In the early part of this century, the company was headed by Edward T. Stotesbury, one of the most influential financiers of his day.

For the new building Stotesbury wanted an Italian palazzo worthy of the Medicis. The design is based on the Strozzi Palace in Florence. It is a solid fortress of rusticated granite blocks, relieved only by massive doors with hammered-steel hinges. Most of the interior was taken up by a single, two-story room opulently decorated to convey the company's prosperity. Above the fourth floor, offices with ornate mahogany paneling faced onto a stone courtyard.

In 1980 the building was converted to offices by J. Nathan and Company. Although the main room was subdivided, the hand-carved, coffered, walnut ceiling is still visible from the second-floor mezzanine. The original vault, with its massive steel lock, is in the basement and is worth seeing.

322 H PR
Alden Park, *1920*
Wissahickon Ave. and School House Lane
Edwyn Rorke
Renovated 1988–93, SRK Associates and John Milner Associates

Alden Park was the first apartment complex in the country built in a parklike setting. The developer, Lawrence Jones, was a wealthy manufacturer who wanted to create a luxury cooperative for families who desired the amenities of a pastoral setting without the responsibility for maintenance.

The complex consists of three buildings located on 30 acres overlooking the Wissahickon Valley. Each building is designed differently, but all are based on the Jacobean Revival style. The Manor is the most elaborate. It has three separate towers linked by an elaborate lobby. Each tower is a reinforced concrete structure finished with rough-textured brick walls offset by

▼
1925
First woman judge,
Violet E. Fahnstock

▼
1926
Sesquicentennial
Exposition opens in
what is now F.D.R.
Park

▼
1926
Franklin Bridge spans
Delaware River

323

324

pink terra-cotta detailing. The lobby is decorated with reproduction period furniture and has a massive fireplace and wrought-iron chandelier.

Among the original amenities of the complex were a nine-hole golf course, a year-round swimming pool with roll-top roof, formal gardens and individual garden plots for residents.

---

323   J   PR

French Village, *1925–28*
Elbow and Gate Lanes, off Allens Lane
Robert R. McGoodwin

Just as Dr. Woodward's trip to London led to the creation of the Lincoln Drive development, his trip to Normandy in 1923 inspired the creation of French Village. The village consists of a series of large houses built along three private lanes. The overall plan and most of the individual houses were designed by McGoodwin, Woodward's favorite architect, who had studied at the École des Beaux-Arts.

Gatehouses flank the ends of Gate Lane and Emlen Street. These private residences mark the entrance to the village with archways that extend over the sidewalks. All of the houses are built of local stone and designed with a common vocabulary of distinctive forms: octagonal and circular stairtowers, hipped roofs with overhanging eaves, tall French doors and broad masses reflecting the spacious interiors. The sensitive and varied relationships of the houses to the landscape and to each other make French Village one of the period's most interesting developments.

ART DECO

Art Deco began as a European movement, taking its name from the International Exposition of Decorative Arts, held in Paris in 1925. The exposition emphasized design that deliberately rejected historic influences and expressed the new machine age. During the decade of its popularity, Art Deco had an enormous impact on the design of such diverse elements as jewelry, trains, furniture and movie sets.

Art Deco's sleek appearance is often referred to as streamlining. Primarily a style of ornamentation, it was influenced by Cubism and by North and South American Indian art. Linear patterns of parallel lines, zigzags or chevrons predominate. On buildings, exterior materials of smooth stone and metal are contrasted by accents of terra-cotta, glass and colored mirrors. Sculpture and lettering were also integrated directly into the architecture. Most Art Deco buildings have a unity of design that carries through to the interior fixtures and furniture.

---

324   E   OP

Fidelity Mutual Life Insurance Company Building, *1925–26*
Pennsylvania and Fairmount Aves.
Zantzinger, Borie and Medary; sculptor Lee Lawrie
Renovated 1983, Environmental Design Corp. and David N. Beck
Ruth and Raymond G. Perelman Building
Renovated 2007, Gluckman Mayner Architects and Kelly/Maiello, Inc.

The Fidelity Building was planned in conjunction with the Benjamin Franklin Parkway. In contrast to the parkway's neoclassical civic buildings, the Fidelity Building was designed in the Art Deco style, popular for commercial buildings in the 1920s and 30s. The sleek appearance, lavish materials, color and ornamentation conveyed a sense of prosperity and confidence in the future.

The Fidelity Building is a fine example of the best characteristics of the Art Deco style. Sculpture and decoration are concentrated around the two massive arched portals, the

▼
1927
Philadelphia General
Hospital dedicated

▼
1928
Broad Street Subway
opens; First autogiro
in U.S. flown at
Willow Grove

325

326

window spandrels and the cornice. Figures of the father and the mother, symbolizing work and home, crown the pilasters. Other figures on the arch symbolize the seven ages and twelve labors of man, and a variety of images decorate the spandrels and cornice. The building was renovated in 1983 for the offices of the Reliance Standard Life Insurance Company.

After Reliance moved the building stood vacant for many years, until it was acquired by the Philadelphia Museum of Art, which restored the original building and added a new wing. The restored lobby with Art Deco details leads to a glass-roofed atrium that links the historic building to the understated new addition. One wall of the atrium is formed by the yellow-brick back of the older building, while the other consists of a wall of split and ground face concrete block that twists as it widens giving the atrium a dynamic character. Galleries for changing exhibits and a café line the atrium. Upper levels contain a library with views of Fairmount Park, conservation studios, workshops, climate controlled storage space and administrative office space.

The Perelman Building beautifully relates a contemporary addition to an historic building.

---

325 L

Lasher Printing Company, *1927*
1309 Noble St.
Philip Tyre

During the 1920s many industrial buildings located on North Broad Street. The Lasher Printing Company was designed by Philip Tyre, an industrial architect who was remodeling the nearby showroom of the Packard Motor Car Company. Tyre designed a concrete urban fortress to accommodate the heavy machinery that the printing industry then required. It is a

unique example of an Art Deco industrial building. The building's rough-textured concrete and straightforward expression of structure and service elements, such as the concrete fire escape, give it a very contemporary character. But the zigzag pattern at the top and bottom levels, originally unpainted, is a clear expression of Art Deco ornamentation.

---

326 L PR

N. W. Ayer Building, *1927–29*
204–12 South 7th St.
Ralph Bencker
The Ayer
Renovated 2006–2008, Wesley Wei Architects and PZS Architects

Although most new office construction was occurring around City Hall, N. W. Ayer and Son, a prominent advertising firm, located its headquarters on Washington Square, near the concentration of publishing companies. Bencker wanted the building to harmonize with its historic surroundings without using borrowed forms. He achieved this by a subdued Art Deco style similar to that of the Fidelity Building.

The blocky mass is given a vertical emphasis by the use of tall, narrow windows and setbacks on the upper floors. This simple form is embellished in the Art Deco manner with decoration based on symbolism related to the building's function. The pylons, extending through the top three floors, terminate in monumental figures symbolizing truth, holding the open book of advertising. Carved birds in flight decorated the lobby and carved bronze panels o the entrance doors depict Egyptian-lookir figures in robes, working in various phase of the advertising industry. Egyptian mc gained popularity after the opening of I Tutankhamen's tomb in 1922.

▼
1928
*Baldwin Locomotive
closes*

▼
1929
*City Planning Com-
mission established*

327

328

327 L OP

Rodin Museum, *1927–29*
22nd St. and Benjamin Franklin Pkwy.
Paul Philippe Cret and Jacques Greber

The Rodin Museum houses the largest collection of Auguste Rodin's work outside France. The museum and collection were the gift of Dr. Jules Mastbaum, who asked Jacques Greber to prepare preliminary plans. Greber, a French landscape architect who drew the final plans for the parkway, invited Paul Philippe Cret to collaborate.

The gateway to the museum is a replica of the Chateau d'Issy, reconstructed by Rodin for his own home in Meudon, France. It leads to a formal garden beyond which the architects placed a small, well-proportioned classical temple on a high podium. The interior walls are decorated with murals by the well-known Philadelphia painter Franklin Watkins.

Several of Rodin's most popular sculptures are incorporated into the architectural composition, including The Thinker and The Gates of Hell, the bronze doors located at the entrance to the museum.

328 D

WCAU Building, *1928*
1620 Chestnut St.
Harry Sternfeld and Gabriel Roth
The Art Institute of Philadelphia
Renovated 1983, Kopple Sheward and Day

Art Deco was an extremely popular style for places of entertainment and, by association, the appropriate style for a radio station. Although Sternfeld studied the Beaux-Arts style under Paul Philippe Cret, he was a master of Art Deco design.

The facade creatively expresses the building's uses. Large glass windows on the second floor originally displayed a Woolworth's store. Horizontal strip windows highlight the office floors. At the top,

the radio studio was expressed by a tower of glass, which glowed blue at night when the station was on the air. Glass and metal chevrons decorate the facade on either side of the tower. The whole composition is tied together by a wall surface of blue glass chips set in plastic.

Roth, a student of Sternfeld's, designed the lobby, which has a coffered ceiling and marble walls with metal strips. The brushed-metal elevator doors and the mailbox are wonderful examples of Art Deco design. The building was renovated in 1983 for the Art Institute of Philadelphia.

329 L

Rodeph Shalom Synagogue, *1927*
615 North Broad St.
Simon and Simon

See facing page.

330 H PR

Abraham Malmed House, *1929*
1021 Hortter St.
Mellor and Meigs

Although architectural design was moving away from historically derivative styles, many wealthy persons still preferred traditional homes. Even after George Howe left the firm, Mellor and Meigs continued to design fine country homes in the pastoral style. This house, built for Abraham Malmed, a manufacturer, is typical of the many beautiful homes they designed in Chestnut Hill and surrounding suburban towns.

A narrow drive, lined by high stone walls, leads into a small forecourt formed by wings of the house. This entrance gives little indication of the building's large size and complexity. The division of the plan into several wings breaks down the size and allows the house to follow the contours of the steep site overlooking Fairmount Park.

329 L

Rodeph Shalom Synagogue, *1927*
615 North Broad St.
Simon and Simon
Restored 2005, Becker Winston Architects
and Martin Jay Rosenblum Assoc., R.A.

The Mikveh Israel Synagogue, founded
in 1740, was the focus for Philadelphia's
Jewish community. In 1802 a group of
German Jews founded a second synagogue,
later known as Rodeph Shalom. It is the
oldest Ashkenazic congregation in continuous existence in the United States.

The new synagogue, built on the site of
an earlier building by Fraser, Furness and
Hewitt, is an outstanding example of the
Byzantine style. Both the exterior and
interior walls are covered with painted
and carved geometric designs executed
by the D'Ascenzo Studios. They also were
responsible for the stained glass in the main
sanctuary and the mosaic floor of the vesti-
bule. The sanctuary has a large pendentive
dome and contains a beautiful ark, supported on marble columns, with intricately
carved doors of painted copper, bronze,
steel and glass.

▼
1930
*Great Depression
begins*

▼
1930
*Philadelphia Athletics
win second consecu-
tive World Series*

▼
1931
*Convention Hall
opens; Empire State
Building completed*

331

332

The facade, of local stone set in tan-colored mortar with brick courses over the windows, blends into the natural setting. The design achieves a medieval character by the steep-pitched roof, polygonal chimneys, gabled dormers and a tower on the facade facing the park.

---

331   C,K

The Drake Hotel, *1929*
1512–14 Spruce St.
Ritter and Shay
The Drake
Renovated 1998, VLBJR Architects

The Drake Hotel was one of many tall build-ings constructed west of Broad Street in the late 1920s. The overall form was influenced by the emergence of zoning laws in the 1920s, which required setbacks on the upper floors of tall buildings. Even today, the tapered silhouette of the Drake is a striking feature on the city's skyline.

Ritter and Shay, one of the city's most versatile architectural firms, covered the steel-frame structure with Pompeian brick and terra-cotta decoration. The Spanish Baroque ornamentation is based on themes related to Sir Francis Drake. Terra-cotta motifs of dolphins, shells, sailing vessels and globes cover the ground floor and reappear on the piers, which rise to an elaborate series of cornices and culminate in a distinctive terra-cotta dome.

---

332   K   OP

30th Street Station, *1929–34*
30th St. and John F. Kennedy Blvd.
Graham, Anderson, Probst and White
Restored 1991, Dan Peter Kopple & Associates

In exchange for land required by the city for the construction of the Benjamin Franklin Parkway, the Pennsylvania Railroad was given tunnel rights from the Schuylkill River to 15th Street. The railroad then built two new stations: Suburban Station, near City Hall, and 30th Street Station, in West Philadelphia. Both buildings were designed by the successor firm to D. H. Burnham and Co.

Only a few railroad stations as grand as 30th Street Station remain in the country today. Like others of the time, it has an enormous interior waiting room. This room is faced with marble and covered with a coffered ceiling painted in red, gold and cream. Natural light enters through glass walls at both ends, which contain catwalks connecting the flanking wings of the building.

The exterior has monumental, columned porte cocheres on the east and west facades. Although classical elements are used on the facade, their simple form indicates a compromise between historical and emerging modern styles.

When completed the station contained a chapel, a mortuary, over 3,000 square feet of hospital space and a landing deck for small aircraft on its reinforced concrete roof.

---

333   C

One East Penn Square Building, *1930*
1–21 North Juniper St.
Ritter and Shay
Residence Inn by Marriott
Renovated 2002, Nobutaka Ashihara Assoc. and John Milner Assoc.

One East Penn Square was built for the Market Street National Bank when Art Deco was at the peak of its popularity. The building is typical of the Art Deco approach to office buildings. The facade is divided into three parts, with a strong vertical emphasis in the brick curtain wall. Polychrome terra cotta ornamentation, derived from Mayan designs, is concentrated

▼
1932
International style
exhibit at Museum of
Modern Art

▼
1932
First woman elected
to U.S. Senate

▼
1933
First dried blood
serum developed;
First Girl Scout cookie
sale

333

334

around the base and along the skyline. The decision to place the banking room on the second floor and reserve the first floor for shops was unusual at the time, and may have influenced the design of the PSFS building.

---

334   J   PR
Schofield Andrews House, *1930–32*
9002 Crefeld St.
Tilden, Register and Pepper

Tilden, Register and Pepper was a very successful architectural firm in the 1920s and 30s. They designed several major Philadelphia buildings, including the University of Pennsylvania Hospital, the Art Deco office building at 1616 Walnut Street and, with Rankin and Kellog, the 30th Street Post Office. Their specialty, however, was residential design.

One of their clients was Schofield Andrews, a resident of Chestnut Hill, for whom they designed several homes. This house is designed in the English country style similar to that used by Mellor, Meigs and Howe. It is beautifully sited on the edge of Fairmount Park. Certain features make the house unique. The doors and gates were imported from Italy, and the courtyard is laid in Belgian block patterned around an ancient grindstone centerpiece. Other notable features, such as the solarium at the end of the drawing room and the automated bowling alley in the recreation room, were added by the second owner, Mrs. Eleanor Widener Dixon, who acquired the property in 1949. In 1969, her son, Fitz Eugene Dixon, gave the property to Temple University, which used it as a conference center until 1986 when it was returned to residential use.

THE INTERNATIONAL STYLE

In the 1920s, European architects created a new architectural style that was an even more dramatic departure from the past then was Art Deco. Many of the originators of this new style taught at the Bauhaus, an important German school of design. Three of its most influential teachers, Walter Gropius, Ludwig Mies van der Rohe and Marcel Breuer, moved to the United States in the late 1930s and became prominent American architects.

This new approach to design was recognized in the United States and named the International style by the 1932 exhibition of architecture at the Museum of Modern Art. Until after World War II, it was the dominant influence in this country and the source of subsequent modern styles.

International style is characterized by a total absence of ornamentation. Most residential buildings have a horizontal emphasis, with flat roofs, ribbon windows and smooth wall surfaces, usually painted white. Commercial structures are also devoid of ornament, emphasize horizontal elements and use such new industrial materials as aluminum or stainless steel for interior and exterior finishes. In addition to its impact on architecture, the International style had a strong influence on the design of furniture and household objects.

---

335   C,K
Philadelphia Saving Fund Society,
1930–32

See pages 126–127.

Philadelphia Saving Fund Society,
1930–32
12 South 12th St.
Howe and Lescaze
Loews Philadelphia Hotel
Renovated 2000, Bower Lewis Thrower

When PSFS decided to build a new headquarters, the directors chose a site near the Reading Terminal and Wanamaker's department store, where they already had a successful branch bank. George Howe was retained as architect. Howe had a national reputation for his pastoral suburban houses but recently had become an advocate of the International style emerging in Europe.

PSFS marked Howe's break with his past. He left Mellor and Meigs and entered into partnership with William Lescaze, a Swiss architect. Together they designed the first International style skyscraper in the country. James Wilcox, president of the bank, supported the design and persuaded the conservative board to accept it.

PSFS is a masterpiece; it is the finest 20th-century building in the city and one of the most important examples of the International style in the country. The exterior form is a sophisticated expression of the different functions within the building. The base contains a retail store on the first floor, with the banking room located above, following Ritter and Shay's successful use of a similar arrangement in the Market Street National Bank building. Bank offices above are set back from the facade of the office tower, which rises to a complicated roof structure and prominent sign. At the rear of the building, elevator shafts and service elements form a separate unit. To emphasize further the contrasting elements of the design, different materials and colors were used. Highly polished gray granite covers the base; sand-colored limestone is used for the facade of the bank offices. The office tower has exposed vertical columns covered with the same limestone and gray brick spandrels. The huge rear wall of the service core is made of glazed and unglazed black brick.

Even though PSFS was built at the height of the Depression, expensive materials and furnishings were used throughout. The stainless steel hardware and most of the furniture were custom designed by the architects, as there was no inventory of modern fixtures in the United States. This was also the second building in the country to be air conditioned. The most dramatic interior space was the high-ceilinged banking room. Subdued colors; polished materials like marble, glass and stainless steel; and gently curved balconies give the room an exceptional quality. The PSFS building was beautifully maintained by the bank. However, in 1992 PSFS was purchased by another bank which became insolvent. The building remained vacant for many years until it was converted to a hotel. The main banking room became the ballroom and the 33rd floor boardroom and enclosed terrace were retained in their original character. New meeting rooms, a spa and parking were included in an addition designed in a sympathetic style.

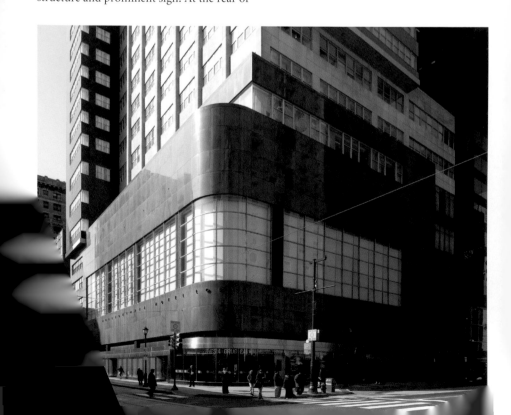

▼
1933
Philadelphia Eagles
football team
founded

▼
1935
30th Street Post
Office opens

▼
1936
Frank Lloyd Wright
designs "Falling
Water," Bear Run,
Pennsylvania

▼
1936
Democratic National
Convention held in
Philadelphia; First
public housing opens

336

337

336   L   PR

Midvale Avenue Row Houses, *1931–33*
3421–75 Midvale Ave.
Robert J. McCrudden

Midvale Avenue was opened in 1889, when
Falls of the Schuylkill was a mill town. The
area was forested with poplar trees and as
late as 1920 was still known as the Midvale
woods. McCrudden, a local developer,
began constructing houses in 1925 and continued until he went bankrupt during the
Depression.

This beautifully designed row was adver-
tised as studio homes because of the English
Tudor-style living room with a balcony
and 14-foot-high beamed ceiling. A large,
leaded-glass bay window floods the room
with light and adds to the distinctive Tudor
character of the half-timbered facade.

337   L

Federal Reserve Bank, *1931–35*
10th and Chestnut Sts.
Paul Philippe Cret
Thomas Jefferson University Health System

The Federal Reserve Bank of Philadelphia,
founded by Congress in 1913, is one of 12
regional banks that make up the central
bank of the United States. These banks
are responsible for managing the nation's
supply of money.

This building is a fine example of Cret's
later style, which was based on classical
principles rather than the use of correct
classical details. Cret placed the public
banking room in a Greek temple form with
a Doric front and placed the private offices
in a three-story "attic" above. The original
bronze light fixtures, gently vaulted ceiling
and bronze grilles of the lobby retain a
classical spirit and are examples of Cret's
meticulous attention to detail.

This facade is enriched by monumental
figures, sculpted by Alfred Boitteau, which
depict Athena, the goddess of wisdom, and
a mighty oak. There are also symbols of the
nation's economic foundation: agriculture,
industry and trade.

Cret added the formal garden in 1941.
His successor firm, Harbeson, Hough,
Livingston and Larson, added the recessed
seventh story from 1952–53.

338   A,B,K

U.S. Customs House, *1932–44*
2nd and Chestnut Streets
Ritter and Shay
Renovated 1993, Ueland Junker McCauley
Nicholson

As the world's largest freshwater port
and, after New York, the nation's busiest,
Philadelphia was the logical site for a new
Customs House when the Hoover and
Roosevelt administrations sought opportunities for public works programs to counter
unemployment. The Customs House took
seven years to plan and build and was one
of the most imposing federal projects in the
Philadelphia area.

A four-story base with classical details
relates the building to the scale of the surrounding neighborhood. The base supports
a fourteen-story, brick and limestone,
cruciform-shaped tower in the Art Deco
style, culminating in an expressive lantern
that suggests a symbolic lighthouse overlooking the port. On the interior, the lobby
and rotunda are among the finest examples
of government-sponsored art of the period.
The design reflects a partnership of artist
George Harding, architect Howell Lewis
Shay and Art Museum director Fiske Kimball. Harding's murals and Shay's rotunda
walls are inspired by nautical imagery
including ships and planes, conch shells, sea
horses and reclining Neptunes. Rich finish-

▼
1937
*Celebration of 150th
anniversary of the
U.S. Constitution*

▼
1938
*Philadelphia enacts
first U.S. wage tax*

▼
1940
*Republican National
Convention held in
Philadelphia*

▼
1941
*Pearl Harbor: U.S.
enters World War II*

338

339

ings include aluminum and bronze stair rails, travertine, painted plaster and terrazzo for walls and floors. A major renovation in 1993 restored the exterior and interior public spaces, added exterior lighting, and modernized workspaces for 30 federal agencies.

339 L   PR
Carl Mackley Houses, *1933–34*
M and Bristol Sts.
Oscar Stonorov and Alfred Kastner
Renovated 1999, Bower Lewis Thrower

Although there had been much public concern about housing conditions for lower-income families around the turn of the century, the provision of housing was considered a private responsibility until the Depression. Even before the U.S. Housing Authority was created, John Edelman, an official of the Philadelphia local of the Hosiery Workers Union, initiated the construction of cooperative housing for factory workers.

Carl Mackley Houses, named for a union member killed in a strike, was located near the mills of Kensington and Frankford. It was the first of many socially responsive housing developments designed by Stonorov. The complex is organized in four parallel rows of three-story buildings, arranged around courtyards connected to one another by walkways passing through the ground floors. The simple structures, influenced by International style housing in Europe, where Stonorov was trained, are enriched by recessed balconies and the use of buff-colored brick and yellow terracotta tiles. The architects were particularly sensitive to the tenants' needs and included such amenities as a swimming pool, rooftop laundries, a cooperative grocery, collective kitchens and dining rooms and a nursery school.

340 L
Mayfair Theater, *1936*
7300 Frankford Ave.
David Supowitz

Streamlining was a favorite mode of design in the 1930s. It was an important aspect of the Art Deco style and reflected America's growing preoccupation with speed and transportation machines. Streamlining had little impact on building design in Philadelphia, but even in conservative cities movie theaters were often designed in this popular style.

The Mayfair was the first movie theater in the city designed in a streamlined manner. Supowitz, the city's outstanding theater designer of the 1930s, transformed the building into a giant sign. The horizontal bands of the curved marquee are repeated in decorative horizontal bands on the wall below, broken by circular display windows. To achieve a sleek appearance, Supowitz used modern materials, including porcelain, structural glass and stainless steel. The Mayfair influenced the design of many subsequent theaters in the city.

341 J   PR
Charles Woodward House, *1939*
8220 Millman St.
Kenneth Day

The Woodward House is one of the few houses in the city designed in the International style. Kenneth Day, the son of Frank Miles Day, received a Beaux-Arts education at the University of Pennsylvania and worked for the neoclassical architects McKim, Mead and White. But in the 1930s his interests in city planning and large-scale housing developments introduced him to the International style then evolving in Europe.

The Woodward House combines International style elements with local building

▼
1945
Atomic bomb dropped

▼
1945
First public demon-
stration of the Slinky,
at Gimbels Depart-
ment Store

▼
1945
First electronic com-
puter operated at
University of Penn-
sylvania

▼
1947
Better Philadelphia
Exhibit at Gimbels
department store

343

methods and materials. The plain, white, painted exterior wall surfaces and narrow windows are typical of the new style. But the pitched slate roof and foundation of local stone are acknowledgments of Chestnut Hill building traditions. On the interior, Day gave each function a separate, spacious room, in contrast to the open plans of contemporary European designers, and linked the two floors with a dramatic freestanding spiral staircase.

342   L

Philadelphia Psychiatric Center, *1949–53*
Ford Rd. and Monument Rd.
Louis I. Kahn

Shortly after completing the Mill Creek project, Kahn designed two wings for the Philadelphia Psychiatric Center: the Pincus Occupational Therapy Building, 1949–50, and the Samuel Radbill Psychiatric Hospital, 1950–53. Both buildings demonstrate Kahn's early experiments with structural systems as determinants of building form.

The Pincus Building is built of steel lally columns and exposed open-web steel joists, with unplastered cinder-block partitions. It was Kahn's last use of metal construction systems. The Radbill Building features a facade that reflects the building's internal functions. The ground floor has large glass areas for the administrative and public rooms, and the upper floors have smaller windows for the nursing and treatment rooms. Cantilevered sunshades above the windows are perforated with collared flue tiles, through which the sun makes patterns on the walls.

Both buildings are interesting examples of Kahn's work during a transitional phase of his career.

343   K   PR

Parkway House, *1952–53*
22nd St. and Pennsylvania Ave.
Gabriel Roth and Elizabeth Fleischer

Parkway House was one of the first postwar luxury apartment buildings in the city. It is an exceptionally fine design, with elements from both the Art Deco and International styles. The form of the building is derived from a remarkable response to the shape and location of the site. Two side wings of the U-shaped plan step down toward the parkway, creating generous terraces for many of the apartments. Other apartments have curved-glass projecting window bays, which are organized in vertical rows on the main facade. These elements create the only decoration on an otherwise plain brick structure and are more characteristic of buildings of the 1930s than the 50s, reflecting Roth's Art Deco background. The building is also noteworthy because it was one of the first in the city designed by a woman architect. With its large apartments, fine design and wonderful views of the city, Parkway House is still one of the city's finest residential buildings.

THE MODERN STYLE

Most American architecture designed since the mid-1940s is called modern, a term that encompasses many different approaches to architectural design. Modern architecture is an evolution of the International style into several different modes of expression, often associated with an individual architect. For example, Ludwig Mies van der Rohe's emphasis on structural expression, particularly exposed-steel construction, and a uniform curtain wall has been the basis for almost all tall office buildings erected in this country from 1950 to the present. The extensive use of exposed concrete in modern buildings derives from the work of the French architect Le Corbusier.

344

Among the few common characteristics of most Modern buildings are the absence of ornamentation, the direct expression of structural systems and the use of muted colors.

344   D,K

Penn Center Complex, *1953–82*
15th to 18th Sts., between Market St. and John F. Kennedy Blvd.
Vincent G. Kling and Assoc. / Emery Roth and Sons / Kohn Pedersen Fox
Renovations to #2 and #3, 1989, 1986, Ueland Junker McCauley

In 1953 the Broad Street Station and "Chinese Wall" of elevated railroad tracks behind it were demolished to make way for the city's first new office buildings since the Depression. The original concept for Penn Center was developed by Edmund Bacon, his City Planning Commission staff and Vincent Kling. They proposed a lower-level pedestrian area, open to the sky, that would connect the subway station and suburban train station with the new shops and office buildings. Real estate considerations by the Pennsylvania Railroad modified the plan, resulting in a lower-level pedestrian area, lighted by small courtyards, and a group of office buildings organized along a street-level pedestrian mall.

Penn Center was significant not for the design of the individual buildings but for the project as a whole. The concept of a separate pedestrian concourse linking transportation, retail and office facilities was innovative at the time and influenced downtown development in many other cities. In Philadelphia, Penn Center created a huge parcel of developable land in the heart of the city. Since the 1950s, nearly all major office development has occurred in or around this complex.

345   E,J

Richards Medical Research Laboratory, *1957–61*
See page 132.

346   H   PR

Hassrick / Sawyer House, *1958–59*
Richard Neutra, addition by Thaddeus Longstreth
3011 Cherry Lane

Local avant-garde metal sculptor, Kenneth Hassrick and his wife commissioned this house on land inherited from her family. The house was built in three stages. The first consisted of a one-story structure with a garage and room above. A studio for Hassrick's sculpture work was added in a second phase and later Longstreth, a student of Neutra's, added a two-story welding studio.

The initial house was typical of Neutra's Southern California style, transplanted to Philadelphia. It had a flat roof and an open sprawling interior plan. Kitchen and living room were one space divided by a suspended kitchen cabinet with huge floor-to-ceiling sliding glass doors opening on to a garden. A unique feature was a built-in cage in the kitchen for Hassrick's pet chimpanzee.

In 1962, prominent attorney Henry Sawyer and his wife purchased the house and the Sawyer family retained ownership until 2003. Relatively few changes were made: the welding studio was converted to a recreation room and the kitchen enclosed. Modifications made to the roof were removed by a subsequent owner.

345   F,K

Richards Medical Research Laboratory,
1957–61
37th St. and Hamilton Walk
Louis I. Kahn

The Richards Medical Research Laboratory
is considered one of the most significant
buildings in modern American architecture.
It was the pivotal project in the career of
Louis Kahn and transformed him from an
influential theoretical architect to one of
international importance. Beginning with
the Richards Laboratory, Kahn evolved a
style of design that emphasized the use of
heavy masonry construction, structural
innovation and building volume, in contrast to the thin, steel-and-glass image of
the International style. In the 1960s this
approach, used by many locally based and
trained architects, was referred to as the
Philadelphia School.

At the Richards Laboratory, Kahn
brought together in a unified design several
concepts developed previously in other
projects. He divided the building into
erved and servant spaces, giving each its

own form and expression. The core tower
of the building is poured-in-place concrete;
it contains such services as elevators, animal
quarters and utilities. The laboratories are
located in three eight-story towers, connected to the core. Each of these towers in
turn is served by smaller brick shafts containing additional services. The laboratories
are open spaces made possible by placing
both services and the structural system on
the periphery of the building. Within the
laboratories, the interlocking grid of supporting precast beams is exposed to allow
for easy connection of utility systems to the
surrounding towers.

Kahn felt that a building should reflect
the way it was built. The innovative precast and poured-in-place concrete system,
designed by August E. Komandant,
articulates the structural principles of the
cantilevered construction while providing
visual interest to the facade.

The Biological Research Laboratory,
added later, follows the same design principles, with some simplification of the
structural system and the addition of projecting study carrels on the upper floors.

▼
1957
Walt Whitman Bridge
opens

▼
1959
Dock Street markets
relocated: Society
Hill renewal begins

▼
1960
John F. Kennedy
elected President

e Kelly marries
ce Rainier

348

347 F,K PR

Hill Hall, *1960*
34th and Walnut Sts.
Eero Saarinen and Associates

Hill Hall, originally a women's dormitory, was planned during the university's expansion in the 1950s. It is the only building in the city designed by Saarinen, one of the country's most influential modern architects.

From the outside the building is a simple, rectangular form. It is made of irregular brick, with recessed windows alternating in a horizontal and vertical pattern, behind which are the bedroom cubicles. This simple, austere exterior gives no indication that the interior focuses on a bright, spacious atrium that extends the full height of the building. Clerestory windows and glass walls above the dormitory floors light the atrium, which has private lounges and balconies opening onto it. The first floor contains a dining area for the dormitory, which is open to other university members and the public.

348 J PR

Margaret Esherick House, *1960*
204 Sunrise Lane
Louis I. Kahn

Kahn designed a number of residences in the course of his career, only a few of which were built. The Esherick house is an outstanding example of a modest building transformed by the use of natural light to define interior spaces. It is built of concrete block covered with stucco. The walls of the street facade are pierced by two T-shaped windows, which provide light to the interior but ensure privacy. By contrast, the rear wall, which faces onto a wooded area and public park, is almost entirely glazed and open to the view. Additional light is brought in by a window placed behind a

freestanding fireplace chimney on the side of the house. The interior rooms, though modest in size, are extremely handsome because of the thoughtful use of natural light.

349 L PR

Guild House, *1960–63*

See page 134.

350 B PR

Society Hill Townhouses, *1962*
3rd and Locust Sts.
I. M. Pei and Associates

When the Dock Street wholesale food markets were relocated to assist the redevelopment of Society Hill, a competition was held to select a housing project to be built on the site. Pei's winning design included three towers and 25 townhouses.

The townhouses were designed to provide a transition between the scale of the apartment towers and the 18th- and 19th-century rowhouses on Third Street. The new three-story houses are clustered around an attractively landscaped parking court in the center of which is the bronze sculpture "Floating Figure," by Gaston Lachaise. The more formal street facades are dark brick, with modest window openings similar to their predecessors and round-arch recessed doorways. But these unornamented, handsome houses do not imitate the Georgian style. The houses were regarded as distinguished contemporary design that respected the historic character of Society Hill. They influenced other groups of new houses in the area, including Bingham Court, on 4 Street, also designed by Pei in 1968.

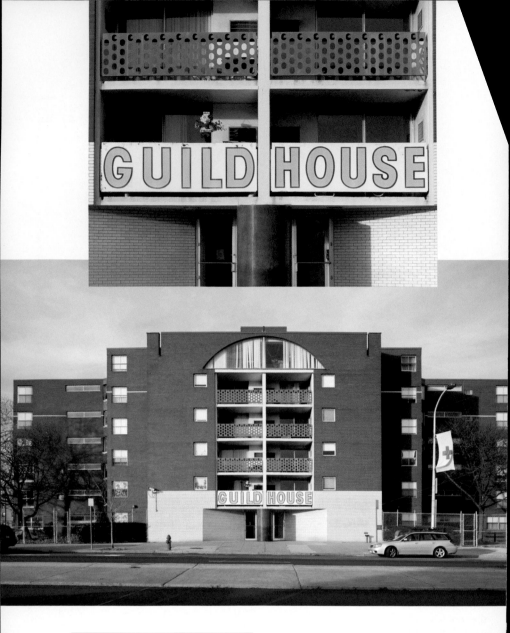

349 L PR

Guild House, *1960–63*
7th and Spring Garden Sts.
Venturi and Rauch with Cope and Lippincott

Venturi and Rauch have transformed
contemporary architecture through their
imaginative use of standard building
materials, popular imagery and historical
references. The Guild House, an apartment
building for low-income elderly persons
designed for the Friends Neighborhood
Guild, is an outstanding example of their
ability to create a distinctive building from
ordinary materials and forms.

The building is dominated by a six-story
entrance facade, designed as a single unit in
the classical tradition. The first-floor base is
faced in white glazed brick; the upper floors
have balconies puncturing the flat facade
and the top floor terminates the composition with the flat arch of the common room
window. From this facade, the building
setback on either side, permitting most
apartments an east, west or south exposure
over small landscaped areas.

The composition of the elevation is particularly skillful in the placement, size and
shape of standard metal windows. A decorative stripe of white brick appears to be
a string course but is broken by windows
rather than defining a floor level. By contrast with the articulated form and varied
windows of the front elevation, the rear of
the building is a flat surface with uniform
windows, in keeping with the ordinary
character of the surrounding housing. On
the interior, apartments are arranged along
a corridor that bends and turns, giving a
more intimate scale and informal organization.

Guild House is a masterpiece of siting,
interior planning and the use of standard
materials to create a building that both fits
its context and is strikingly new.

▼
1963
President Kennedy assassinated

▼
1965
Community College of Philadelphia opens

▼
1966
Venturi's Complexity and Contradiction in Architecture published

351

352

351   J   PR

Vanna Venturi House, *1962*
8330 Millman St.
Venturi and Rauch

Venturi's house for his mother is now considered a classic of contemporary architecture and one of the earliest expressions of post-Modern design concepts. The house reflects the firm's interest in applied decoration, historical references and the use of traditional elements in a nontraditional manner.

At first glance the house seems very simple. It has a large, sloping, gabled roof, deliberately reminiscent of 19th-century Shingle style. The smooth, flat stucco facade is nearly symmetrical, but the symmetry is broken by the placement of windows, and the roof is split by a deep recess, similar to the incomplete pediments of Baroque buildings. Other motifs used in a novel manner include the applied arch over the entranceway and the overscaled molding.

On the interior, complexity is achieved through the use of a few simple devices. Diagonal walls, to accommodate circulation, break the simple spaces of the rooms, and the stair to the second floor is distorted by the dominant chimney of the central fireplace.

Traditional elements used in a new way give the house a liveliness that is unified by its overall form and plain stucco exterior. Even today, the house seems remarkably innovative.

352   C,D

Municipal Services Building, *1962–65*
15th St. and John F. Kennedy Blvd.
Vincent G. Kling and Associates

Plans for a new city office building on Reyburn Plaza were put forward before the Depression, but the proposal was not implemented until after new private office buildings were completed in Penn Center. The new building was part of a larger redevelopment effort that included an underground parking garage and public plaza to the west.

The Municipal Services Building forms a backdrop for a new plaza on the west side of City Hall. The design extends the lower-level pedestrian concourse created in Penn Center, with connections to City Hall, the parking garage and subway stations. Within the building this lower level contains the offices of city agencies with the greatest public use. Two-story light wells in the building lobby and a sunken garden to the east allow natural light to reach the lower level.

The office tower has a cruciform plan created by cantilevering the floors above the lobby. Carefully detailed panels give the facade a rich masonry character, which complements City Hall. Advanced energy-saving features included double glazing in the windows and the separate heating and cooling zones for each face of the building. The Municipal Services Building is typical of the many carefully designed buildings by the Kling firm in the Penn Center area.

353   J   PR

Dorothy Shipley White House, *1963*
717 Glen Gary Dr.
Mitchell / Giurgola Associates

Mrs. White, an artist and author, wanted a house that would accommodate a private studio for painting and writing, a place for entertaining and ample space for her large collection of antiques, art objects and books.

The house is located on a high knoll overlooking the Wissahickon Valley. From the street it appears to be a modest group of plain rectangular volumes, with relatively few visible windows. This reflects the asymmetrical plan, which consists of separate

355

rooms linked by an entrance hall with a studio above. Each room is designed to meet the specific requirements of the client's work and collections. The principal rooms have high ceilings and are lit by square clerestory windows, which ensure privacy and allow ample wall space for storage and display. As in Kahn's Esherick house, the private side of the house away from the street is more open to the light and view. The White house is an excellent example of Mitchell / Giurgola's fine sense of proportion and scale.

354   C

1500 Walnut Street Addition, *1963*
15th St. below Walnut St.
Bower and Fradley

The office building at 1500 Walnut Street, designed in 1928 by Ritter and Shay, is a good example of the firm's restrained Art Deco style. Bower and Fradley's addition respects the basic form of the older building in spite of its distinctively contemporary glass curtain wall. This is one of the city's best examples of the type of finely detailed curtain wall made popular by Mies van der Rohe. It is used in a very sophisticated manner. The height and certain indentations on the new facade respond to cornice lines of the older building. Inset panels beneath the windows and larger windows at the corners create a richer expression than the normally flat, uniform curtain wall of most commercial buildings.

This was Bower and Fradley's first commission, and it established the firm's reputation for thoughtful and distinctive design.

355   L

Police Administration Building, *1963*
Race St. between 7th and 8th Sts.
Geddes Brecher Qualls Cunningham

The Police Administration Building is one of the most unusually shaped structures in the city. It was built as part of the Independence Mall urban renewal project to provide offices and facilities for the Philadelphia Police Department, replacing those in City Hall. The unusual form, which consists of two circular units linked by a curved center section, was selected for its efficient use of floor space.

The building is notable for its innovative, precast concrete structural system, designed by August Komendant. The building is made of over 2,000 pieces of precast white concrete. The panels that make up the facade are structural units and also carry mechanical systems for heating and air conditioning.

356   F

University Parking Garage, *1963*
3201 Walnut St.
Mitchell / Giurgola Associates

In the 1960s, the University of Pennsylvania planned a decentralized system of parking garages to serve the campus. This first garage demonstrates Mitchell / Giurgola's use of creative structural systems as a source of architectural form and expression. The form of the garage is determined by the two-level site and by the system of ramps, which creates a continuous spiral within the building. The main elevations consist of deep, heavy, diagonal concrete trusses that support beams spanning 60 feet over the parking areas to a row of central columns. The light-colored concrete shows the patterns of its formwork.

High end walls, shaped by the ramps and exit stairs, rise above the garage to accom-

▼
1968
*Martin Luther King
assassinated*

▼
1968
*Black students
admitted to Girard
College*

356

358

modate a planned (but never constructed) addition. The walls are clad in purple brick and provide a counterfoil to the heavy, colorless concrete of the main structure.

In 1968 the architects designed a second garage, on South Street. This building, with its thin, precast components and massive brick end walls, is an interesting contrast to the Walnut Street garage.

357 L

Ukrainian Cathedral, *1963–66*
816 North Franklin St.
Julian K. Jastemsky

East Poplar was one of the city's early urban renewal areas designed to remove deteriorated housing and provide new housing and community facilities. To keep the stabilizing Ukrainian population in the area, the city made land available for construction of a Ukrainian cathedral. It is the largest in the country and serves 300,000 Catholic Ukrainians of the Byzantine Rite.

The cathedral is a contemporary interpretation of Byzantine architecture, with a central domed space for worship. The exterior of the dome is covered with Venetian tile of glass fused with gold, making it a very visible landmark in the area. The concrete walls supporting the dome are shaped in graceful arches, within which are stained-glass windows. The interior is richly decorated and includes a figure of Christ worked in mosaic on the dome.

358 B,K PR

Society Hill Towers, *1964*
2nd and Locust Sts.
I. M. Pei and Associates

By the 1940s, Society Hill was one of the city's worst slums. Most of the 18th-century houses were in dilapidated condition, and the area was dominated by the wholesale food market. As part of a comprehensive plan to redevelop the area, the food markets were relocated to a new food distribution center, in South Philadelphia.

A competition was held to select a housing design for the site that would symbolize the renewal of the area. Pei's winning entry included the townhouses on Third Street and three tall apartment buildings located on the axis of Second Street. The buildings are constructed of poured-in-place concrete, divided into meticulous rectilinear units that are both the structural frame and the facade. Each apartment has floor-to-ceiling glass windows, which provide dramatic views of the river and the city. The entrance court contains the sculptural group "Old Man, Young Man, The Future," by Leonard Baskin.

359 A

Rohm and Haas Building, *1964*
6th and Market Sts.
Pietro Belluschi with George M. Ewing Company

Rohm and Haas, founded in 1909, is one of the country's leading chemical processors and the producer of plexiglass. When the company outgrew its headquarters on Washington Square, it became the first private investor to build on Independence Mall. The mall and facing blocks on either side were cleared of older buildings as part of the city's urban renewal program. New buildings were expected to be of contemporary design to contrast deliberately with the Georgian style of Independence Hall.

▼
1968
U.S. Mint, fourth in
Philadelphia history,
dedicated on
Independence Mall

▼
1969
First man walks on
the moon

▼
1970
Penn Central Railroad
goes bankrupt

360

The Rohm and Haas Building was designed by Belluschi, then dean of the School of Architecture at M.I.T. He advocated the use of subdued color tones, resulting in a handsome, restrained, nine-story structure of concrete faced with dark bronze sunscreens and spandrel panels. Belluschi used plexiglass, manufactured by the company, for the sunscreens and spandrels and for the prominent lighting fixtures, designed by the Bauhaus artist Gyory Kepes, in the ground floor lobby and bank.

360   D,K

United Fund Headquarters, *1969*
Benjamin Franklin Pkwy. between 17th and 18th Sts.
Mitchell / Giurgola Associates

When the Benjamin Franklin Parkway was built, the city adopted elaborate design controls, in part to ensure that buildings east of 18th Street would create a narrow urban space. Mitchell / Giurgola's United Fund building is faithful to the intent of the parkway controls and illustrates the firm's sophisticated response to the urban context.

The small, seven-story structure conforms to its trapezoidal site. Each elevation responds to the unique conditions of its orientation. The north side is a curtain wall of gray-tinted glass, which allows maximum light for the office floors. The west wall is shielded from the sun by horizontal concrete sunscreens. The south wall, of structural concrete, has deeply recessed windows that block the south sunlight but afford views of Logan Circle.

The different character of each elevation was a dramatic contrast to the uniform exterior design of most contemporary buildings and reflected a concern for environmental conditions that would not become prevalent in architecture until the late 1970s.

361   B   PR

Franklin Roberts House, *1969*
230 Delancey St.
Mitchell / Giurgola Associates with Roy Vollmer

As part of the Society Hill urban renewal program, many 19th-century buildings were demolished and vacant land made available for new construction. The Roberts house is one of the better examples of a new house designed in a contemporary style sympathetic to its historic neighbors.

The austere brick facade is similar in scale and material to the adjacent 18th-century houses. It has fewer windows, however, and these are highly placed to ensure privacy in a manner that is reminiscent of Mitchell / Giurgola's White house. Behind the modest facade, the L-shaped plan focuses on a two-storied, skylit living room. A cantilevered library and balcony overlook the living area, which opens onto a large courtyard visible through the rear glass wall.

Mitchell / Giurgola also designed the Zebooker house, at 110–12 Delancey Street, which has a brick facade similar to its neighbors but uses large windows to create a contemporary contrast.

362   F   OP

International House, *1970*
3701 Chestnut St.
Bower and Fradley
Renovated 1983, 1992, Dagit / Saylor Architects

In 1908, Dr. A. Waldo Stevenson began informal meetings with foreign students in his West Philadelphia home. These led to the establishment of the International Students House in 1918, the first such organization in the country.

When expanded facilities were required in 1965, a competition was held to select the design for the new building. Bower and

1972
Richard M. Nixon first
U.S. President to visit
China

▼
1974
Episcopal diocese
ordains first women
priests

362

363

Fradley's winning design was considerably modified. The final design is composed of two major elements. The eight upper floors contain single rooms arranged in suites of 10, an organization that is articulated on the facade. The stepped floors of the lower levels are shaped by a dramatic interior arcade that runs the length of the building. Restaurants and shops are located on the first floor, with social and educational facilities and apartments on the upper five levels that overlook and form the roof of the arcade.

The building is an excellent example of poured-in-place concrete construction with exposed formwork patterns.

363   K

Philadelphia Electric Company, *1970*
2301 Market St.
Harbeson, Hough, Livingston, Larson

Electricity was introduced to most Philadelphia homes after World War I but did not increase in use dramatically until the 1920s, when the electrification of trolleys, suburban railroads and subways added to normal demands. Philadelphia Electric built new stations and expanded old ones. One of these later provided the location for its headquarters building.

A three-story building on the site was renovated to adjoin a new 23-story office tower. The tower is one of the few excellent examples in the city of buildings designed in the style of internationally famous contemporary architect Ludwig Mies van der Rohe. Structural steel columns, placed on the two long sides of the rectangular floor plan, are expressed on the facade and emphasize the height of the building. They are sheathed in black aluminum, matching the spandrel panels and windows, which are carefully divided into individual units to give scale to the tall facade.

A dramatic, illuminated billboard surrounding the top four floors carries messages appropriate to the season or current events. Because of its location on the western edge of downtown, it is a highly visible and handsome landmark on the city skyline.

362   B

Penn Mutual Life Insurance Company Addition, *1969–70*
See page 140.

365   A

Federal Reserve Bank, *1973–76*
6th and Arch Sts.
Ewing, Cole, Cherry, Parsky

When the Federal Reserve Bank outgrew Cret's neoclassical building on Chestnut Street, a site on Independence Mall was selected for its new headquarters. The new building contains the offices of the Federal Reserve and other government agencies, as well as specialized banking facilities for the storage and disposal of currency. One of the vaults is as long as a football field and holds millions of dollars.

Fine materials were used for interior and exterior finishes, conveying a monumental dignity and elegance that is unique in recent government buildings in the city. The meticulously detailed exterior is covered in polished pink granite panels set flush with horizontal banks of windows of varying sizes. A large vertical window divides the facade in half, reflecting the large entrance court within the building.

The spacious court is eight stories high, sheathed in travertine and covered with a skylight. Suspended in the court is a 10-ton mobile, the largest in the world, designed by Alexander Calder.

362   B

**Penn Mutual Life Insurance Company
Addition,** *1969–70*
Walnut St. between 5th and 6th Sts.
Mitchell / Giurgola Associates

Penn Mutual's headquarters have been
located on this site since the 19th century. The original, cast-iron structure
was replaced by the current headquarters
building in 1913, which was added to
in 1931. When the company decided to
expand again, they wanted a new addition
that would connect to each floor level of the
existing building.

Mitchell / Giurgola's design again
demonstrates the firm's responsiveness
to the urban context. In addition to the
constraints of a small site, the design had
to incorporate the 1838 Egyptian Revival
facade of John Haviland's Pennsylvania
Fire Insurance Co. The north facade, facing
Independence Hall, is a continuous plane
of dark glass rising to a concrete roof structure. An observation deck on the roof, no
longer in use, is reached by an exterior
elevator expressed by concrete piers. At

the ground level the glass facade steps back
to allow Haviland's facade to stand in its
original location, serving as a screen to the
entrance courtyard.

In keeping with the firm's earlier work,
each facade responds uniquely to its environment. The east wall has cantilevered
concrete sunscreens and large recessed
windows, the south wall is tinted reflecting
glass and the west wall has indentations
responding to the older building. Because
of the small site, a special structural system
was designed to simplify construction. Steel
columns on the east wall support paired
steel trusses, which span the full width of
the building and support steel decks for the
floors. The steel is covered with concrete.
This system takes advantage of the high
ceiling heights, resulting from the require-
ment to connect with floor levels of the
existing building, and provides column-free
office floors in the addition.

The overall composition provides a beautiful backdrop for Independence Hall.

▼
1974 & 1975
Flyers win Stanley Cup

▼
1975
Southeast Asian refugees begin to arrive in city

▼
1975
Microsoft founded by Bill Gates and Paul Allen

366

367

---

366   A   OP
Franklin Court, *1973–76*
312–22 Market St.
Venturi and Rauch with John Milner Associates

Benjamin Franklin built his own house and print shop in the courtyard behind a row of tenant buildings on Market Street. Although the tenant buildings survived, Franklin's house, except for sections of the foundations, was destroyed. Lacking sufficient evidence to reconstruct the house faithfully, the National Park Service commissioned the architects to design an interpretive complex. The resulting project is one of the most imaginative historic restorations in the country.

The complex consists of four elements: the restored Market Street buildings, a garden, the "ghost structures" representing the house and print shop, and an underground museum. The most original aspect of the design is the white tubular-steel frames outlining Franklin's original buildings. The plans of the house and print shop are inlaid in the paving beneath the frames, supplemented by quotes from Franklin and his wife cut into the slate paving. Beneath the ghost structure and 18th-century garden is a museum, reached by a long, sloping ramp. The museum contains imaginative exhibits about Franklin's life and accomplishments. The restored Market Street buildings also interpret Franklin's activities; one contains a post office and another a print shop. Of particular interest is the building west of the entrance archway, which has been left unfinished on the inside so that it is possible to see the original construction details.

367   B
Old Pine Community Center, *1974–77*
4th and Lombard Sts.
Friday Architects

The Third Presbyterian Church, informally known as the Old Pine Street Church, was built in 1766 and extensively remodeled during the 19th century. The community center to the south was built to serve a number of local organizations, including two churches, a historical society, an elementary school and the community at large. It contains a nursery school, community room, gym and historic archives.

The design incorporates historical elements of different periods into a wholly original composition. Flemish bond brick and white trim, typical of the colonial neighborhood, are combined with glass block and ziggurat ornamentation derived from the Art Deco style. A portion of the site is developed as a small park, with a miniature amphitheater surrounded by a terrace decorated with mosaics created by community organizations in the area. The interior shows the architects' fondness for decorative patterns and imaginative details in the tile work of the lobby and the common room, which has a trompe l'oeil Persian rug with fringe set in tile.

---

368   C,K   OP
The Gallery, *1974–77 /1982–83*
Market St. between 9th and 11th Sts.
Bower and Fradley / Bower Lewis Thrower and Cope Linder Associates

In the late 1950s, the City Planning Commission proposed the construction of a new retail and office complex east of City Hall over a rail tunnel connecting the Pennsylvania and Reading railroad lines. In 1964 the city and business community adopted a plan for a six-block-long skylit pedestrian mall, one level below the street, with retail

▼
1976
*Bicentennial celebra-
tion; Flyers win Stan-
ley Cup*

▼
1977
*John Neumann,
fourth bishop of
Philadelphia,
canonized*

▼
1980
*Phillies win World
Series*

368

370

shops connecting existing department
stores at either end.

This ambitious proposal was eventually carried out by the city and the Rouse
Company, one of the most innovative
retail developers in the country. It was one
of the first downtown enclosed shopping
malls in an American city. A dramatic skylit
pedestrian mall connected four levels of
retail stores. The entrance at 9th Street has a
stepped, glass-covered atrium leading to the
multilevel mall. Fountains, special displays
and glass-enclosed elevators enliven the
public areas. The second phase of the mall
opened in 1983 and included a new department store, a major office building and a
new underground rail station with a colorful wall mural designed by the architect
David Beck. The total complex, running
from 8th to 11th streets, combines the
excitement of the city with the successful
marketing techniques of suburban shopping centers.

369   F,G,K
ISI Building, *1978–79*
3501 Market St.
Venturi Rauch and Scott Brown

The four-story office building of the Institute for Scientific Information is part of the
University City Science Center, a research
complex sponsored by most of the colleges and universities in the Philadelphia
area. The ISI Building is a straightforward,
inexpensive structure with a typical office
layout. It is noteworthy because it is a lit-
eral expression of Venturi Rauch and Scott
Brown's concept that buildings should
be viewed as "decorated sheds." In this
instance, the decoration consists of a symmetrical pattern of brightly colored tiles
set in long horizontal bands on the main
facade. The entrance is marked by porcelain

enamel panels decorated with a bold floral
design similar to that used by the firm for
the facade of a Best store in suburban Philadelphia.

370   D
**Insurance Company of North America
Annex,** *1979*
17th and Arch Sts.
Mitchell / Giurgola Associates

The Insurance Company of North America,
organized in Independence Hall in 1792,
is the oldest stock and marine insurance
company in the country. In 1925 the company built its new home office at 16th and
Arch streets. The Georgian Revival building
designed by Stewardson and Page was converted to residential use in 2002.

Mitchell / Giurgola's addition is designed
with the firm's usual sensitivity to adjacent
buildings. But the use of a sleek, pale-green
aluminum and the strong horizontal character of three sides of the building give it a
different and a more sophisticated appearance than the firm's earlier buildings.

The design incorporates many of the
firm's standard devices. The north wall is
essentially glass, with a clear expression
of structural columns and beams. The
south, east and west walls have long
horizontal aluminum sunscreens protecting the deeply recessed glass windows.
The mechanical equipment floor at the
15th level is clearly expressed by a wide
aluminum band on the facade, which
corresponds to the cornice height of the
1925 building, visually connecting the two
structures. Portions of the facade are set
back to mark the corner entrance and allow
the structural grid to stand free. Although
crowded into the urban fabric and difficult
to view, the building is one of the most
handsome office structures in the area.

▼
1980
John Lennon fatally shot

▼
1983
Sixers win NBA championship

▼
1983
Wilson Goode elected first black mayor

371

372

371 K

The Atrium, *1982*
Market St. between 19th and 20th Sts.
Cope Linder Associates

Most recent office buildings have been built to the maximum height allowed by the city's zoning ordinances. Rouse and Associates created a prestigious office setting by constructing a low, eight-story structure around a skylit atrium extending the full height of the building. This atrium is designed as if it were a gigantic interior greenhouse. Hanging plants on the end walls complement the lush tropical landscape of the main floor. The predominantly glass walls facing the atrium have balconies and small terraces projecting into the space. Terraced, landscaped courts step down to the lower-level offices of the Philadelphia Stock Exchange, the building's principal tenant. Large windows allow visitors to watch the activities on the exchange floor.

On the exterior, the curtain wall has horizontal windows and spandrels, which change dimension to accent the center. Corner entrances are created by simple setbacks within the building volume.

THE POST-MODERN STYLE

In recent years many American architects have expressed dissatisfaction with Modern architecture. References to historic styles have become more acceptable, often interpreted in an abstract manner or used in a way that reflects their borrowed nature. One of the principal sources of this post-Modern movement is the work and writings of the Philadelphia architectural firm Venturi Rauch and Scott Brown.

Post-Modern buildings are characterized by a greater use of ornamentation and color, richer materials and an eclectic combination of elements from previous architectural styles.

372 D

Alfred J. D'Angelo Pavilion, Magee Rehabilitation Hospital, *1982–83*
15th and Race Sts.
Dagit / Saylor Architects

In 1958 the Magee Hospital constructed a modest facility to serve physically handicapped patients. The recent six-story addition, which more than doubled the hospital's size, is one of the earliest buildings in the city designed in a post-Modern manner.

Although modest in scale, the hospital addition skillfully unites the old and new buildings into a single composition. This is achieved by a continuous rusticated granite base, and by the horizontal bands of molded brick and projecting second-level terrace, which extend over both facades. The overall appearance of the building is reminiscent of designs of the 1930s, a feeling that is enhanced by the use of glass block, horizontal bands of brick and square windows.

▼
*1984
Macintosh computer
introduced*

▼
*1984
Kevin Bacon stars in
Footloose*

373

374

---

373   D,K
Four Seasons Hotel and One Logan Square,
1982–83
Race St. between 18th and 19th Sts.
Kohn Pedersen Fox

The strict controls for the Benjamin Franklin Parkway limit the height of any building on Logan Circle to 80 feet. In the early 20th century, new buildings in the neoclassical style for the Free Library, the Family Court and the Franklin Institute all adhered to the height limitation. One parcel remained undeveloped until the Insurance Company of North America commissioned this exceptional design for a hotel and office complex.

To follow the parkway controls, the architects placed the seven-story hotel on Logan Circle and the 30-story office tower to the rear, with a courtyard between the two buildings. Both buildings are faced with polished granite, giving the complex an elegant character. Light-colored granite is used on the hotel to match the color of the Franklin Institute; the office building is a darker tone. Fine materials, equally well detailed, are used in the public spaces on the interior of both buildings.

---

374   K   PR
University City Family Housing, *1982–83*
Market St. between 39th and 40th Sts.
Friday Architects

In the late 1970's, the federal government required some new low income housing be built in locations that would promote racial and economic integration. Neighborhood opposition to this policy often led to the selection of sites in unusual locations.

This imaginatively designed low income housing complex creates a sense of place for residents to overcome its predominantly institutional and commercial surroundings. The strikingly simple yet original design shows an appreciation for vernacular

architecture while also incorporating Victorian motifs from West Philadelphia houses. Most of the houses are arranged in rows perpendicular to Market Street, with small backyards and common entrance courts. The courts are framed by entrance arches and by a long row of houses on the southern edge of the site, giving privacy to the common open space. Brick is used for the facades facing the entrance courts, which also have Queen Anne style wood porches with decorated gables and bay windows. On the back the houses are covered in green aluminum siding, symbolizing the garden side of the building.

In 1992, this project was selected by the Foundation for Architecture as the best designed low income housing complex of the previous ten years.

---

375   L
Shelly Ridge Girl Scout Center, *1984*
330 Manor Road
Bohlin Powell Larkin Cywinski

As late as the 1990's, Upper Roxborough retained a largely rural character made possible by the dedication of large tracts of land as a nature center and the preservation of previous farmland. The 88 acres of woods and deep ravines of Shelly Ridge provided the Girl Scouts with a wilderness setting for a summer camp virtually within the city limits.

To preserve the one large open space on the site, five new buildings were grouped around its edge in an informal composition with an existing barn. The buildings derive their form from the barn, traditional wood-frame cabins of summer camps playfully interpreted, and an innovative use of passive solar energy. Gray clapboard, green gables, bright red trim, and red columns with undulating gray capitals marking the entrances to buildings, provide a unifying vocabulary.

▼
1985
*Police drop bomb on
MOVE house; 11 chil-
dren and adults killed,
62 homes destroyed*

▼
1985
*First U.S. Pro Cham-
pionship Bicycle Race
climbs the "Man-
ayunk wall"*

▼
1986
*HIV virus identified;
thought to be cause
of AIDS*

375

376

The main building, triangular in plan, has a twenty-five foot high timber-framed Trombe wall with brick in-fill panels that store heat in the early part of the day for release in late afternoon. Exposed structural timber trusses cover a spacious interior with a prominent free-standing Rumford fireplace and adjacent stepped seating and performance area. A semi-circular wall facing south creates a warming area and also serves as a sun dial. The caretaker's house has a central two-story space allowing heat from a wood burning stove with exposed pipes to rise to the second floor. Exaggerated south facing dormer windows allow deep penetration of natural light.

---

376   E,K   OP

George D. Widener Memorial Tree House,
1985
The Philadelphia Zoological Gardens
34th St. and Girard Ave.
Venturi, Rauch and Scott Brown

The 42 acre Philadelphia Zoo contains an interesting collection of buildings by some of the city's most distinguished architects. (See page 181.) One of the most interesting areas is the Children's Zoo where animals are free to be touched and fed. When the Children's Zoo was redesigned in the 1980's to foster a greater understanding of the natural world, the 1876 Antelope House designed by George Hewitt was trans-formed into a central feature. Six separate environmental settings were created within the Victorian structure, each designed to enable participants to view these environ-ments as their natural inhabitants would. A large cell honeycomb, for example, allows children to experience what it would be like to be a bee. Fiberglass, rubber, insulation and other artificial materials were used to create life-like trees, vegetation and animal forms of exaggerated size. The building

derives its name from a 24 foot high, 16 foot wide artificial ficus tree which projects through the roof of the existing building into an added cupola.

Not just for children, the Tree House is one of the city's most popular interior spaces and the site of many fundraising events.

---

377   L

Renfrew Center, *1986*
475 Spring Lane
Atkins, Voith and Associates

The 27 acre Renfrew farm was originally the estate of Mrs. Samuel F. Houston for whom Robert McGoodwin designed an ele-gant manor house modeled after a late 17th century French chateau. When the farm was purchased for a clinic to treat bulimia and anorexia nervosa, the manor house was adapted to administrative and therapeutic offices and a new building added for dormi-tory and dining facilities.

The residential building is set into the hillside, providing a commanding view of the farmland as well as good views of the original house. The long, thin building has its narrow end toward the manor house to minimize impact. Its scale, roof silhouette, pattern of windows, arched central bay and exterior masonry details are all derived from the manor house, but used in non-imitative ways. On the interior, the building has a residential character while main-taining the standards required of a medical institution. A pair of spacious living rooms behind the large bay window and a wide grand stair provide a central focus. Rooms for 42 residents are provided on two floors. The exterior is stucco over concrete block. Cast stone is used for the water table, still course, cornice, quoins and entrance col-umns reflecting the details and character of the manor house.

378

379

---

378   C,D

**The Graham Building / One Penn Square
West,** *1986*
30 South 15th Street
Cope Linder Associates

The area immediately west of City Hall
once contained a concentration of large and
ornate movie theaters. After the development of Penn Center, the demand for office
sites coupled with the decline in theater
attendance led to the eventual demolition of
these marvelous movie palaces.

This office building, on the site of the
former Goldman Theater, turns a difficult
location into a thoughtful example of urban
design. Taking advantage of an adjacent
small street, the main entrance is located
at the corner and marked by a cylindrical
tower of glass rising the full height of the
building. The masonry walls appear to be
a screen set in front of the glass facade.
Window openings, cornice lines and floor
levels of the main facade respond to the
adjacent office building, providing continuity in scale without imitating the older
forms. The lobby creates a gracious transition from the corner entrance to the central
elevator core through an oval space with a
small fountain.

---

379   L

**Philadelphia Industrial Correction
Center,** *1986*
8301 State Road
Jacobs / Wyper Architects and
The Ehrenkrantz Group

Prisons have been part of Philadelphia
society since the first was built at 5th and
Walnut Streets in 1778. Most have been
located on the outskirts of the city at the
time they were built and some, such as
Eastern State Penitentiary, set innovative
standards for prison reform for their times.
This prison follows in that tradition. The

site, in the far northeast section of the city,
was a garbage dump close to other prison
facilities.

The design is based on an innovative
approach to improving the quality of prison
life and reducing potential for conflict. This
is achieved by reducing barriers between
inmates and officers and by grouping
inmates in small clusters. The basic unit
of the prison is 50 cells organized on two
floors around a double-height dayroom
with access to outdoor recreation. Inmates
spend their entire time within this unit,
thereby minimizing contact and the potential for conflict among the 650 inmates. A
generous use of natural light in the corridors and brightly painted common rooms
adds to the non-threatening character. The
lobby visiting area, with marble wainscot-
ting and picture windows, was deliberately
designed to provide an atmosphere that
would not intimidate visitors.

A well equipped gymnasium, shops
and classrooms are grouped behind a
semi-circular rusticated stone and brick
colonnade. The semi-circular motif also
interrupts the stone and marble wall that
masks the facility from its neighbors,
providing an entrance courtyard for the
complex.

---

380   K

Commerce Square, *1987, 1992*
Market St. between 20th and 21st Sts.
Pei Cobb Freed & Partners

As office sites close to City Hall became
more difficult to acquire, developers began
to look farther west along Market Street and
Kennedy Boulevard. Commerce Square,
the most distinctive of the new office buildings in this area, created a civic setting as
well as office center in an area with few
surrounding amenities. The heart of the
project is a handsome landscaped public

380

383

plaza designed by Hanna-Olin Ltd. The plaza contains a circular fountain surrounded by tree-shaded outdoor cafes and retail shops. The granite paving inset with red pavers and black squares extends the materials and patterns of the towers.

The twin 40-story office towers, built in two phases, are set back in a series of slabs to reduce their scale and allow natural light to reach the courtyard most of the day. The 45 foot height line of the lower slab and ground floor arcade create a pedestrian scale. Each slab is topped by a parapet with geometric openings lightening the edge of the building at the skyline. Horizontal bands of gray glass and gray Caledonia granite inset with squares of darker granite also help to reduce the scale, except along the short sides of the towers where paired square windows form a vertical seam emphasizing the height.

381   D,K
One Liberty Place, *1987*

See page 148–149.

382   L
Frankford Post Office, *1988*
4410 Paul St.
Agoos / Lovera Architects

Early growth in Philadelphia expanded north and south along the Delaware River, rather than westward as William Penn intended. Frankford, one of the earliest settlements outside the official city-limits, still retains buildings from the 18th century. In the 19th century, Frankford, like much of area north of downtown, was the site of many manufacturing plants. The neighborhood post office draws inspiration from this mixed architectural heritage.

The building consists of two simple parts: a service area for customers and a work area to sort and distribute mail. The clere-

story monitor over the work area is a form common to industrial buildings in the area while the small gable roof over the entrance to the public spaces reflects a nearby church. The main facade and exterior walls of traditional red brick are residential in scale and use glazed headers, typical of colonial houses, to create a decorative pattern. Exposed, brightly painted duct work in the public areas gives the interior a simple but playful character.

383   G   PR
Gaither House, *1988*
3601 Baring St.
Atkins, Voith and Associates

Powelton Village developed in the 1850s when horse drawn carriage lines were extended to West Philadelphia. Most of its housing took the form of suburban villas in the Italianate style, influenced by the work of Samuel Sloan, with later 19th century houses influenced by such architects as Wilson Eyre. This three story house, on a tight corner site, reflects these local influences but interprets them in an original manner.

The main living areas are located on the second floor. This provides room on the first floor for a two car garage while giving the living areas a greater amount of natural light and better views. The double-height living room, with a large fireplace, is brightly lit by a south-facing bay window. Bay windows also provide light to the dining room and master bedroom. Like many of the older houses in the area, the exterior is a combination of two materials, brick on the first floor and stucco above with a sloping slate roof. The house is a sophisticated contemporary interpretation of the suburban villa.

386
Two Liberty Place, *1990*

381
One Liberty Place, *1987*

388
Mellon Bank Center

---

381   D,K

One Liberty Place, *1987*
1650 Market St.
Murphy / Jahn

---

386   D,K

Two Liberty Place, *1990*
Murphy / Jahn with Zeidler Roberts
Partnership
16th to 17th Sts., Market to Chestnut Sts.

---

387   D,K   OP

**The Shops at Liberty Place and
The Westin Philadelphia Hotel,** *1990*
Zeidler Roberts Partnership
16th to 17th Sts., Market to Chestnut Sts.

When new office buildings were developed
west of City Hall in the 1950s, an informal
"gentleman's agreement" limited new
buildings to a height no greater than the
491 foot City Hall tower, thereby enabling
the statue of William Penn atop the tower
to preside symbolically over the city. Wil-
lard G. Rouse's proposal to build a higher
office building sparked controversy and
extensive public debate before receiving
City Council approval.

Initially intending only to build a single
building, Rouse commissioned Wallace,

Roberts and Todd to develop an approach
to the entire block. Their master plan envisioned two tall office buildings, retail shops,
a hotel and underground parking all of
which were completed by 1990.

One Liberty Place, at a height of 960 feet
to the top of its spire, is the tallest building
in the city and the most striking landmark
day or night. The 61-story tower is set on a
three story podium which creates a pedestrian scale at the ground level. This podium
is sheathed in blue-gray polished granite
interrupted by bay windows for retail shops,
and a four story entrance portico. The
tower has a silver-blue aluminum grid
which holds horizontal bands of blue glass
and gray granite at the corners. The central
portion of the facade is silver metallic glass
interrupted by bands of gray granite at
every fourth floor, giving scale and decoration to the facade. This combination of
silver and blue glass gives the building a
delicate, shimmering quality in spite of its
massive size.

The top of the building, sheathed entirely
in glass, is formed by the repetitive use of a
gable form, resulting in a silhouette reminiscent of the Chrysler building. Linear
bands of light along the gable edges give the

building a striking presence on the skyline of the city at night.

Due to the height of the building, special consideration had to be given to the structural system. The elevator shafts and emergency stairs create a central vertical core which is connected to four major columns and eight super-columns, located in pairs at the corners of the building. The super-columns are tied back to the core by four story high trusses at three different intervals in the height of the tower. This system acts much like the riggings on a sailboat, adapting to changing directions and velocity of winds.

Two Liberty Place uses the same architectural vocabulary but in a more subdued fashion. It also has a three-story podium sheathed in the dark blue-gray polished granite, with generous windows for the lobby. The rectilinear tower plan is less elegant than One Liberty Place, due to the need to expand floor areas to suit the requirements of the building's tenant. The facade continues the pattern of silver metallic glass in the center with bands of masonry and blue-tinted glass at the corners, but use darker masonry. A single gable roof, also illuminated on its edges, crowns the tower.

One and Two Liberty Place are connected by an elegant two-story arcade of retail stores. Corner entrances lead to a glass enclosed rotunda surrounded by two levels of shops and a large food court. Along Chestnut Street, the facade is divided into bays similar in width to the older stores along the street. Elements and materials from the towers are repeated, giving continuity to the entire design; silver-blue aluminum window mullions incorporate the gable form. The 290-room Westin Philadelphia Hotel is located above the retail arcade. The hotel's simple, masonry wall surface and uniform window pattern are a neutral foil to the office towers.

Liberty Place is an outstanding achievement of both urban design and architecture. Its dramatic break with the past, carried out at such a high standard of excellence, offered Philadelphia a symbol of new possibilities and civic pride.

▼
1989
Berlin Wall falls

▼
1990
*Population of Phila-
delphia declines to
less than population
in 1920*

▼
1990
*Communist Party
relinquishes control of
the Soviet Union*

384

385

---

384 D

Two Logan Square, *1988*
100 North 18th St.
Kohn Pederson Fox

When Kohn Pederson Fox designed One
Logan Square and the Four Seasons Hotel,
the Benjamin Franklin Parkway design controls encouraged a simple and understated
architectural expression. Freed from these
controls for an expansion of the office space
on an adjacent site, the architects produced
an exuberant example of post-Modern
design.

The 34-story office tower is set on a
heavily masonry base of pink and gray
granite corresponding in materials and
character to the adjacent office building and
hotel. However, doorways and windows
are surrounded by an almost Mannerist
interpretation of such classical details
as quoins, keystones and cornices. This
effect continues in the ornate lobby of
gleaming white, gray and green striped
marble. In contrast to the masonry base,
the tower consists of vertical strips of gray
and silver glass emphasizing the height
of the building. The top five floors are
set back and terminate on the skyline in
a pedimented roof giving these floors the
appearance of a separate structure.

---

385 B

**Center for Judaic Studies, University
of Pennsylvania,** *1988*
420 Walnut St.
Geddes Brecher Qualls Cunningham

Dropsie College, founded in 1911 and
originally located in North Philadelphia,
was the only center for Judaic studies in
the country. A generous gift from Walter
F. Annenberg resulted in the move to a
new location near Independence Hall and a
subsequent affiliation with the University of
Pennsylvania. The center is a post-doctoral

research institution for the scientific study
of the history, culture, literature and reli-
gion of Judaism, and of Christianity and
Islam in the Middle East.

The building is shaped by its simple
program. The window pattern of the main
facade reflects the individual offices behind;
the west side, overlooking one of the pedestrian walkways through Society Hill, has
a large bay window providing light to the
reading room, the principal room of the
building. Large dormers on the roof let light
into the conference facilities.

The building incorporates references to
traditional elements and materials in the
surrounding area. The dormers are typical
of colonial row houses, though here much
larger in size. The brick and limestone
facades are consistent with other institutional buildings in the area.

---

386 D.K

Two Liberty Place, *1990*
See pages 148–149.

---

387 D,K   OP

The Shops at Liberty Place and
The Westin Philadelphia Hotel, *1990*
See pages 148–149.

---

388 D,K

Mellon Bank Center, *1990*
1735 Market St.
Kohn Pederson Fox

City Council approval of One Liberty Place
paved the way for other office buildings
exceeding the height of City Hall tower.
However, dense development west of City
Hall made finding suitable sites difficult.
The site for the Mellon Bank Center was
created by relocating a bus terminal and
demolishing a parking garage built in the
1950s for Penn Center.

▼
1991
*Robert Venturi named
laureate of the Pritz-
ker Architecture Prize*

▼
1991
Gulf War with Iraq

▼
1991
*USSR dissolves;
Commonwealth of
Independent States
established*

389

The large site allows the 53-story office tower to take the form of a gigantic, free standing obelisk on axis with the City Hall tower. The five-story base is sheathed in granite, with modestly articulated ornamentation, somewhat similar to the Four Seasons Hotel. The tapering tower has central bays of vertical columns expressing the structural system of the building, rising to a projecting cornice. A lattice, pyramidal structure, housing the building's cooling system, tops the tower and completes the obelisk analogy. Lobbies with walls and floors of polished marble open to both Market Street and Kennedy Boulevard. The lower level contains retail shops and connects to the underground concourse leading to the subway and commuter rail stations. A public winter garden for exhibits and displays, accessed from this lower level, is housed in a small glass structure between the tower and an older office building.

389   L   OP
Mandell Futures Center at the Franklin Institute, *1990*
20th St. and Benjamin Franklin Parkway
Geddes Brecher Qualls Cunningham

When The Franklin Instituteoutgrew its original building on South 7th Street became too small, it erected a sprawling neoclassical structure designed by John T. Windram on the newly completed Benjamin Franklin Parkway. Only a portion of Windram's design was completed, leaving the Memorial Hall, with its enormous marble statue of Benjamin Franklin, isolated from the museum galleries. The 1990 addition completes the circulation scheme and connects the Memorial Hall and old galleries to a new exhibit area.

The new exhibit areas are reached through a central atrium which also contains a cafe and museum shop. In the center, on the central axis of the original building, a bright yellow column with skylight above symbolizes the difference between neoclassical and Modern design. The atrium also provides access to the Tuttleman Omniverse Theater with its huge, multi-screen Imax theater.

The exterior of the building is a deliberate contrast to the classicism of Windram's design. Geometric volumes, handled in a straight forward Modern style, are shaped to reflect the different interior functions.

390   D,K
Bell Atlantic Tower, *1991*
17th and Arch Sts.
The Kling-Lindquist Partnership

The Bell Atlantic Tower *(see pages 148–149),* is a contrast to its predecessors in almost every way. The form and location of the building were influenced by the special design controls along the Benjamin Franklin Parkway which limit the height of buildings within 200 feet of the Parkway. To avoid the line of controls, the office tower was located on the southern edge of the site and designed with stepped-back corners. This left the northern portion of the site for a large landscaped park and fountain.

The 53 story building is easily distinguished by its rectangular shape, flat roof and warm red color. The facades are formed by projecting the stepped-back corners into a series of stepped slabs creating terraces at the top of the building and culminating in the flat roof. This breaks down the scale of the broad facades while giving the ends a narrow, graceful silhouette. The stepped-back corners and narrow floor plan create 16 corner offices per floor and allow an unusual amount of natural light to reach all interior spaces.

One of the most appealing qualities of

▼
1991
*Old-fashioned trolley
service ended on all
SEPTA routes*

391

392

the building is its color. Factory-built red granite panels with gray-tinted glass reflect the brick color of traditional Philadelphia architecture. Honed granite spandrels accent the facade and polished granite surrounds the entrance porticos. The top of the building is more glass than masonry and is the source of a cascade of light at night.

The building's structural system consists of a central structural core connected to four major columns and four super-columns. Five story high vierendeel trusses give stability to the broad facades and two story vierendeel girders tie the super-columns back to the central core.

The choice of materials and simplicity of form give the building a refined elegance and lasting presence on the Philadelphia skyline.

391   F
Clinical Research Building, University of Pennsylvania, *1991*
36th St. below Hamilton Walk
Payette Associates and Venturi, Scott Brown and Associates

The closing and demolition of the Philadelphia General Hospital provided a large site for the expansion of the University of Pennsylvania Hospital. This building contains state-of-the-art wet laboratory and research space for Penn's School of Medicine. The plan of the building places human activities at the edges to take advantage of natural light and views. Offices along the long sides of the building and lounges and seminar rooms at the end of each floor surround the interior laboratory spaces. The exterior treatment of patterned brick and cast-stone window surrounds is similar to older buildings on the Penn campus. However, both the bricks and windows are larger than usual to reduce the sense of the building's size. The top story, housing mas-

sive mechanical equipment, is differentiated by great louvers of porcelain enamelled steel. It also carries a giant rendering of Penn's shield giving visual identity at great distance.

392   G
LeBow Engineering Center and Center for Automation Technology, Drexel University, *1992*
Market Street between 31st and 32nd Sts.
The Kling-Lindquist Partnership

Since its founding in 1891, Drexel University has grown from a single building to a campus covering many city blocks and serving over 8,000 students.

This complex consists of two buildings organized as a single composition. The LeBow building houses several engineering departments and laboratories; the CAT building features labs for computer-driven manufacturing technology as well as facilities for chemical and architectural engineering. Within each building most labs face outward with views of the city, while offices and public areas face inward on a landscaped courtyard.

On the Market Street facade, large windows set behind a ground floor arcade allow the computer lab to be visible to passers-by. Two story high windows add scale to the building while providing north light for third and fourth floor labs. Round windows mark the mechanical systems floor. On the courtyard side, both buildings have a mixture of materials and fenestration. Orange brick, traditional for Drexel buildings, and strip windows enclose lab spaces, classrooms and offices. Curved glass and metal curtain walls bring light into stairwells, lounges and lobbies as well as a demonstration room and computer lab in the CAT building.

▼
1992
*Former Mayor Frank
L. Rizzo dies after
winning Republican
nomination for mayor*

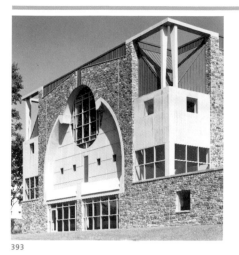

393

394

393 L	394 F OP

St. Joseph's University Chapel, *1992*
City Line Ave.
Francis Cauffman Foley Hoffmann
Architects

St. Joseph's College was founded in 1851 to serve the expanding middle class neighborhoods of North Philadelphia. When the college moved to its present location in 1927, the small population of commuting students and the lack of residential development in the surrounding area did not justify the construction of a chapel. However, by the 1990s an expanded student body, resident dormitories and established residential neighborhoods prompted the addition of a chapel.

The university administration wanted a building that would be central to student life in the 1990s and sufficiently prominent to be inviting to surrounding residents. The chapel is sited between the playing fields and the student union. The exterior is boldly contemporary in design, with relatively little religious symbolism. Wissahickon schist is offset with limestone frames and panels. Large circular windows on all four sides and concrete arches suggest the main sanctuary space within.

The spacious main worship space is framed with three-story Gothic arches supporting a vaulted ceiling that culminates in a sky-lit Greek cross. Stained glass depictions of religious themes, set in the large circular windows, provide an element of traditional symbolism.

The handsome chapel is enriched by a pipe organ built by the Hook Co. in 1868, which was rescued from a deteriorating North Philadelphia church.

Institute of Contemporary Art, *1992*
36th and Sansom Sts.
Adele Naude Santos and Associates with
Jacobs / Wyper Architects

The ICA building contains two floors of gallery spaces linked by a ramp which is visible on the main facade. The galleries are windowless, with exposed beams and ductwork, providing simple, flexible space for exhibits. The second floor gallery is divided into four quadrants by cruciform shaped girders supported by a massive column. One quadrant has a 30 foot high ceiling and skylight. In contrast to the galleries, the lobby is entirely enclosed in glass to be open and inviting to visitors. Stairs rise to a mezzanine level with access to a sculpture garden.

The sleek exterior harks back to the tradition of the International style. Ribbon windows and aluminum cladding are treated as simple flat surfaces; the free standing column at the corner is a clear historic reference, but in this case to the work of Le Corbuiser and the International movement.

395 L

The Caring Center, *1992*
3101 Spring Garden St.
Friday Architects

When the ISI Caring Center's initial sponsor decided to close its day care business, concerned parents formed a nonprofit corporation to carry on what had become a tradition of excellent child care.

The exterior is an immediate indication of the parents' and architects' commitment to make the center fun for children, without making it uncomfortable for adults. A colorful orange corrugated aluminum facade is decorated on two sides with green tadpoles growing into frogs, symbolizing the dif-

▼
1993
*Phillies win National
League pennant*

+
1994
*350th anniversary of
the birth of William
Penn*

395

396

ferent stages of a child's growth. The motif is carried through into the lobby which has a floor pattern in the design of a lily pond. Small details throughout the building reflect similar thoughtfulness about children's interests: child-height bubble windows provide great views to the world outside, cloud fixtures hang from high ceilings and a window in the stairwell allows children to observe the workings of an institutional kitchen. An outside playground provides off-hours recreation for neighborhood children.

396   L   PR
Latimer Street House, *1993–94*
1200 Latimer Street
David Slovic Associates

Most new houses built in Center City in the 1960's and 1970's respected the scale and traditional character of brick row-houses. This house is a startling and deliberate departure from that tradition in virtually every respect.

Every aspect of the exterior exaggerates its difference from its neighbors. The low, two story building is a contrast to the taller, narrow row-houses on the block. This horizontal character is emphasized by the use of dark green slate panels covering the first floor and a white stucco band covering the upper floor.

The house is organized around a courtyard that divides the building into two sections. The larger section contains living areas on the first floor with a bedroom mezzanine above, connected to a roof terrace by a suspended stair. The smaller part of the house on the other side of the courtyard contains a guest suite and studio for the owners.

The inward focus of the plan reduces the need for exterior windows resulting in facades of large, blank wall

surfaces interrupted by only a few windows asymmetrically placed and by protruding structural steel elements.

The house also abandons the post-Modern interest in ornamentation in favor of a style that combines elegant materials and details with stark industrial simplicity.

397   C,K   OP
Pennsylvania Convention Center, *1993–94*
Arch to Race Sts., 11th to 13th Sts.
Thompson, Ventulett, Stainback & Associates with the Vitetta Group, Kelly / Maiello Architects and Planners, and Livingston / Rosenwinkel P.C.

As the convention industry in the United States grew in economic importance, Philadelphia's political and business leaders recognized that the convention center in West Philadelphia was poorly located and too small to compete with other cities. A site for a new center was selected in the heart of Center City.

The center is located in two separate structures: the main meeting and exhibition area is in a new building north of Arch Street, while the Grand Hall, Ballroom and other meeting rooms are located in the historic Reading Terminal train shed. The major convention spaces are on the second level of the new building spanning 12th Street to provide a continuous floor area. Since all the functions are interior ones, the building is a simple box, relieved on the east and west facades by curved bay windows that reduce the building's scale. Folded roofs, large entryways and sculptural features for flags and lighting, mark the limestone and granite-faced main facade along Arch Street.

The train shed contains a spectacular Grand Hall, ballroom and meeting spaces. These new facilities take the form of a

▼
1999
*Mohammed Ali se-
lected Sportsman of
the Century*

▼
1999
*Google begins opera-
tion*

▼
1999
*Anna C. Verna elected
first woman president
of City Council*

398

399

building within a building to preserve the visual continuity of the original shed roof. Long skylights between the iron trusses allow natural light to flood the space, consistent with the original roof design. A few features recall the past functions of the train terminal; the dispatcher's box overhead has been retained and pairs of stainless steel bands imbedded in the terrazzo floor symbolize train tracks. Building in the shed was completed without halting operation of the Reading Terminal Farmers Market below.

398   F,K

Roy and Diana Vagelos Laboratories, University of Pennsylvania, *1997*
34th Street at Locust Walk
Payette Associates with Venturi, Scott Brown and Associates

The Vagelos building is a continuation of the approach to laboratory design previously undertaken by the collaborating architects for Penn's Clinical Research Building (393, page 152). The plan of the building is similar, with flexible laboratory space in the center and offices, study and common areas along the perimeter of the building thereby gaining natural light for these spaces. The exterior envelope also follows the Clinical Research Building with large windows and a similar use of brick and incised cast-stone that provides subtle details when seen close up. The tall top story, for mechanical equipment, provides a cap to the building that recalls the strongly articulated cornice lines of historic buildings on Penn's campus.

Several variations enrich the main facade: a large window illuminating a lecture room relieves the mass of the top story and corner windows help to break the mass of the laboratory block. The first-floor arcade interprets a classical arcade in a Venturi manner: irregularly spaced columns have

flat capitals articulated only on the sides. The Vagelos lab shows how a few simple elements in the hands of a master architect can result in an exceptional building.

399   G   PR

North Hall, Drexel University, *1999*
3200 Race Street
Michael Graves Associates and Burt Hill Kosar Rittleman

Drexel Institute, founded in 1891, became a fully accredited university in 1969. In the following decades, the university further expanded its academic offerings and began to provide on-campus residences for what was once a commuter student body. By the early part of this century, over 3,200 of Drexel's 13,000 full and part-time students lived in on-campus housing.

North Hall, one of the new residential facilities, provides four-to-six person suites for 500 students. Accommodations are organized in two six-story wings joined together by a circular stair tower that also houses the lobby and public gathering areas. The exterior reflects the colorful treatment characteristic of Graves's work. The stair tower and top floor of both wings are painted blue, providing a unifying element to the complex. The darker red of the first floor reflects the row-house character of the surrounding neighborhood, while the peach color of the intermediate floors helps reduce the mass of the building. Vertical organization of windows, as well as the introduction of larger recessed window openings for the living rooms of each suite, also help relate the scale of the dormitory to the surrounding residential area.

403
Kimmel Center for the Performing Arts

See page 161

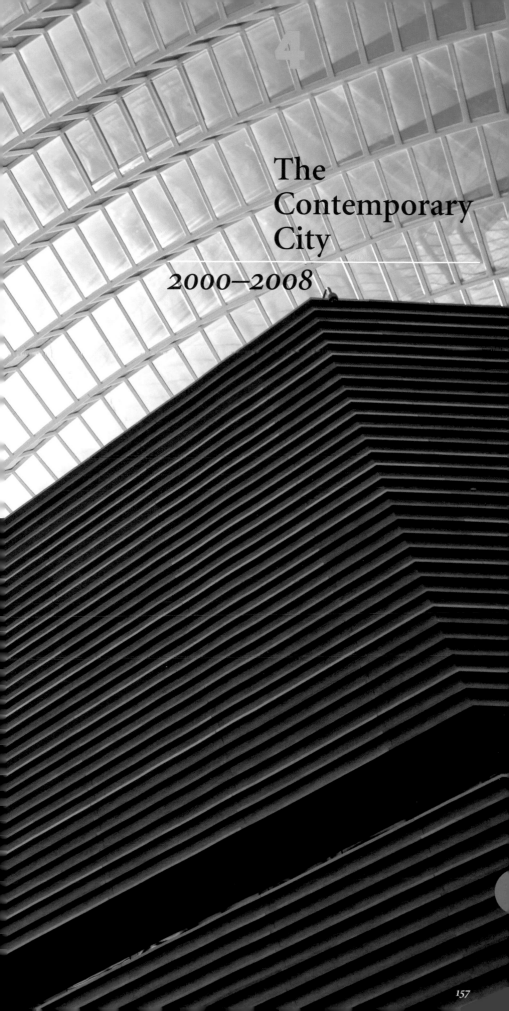

4

The Contemporary City

2000–2008

The Contemporary City

As the first decade of the 21st century began, Philadelphia was a city divided by geography, economy and race. Overall the city continued to lose population, fueled by the loss of 180,000 white residents in the 1990s that resulted in a majority "minority" population by the year 2000. Jobs within the city decreased as well while the surrounding region grew in both jobs and population. As they had for decades, inner city neighborhoods showed the impact of these shifts with blighted conditions and an estimated 29,000 vacant houses.

In contrast, Center City Philadelphia, the two-square mile downtown of William Penn's original plan, began to realize the benefits of plans begun at the end of the 20th century. New civic and cultural facilities were completed, older historic office buildings were converted to apartments and condominiums, and population began to grow. So prosperous did Center City appear, National Geographic's travel magazine labeled Philadelphia "the next great American city."

Three factors contributed to Center City's revitalization. First, the completion of the Pennsylvania Convention Center in 1994 provided a base for expanding the city's hospitality industry. New hotels, many resulting from the conversion of historic office buildings, added thousands of new rooms in the early years of the century. These were followed by the completion of the ambitious master plan for Independence Mall with a new Visitor Center, Liberty Bell Center and a second attraction to complement Independence Hall—the National Constitution Center. New programs for visitors augmented these physical facilities – tour guides in colonial dress, story tellers, a children's recreational area in Franklin Square and an abundance of bus, trolley and even amphibious boat tours.

Frank Gehry's "Ultra Cube" reflects the metallic color and shape of his titanium-covered Guggenheim Museum in Bilboa, Spain. Made of silver-colored plastic resin, it functions both as a small table and a stool.

Second, the emphasis on cultural attractions saw the completion of a new regional performing arts center and other improvements along South Broad Street. By 2008, an additional theater was constructed there. On the Benjamin Franklin Parkway the Philadelphia Museum of Art opened the Perelman Building to house expanded space for the museum's collections and administrative offices in a restored Art Deco office building with a striking new addition. Efforts to bring the Barnes Foundation's art collection from its home in Merion to the Parkway seemed headed for success, leading to the selection of Tod Williams and Billie Tsien of New York as architects for the project.

Probably the most important, and perhaps least expected, change in Center City was a boom in residential development spurred in part by the 1997 10-year tax abatement for conversion of older office buildings and the extension of that program in 2000 to new residential construction. From the introduction of the tax incentives to 2007, over 10,000 new housing units were added to Center City and adjacent neighborhoods. Nearly two-

Although part of Ralph Rucci's 2001 ready-to-wear collection, the "Stingray Swan" floor-length strapless evening dress has a graceful elegance. The gown's subtle texture comes from the use of contrasting materials—navy silk gazar and double-faced duchess satin, with an ostrich spine accent at the bust.

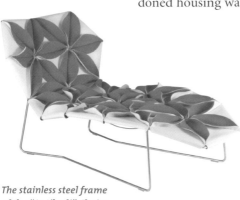

The stainless steel frame of the "Antibodi" Chaise, by Patricia Urquiola of Spain, is covered with PVC, polyurethane and felt in a lavish and playful, red poinsettia design.

thirds of these were the result of $2 billion of investment in the preservation and adaptive use of historic buildings. As a result, the population of Center City grew, which, in turn, supported new restaurants, stores and other businesses.

However, this boom in Center City residential development was not without its negative consequences. By 2006, the shift from rehabilitation to new construction resulted in proposals for many condominium towers out of scale and character with the historic neighborhoods in which they were located. Community associations sought to protect their neighborhoods with special height limitations, neighborhood master plans, design guidelines and opposition to the zoning variances liberally provided by the City to take advantage of these development opportunities. By 2007, the lack of oversight and planning led to cries for a return to the strong government planning of the 1960s.

These Center City changes were the result of the initiatives of former Mayor, and later Governor, Edward G. Rendell. Although Mayor John F. Street (2000-2008), the city's second African American mayor, facilitated the development of such large civic projects as new football and baseball stadiums, he chose to focus his primary attention on blighted inner city neighborhoods. In 2001, Mayor Street proposed an ambitious $300 million bond issue to support a Neighborhood Transformation Initiative designed to eliminate vacant houses, clean vacant lots and assemble land for new housing development. Over the five years of the program, vacant and abandoned housing was reduced to approximately 7,500 structures, many vacant lots cleaned and landscaped, and some sites assembled for new housing construction. But the success of the Neighborhood Transformation Initiative was widely debated and no neighborhoods were actually transformed as a result of its programs.

Of greater significance for many neighborhoods was the demolition of high-rise public housing that occurred throughout the city during this same period. Over 10,000 public housing units were demolished and replaced by 4,000 units of new rental and mixed income housing. This reduction in density had positive impacts on many neighborhoods in North, West and South Philadelphia.

Neither the Center City successes nor the neighborhood programs had a significant effect on overall trends. Philadelphia's population declined from 1,517,550 in 2000 and declined further to 1,449,634 in 2007—slipping in rank to the sixth largest city in the country. Low- and moderate-income households increased in number and the median household income ranked in the bottom

Distinctive product design has characterized Apple, Inc. since the Macintosh computer was first introduced. The iPhone's sleek design uses a touchscreen face to allow quick access to phone, Internet, maps, music, video and thousands of other applications.

quarter of the large U.S. cities. Employment in the city declined from 2000 to 2008 to only 26% of the regional employment. Of particular significance was the nearly 18% decline in employment in the office sector, reflecting the decentralization of office employment in the region and requiring many residents to commute to jobs in the suburbs. No new office buildings were constructed in or adjacent to Center City until 2005, and then a special state tax incentive was needed to make the first attractive to tenants, most of whom moved from other office space in Center City. Similarly, in spite of the heavy investment in tourism, the number of visitors to Philadelphia remained relatively unchanged, leading to a call to double the size of the convention center to be more competitive with other cities.

In 2007, attention shifted to Philadelphia's two waterfronts and to plans for reform of the zoning and development approval processes. With the support of the William Penn Foundation, a major new plan was created for the Central Delaware River Waterfront suggesting opportunities for new housing and ways to reclaim the riverfront for public use. Along the Schuylkill River, the completion of parks and bike and walking trails transformed the east side of the river, while the University of Pennsylvania announced ambitious plans to expand to the western edge of the river. Public interest in reform of city government led to the creation of a commission to revise the City's zoning code. A focus on planning policies in the 2007 mayoral campaign contributed to the election of former City Councilman Michael Nutter who championed new investment in the city's parks, in cultural organizations and a strong emphasis on long range planning.

The national housing crisis slowed residential development in Philadelphia significantly in early 2008. However, the city continued to move forward in other ways. Along North Broad Street, the demolition of 19 historic buildings prepared the site for the expansion of the Pennsylvania Convention Center. In anticipation of its completion, historic buildings that previously might have been considered for condominiums became hotels. The city's tallest office building—the 975-foot high Comcast Center—was completed, only to have an even taller, 1,500-foot high office building immediately proposed for a nearby site. Cultural and educational institutions moved ahead with significant new buildings designed by nationally and internationally prominent architects. Even with concerns raised by turmoil in the financial markets near the end of 2008, this continued growth and the spirit of reform generated by a new mayor sustained a feeling of optimism about Philadelphia's future.

▼
2000
George W. Bush wins
controversial presi-
dential election

▼
2001
Jetliners topple World
Trade Center towers

401

403

---

401 L
Module VII, *2000*
University of Pennsylvania
34th St. and University Ave.
Leers Weinzapfel Architects

Prior to the Modern movement, power
plants were often the subject of impressive
architectural design. The University of Pennsylvania's first power plant, constructed in
1891, was designed by the Wilson Brothers,
one of the 19th century's most prominent
architectural firms. The Central Chiller Plant
(Module VII) returns to this tradition with
a building that respects its industrial function while creating a distinctive architectural
statement and a visual gateway to the university campus.

An elegant continuous stainless steel
screen wall defines a large elliptical form that
wraps around the chiller plant. Except for
the large units that protrude above and indicate the structures function, the mechanical
equipment within is hidden by the screen
during the day. At night brightly lit and
colored pipes are visible through the screen,
creating a distinctive visual image. The site
was also able to accommodate a lighted baseball field with grandstand seating.

---

402 A,K OP
Independence Visitor Center, *2001*
6th and Market Sts.
Kallman McKinnell and Wood

In 1995, the National Park Service proposed
rebuilding the three-block mall in front of
Independence Hall that had been created in
the 1950s and 60s. After considerable public
debate, a master plan developed by the Olin
Partnership was adopted. The new plan
provided sites for three new buildings along
the western edge and at the end of the mall,
along with a new landscape plan for the first
two blocks.

The Visitor Center creates a "garden wall"
along the western edge of the second block

of the mall as indicated in the master plan.
Brick piers with vine covered trellises form
porches with large glass windows facing
onto the park. To further extend the garden
wall concept, the roof is sheathed in copper,
which will turn green with weathering.

The narrow Market Street frontage contains the entrance to the building and a
bookstore on the first floor, with an expansive outdoor viewing terrace on the second
floor also covered with a trellis. The interior
plan is organized around a central skylight
walkway extending the full length of the
building, opening into a large exhibit hall
with services for trip planning, and information on visitor attractions. A glazed cupola
in the center lets light into the exhibit area
and marks the entrance from the east. The
western side of the building contains rooms
for audiovisual presentations and meeting
spaces.

---

403 C,K OP
Kimmel Center for the Performing Arts, *2001*
Broad and Spruce Sts.
Rafael Viñoly Architects

In 1992, the Central Philadelphia Development Corporation created a plan for a
performing arts district along South Broad
Street, extending from the Academy of Music
south to Catharine Street. The central feature
of the plan was a new concert hall for the
Philadelphia Orchestra, an idea that was later
expanded into the Kimmel Center.

Beneath the huge, folded plate-glass,
barrel-vaulted roof, the Kimmel Center
contains a 2,500-concert hall and a 650-seat
recital hall. The concert hall is in the shape
of a cello with interior surfaces covered in
mahogany. The recital hall, with a revolving
stage to accommodate a variety of performance types is enclosed in a metal clad cube
and finished on the interior with light woods
and warm-colored fabrics. Each performance
facility is treated as free-standing building

▼
2001
Apple iPod introduced

▼
2002
Edward G. Rendell
elected governor of
Pennsylvania

404

405

with the irregular space between them defining an indoor public plaza lit by the all-encompassing glass and steel vaulted roof. Upper levels contain indoor rooftop gardens and a restaurant.

On the exterior, a three-story base of plain brick volumes with large expanses of glass windows reflects the material, if not the scale, of the surrounding neighborhood.

404 L

NovaCare Complex, *2001*
1601 Pattison Ave.
Michael Graves Associates and Wirt-Vitabile Architects

When the Art Deco U.S. Naval Hospital was demolished, its site become available for development. The Philadelphia Eagles professional football team formed a partnership with NovaCare to create a facility to serve both their needs. It is a team training center for the Eagles as well as an outpatient physical therapy center.

The L-shaped plan consists of a two-story brick structure housing the Eagles administrative offices, meeting rooms, an auditorium and a cafeteria that opens onto a terrace overlooking the practice field. The terrace is covered by an arched roof supported by a colonnade that gives scale and character to the simple building as seen from Pattison Avenue.

The one-story wing contains lockers, training and physical therapy facilities. A state-of-the art weight room under an arched roof with exposed trusses and generous windows also overlooks the practice field.

405 F

Melvin J. and Claire Levine Hall, *2003*
University of Pennsylvania
3340 Walnut St.
Kieran Timberlake Associates

This teaching and research facility for the School of Engineering and Applied Science deftly connects each level of three engineering buildings and creates a central courtyard out of a former service yard that also serves as a common point of orientation. The building contains research labs, offices, meeting spaces, a cyber café and 150-seat auditorium.

The design of the façade facing the courtyard combines an innovative curtain wall system with a brick frame that links the strikingly new design to the character of the adjacent older buildings. The facade is a pressure-equalized ventilated curtain wall system that is highly energy efficient. The triple-glazed wall uses return air to ventilate an inner cavity that also includes adjustable blinds. This approach allows abundant interior light while minimizing energy consumption. The curtain wall was pre-assembled off site for installation; it is the first use of this technology in the United States. The pattern of mullions framing the transparent and translucent glass of the façade is based on the Golden Section, a ratio used in buildings dating back to the Egyptians and Greeks.

The interior contains a double-height entrance lobby leading up to laboratory floors. To allow for long-term flexibility, 14-foot-high floor heights with exposed mechanical systems create loft-like spaces easily adapted to changing needs.

406

408

---

406 A,K OP
Liberty Bell Center, *2003*
501 Market St.
Bohlin Cywinski Jackson

The new master plan for Independence Mall required the demolition of Mitchell / Guirgola's Liberty Bell Pavilion and the construction of a new facility to house the Liberty Bell. Cast in 1753, the bell originally hung in the tower of Independence Hall. The name derives from the biblical inscription on the bell "Proclaim liberty throughout all the land and unto all the inhabitants thereof."

The new facility consists of three components: a covered outdoor entrance area, an exhibit hall, and the pavilion that houses the bell. The exterior forms a wall along the western edge of the mall, similar to the Visitor Center, with sun shading trellises protecting large glass windows facing onto the park. On the interior, a long undulating granite wall leads visitors through exhibits about the bell up a slightly inclined floor to the bell pavilion.

The pavilion is set at an angle to provide an unobstructed view of the tower of Independence Hall through a tall glass window. The bell is framed by curved walls of carrera white marble and is dramatically illuminated at night and easily visible through the large window facing Independence Hall.

The house in which George Washington lived while he was president was located in front of the entrance to the building. Research documenting the presence of slave quarters at the house led to a decision by the National Park Service to commemorate the house and this fact in an exhibit facility to be built on the site.

407 L OP
Lincoln Financial Field, *2003*
1020 Pattison Ave.
NBBJ Sports and Entertainment, Agoos / Lovera Architects

When the 1971 Veterans Stadium no longer served the needs of sports teams, separate new facilities were constructed for football and baseball. Lincoln Financial Field—popularly known as "The Linc"—was constructed for the Philadelphia Eagles football team.

The design of the stadium is similar to others recently built for National Football League teams. Most of the seating is located along the sidelines, creating a relatively intimate setting for a large stadium by placing seats only 60 feet from the field with three tiers of grandstand seats above. Three open plazas at the corners provide entry to the stadium and allow for views of the city skyline. The profile of the stadium is enhanced by dramatic canopies over the upper decks that provide shelter and are intended to direct crowd noise back to the field. The steel, glass and brick structure seats 68,500 and has two 27-by-96-foot video boards located above the end zones.

408 A,K OP
National Constitution Center, *2003*
525 Arch St.
Pei Cobb Freed and Partners

The Constitution Center is the third of the new buildings proposed in the Independence Mall master plan. It is the first museum dedicated to telling the story of the U.S. Constitution and its adoption in 1787.

The Center is a deliberate contrast to Independence Hall at the south end of the mall. It is a low, two-story building of pale Indiana limestone with large glass windows opening onto a two-story grand entrance hall. The building also frames the western edge of the mall, with a triangular restaurant space creating a diagonal link and entrance from Arch

409

Street. Four-foot-tall letters on the east portion of the façade contain the opening words to the preamble to the Constitution, "We the People…"

Half the building consists of conference and meeting spaces and half consists of interpretative exhibits about the Constitution, designed by the noted exhibit designers, Ralph Appelbaum Associates. A 350-seat, star-shaped theater with a 360-degree screen uses film, live actors and video projection. The Center houses over 100 interactive exhibits as well as 42 life-size bronze statues of the 39 signers and three dissenters to the Constitution.

409 L OP
Citizens Bank Park, *2004*
One Citizens Bank Way and Pattison Avenue
Ewing Cole Cherry Brott, HOK Sport

Citizens Bank Park, the second sports facility built to replace Veterans Stadium, provides a ballpark for the Philadelphia Phillies baseball team. Although it seats 43,500 fans, the ballpark has an intimate scale on both the exterior and interior.

The exterior is constructed of multiple shades of red brick, trimmed with pre-cast concrete and limestone, and topped by a green roof with a copper patina finish. Black accent bricks in the shape of baseball diamonds spell out "Philadelphia" along the Pattison Avenue façade. Four outdoor plazas at the corners for public events reflect the four historic squares of William Penn's original city plan.

The entrance to the seating area is framed by twin light towers, and provides an open view to the playing field, which is set 23 feet below street level. The grass field is surrounded by three seating decks and roof top bleachers with a view of the city skyline. Several seating decks have concourses that wrap completely around the park, providing a variety of different viewing opportunities. A special outfield entertainment area contains picnic benches, concession areas and allows a clear view of the bullpens.

A special feature of the park is a 100-foot tall sign with a gigantic Liberty Bell that rings, swings and lights up whenever a Phillies player hits a homerun.

410 G
Edmund D. Bossone Research Enterprise Center, *2005*
Drexel University
3128 Market St.
Pei Cobb Freed and Partners, Burt Hill Kosar & Rittlemann Associates

The Bossone Center houses the growing research program of Drexel's College of Engineering and other departments as well. The building provides teaching laboratories, support spaces, conference rooms, offices and a 300-seat auditorium.

The predominantly glass façade along Market Street extends the wall of the adjacent LeBow Engineering Building, terminating dramatically in a narrow point adjacent to the Paul Peck Center. The seven-story atrium behind contains the main lobby and a dramatic stair leading to the laboratory wing; it also shields an upper-level terrace.

The laboratory facilities are located in a simple, rectangular building set perpendicular to Lancaster Avenue to create a garden adjacent to Paul Peck Center. Alternating bands of glass and brick allow light into the labs along the perimeter of the building. A three-story atrium in the center, lit from above by a 70-foot-high prism, provides a community gathering space.

Special consideration was given to energy saving features. The cooling system incorporates ice storage to reduce consumption; a heat-recovery system retains heat from the laboratories and channels it back into the building.

▼
2005
Hurricane Katrina
devastates Mississippi
and Louisiana

▼
2005
Salvador Dali exhibit
attended by 400,000

413

411 K

Cira Centre, *2005*
See page 166.

412 B PR

Delancey Street House, *2005*
330 Delancey St.
Christopher Scalone Architect

The redevelopment of Society Hill in the 1960s encouraged contemporary design for new houses to be built on vacant lots created by the demolition of older buildings. This house follows in that tradition, with the added challenge of building a single-family house on a 60-foot-wide lot in a context of 16-foot-wide rowhouses. An imaginative solution was achieved by breaking the house into three sections and by interpreting historic elements of houses in the neighborhood in a contemporary manner.

The three-story east portion of the house consists of red brick in a Flemish bond pattern on a limestone base and is capped by a bracketed wood cornice. The middle section, two stories high with an outdoor roof terrace, is constructed of brick in a standard bond with a limestone first floor and is topped by a stainless steel bracketed cornice that is also a planter for the roof terrace. The west portion is set back 15 feet, thereby diminishing the scale of the house while creating a courtyard entrance visible through a decorative metal screen.

The house fits well in its historic setting through the use of architectural details that are contemporary in character, but also reflect historic patterns.

413 L PR

One Hancock Square, *2005*
1001 N. Second St.
Erdy McHenry Architecture

Northern Liberties is one of the oldest sections of Philadelphia, first established as an independent district in 1771; it was considered one of Philadelphia's first "suburbs." In recent years the neighborhood has become a center for local artists and musicians and the setting for a number of innovative architectural projects. Hancock Square is one of the largest and most dramatic.

The 380-foot long, six-story apartment building provides high ceilinged retail spaces on the first floor with apartments above. Two 12-foot-wide, bi-level apartments are stacked on top of one another to create a three-story block served by one internal corridor. Although narrow, the apartments feel spacious due to the expansive glass walls. The 12-foot module and the one- and two-story components of the apartments are articulated on the façade through concrete bearing walls and horizontal floor slabs. This expression of the interior plans helps to reduce the scale of the building as do strategic cuts in the roof line, voids cut into the façade and the angular configuration of the narrow northern end of the building. The architectural character is remarkable for a building constructed on a limited budget.

414 F

McNeil Center for Early American Studies,
2005
3355 Woodland walk
(34th and Walnut Sts.)
Robert A. M. Stern Associates

Robert A.M. Stern's three buildings in Philadelphia are a commentary on the eclectic nature of architectural design in the early 21st century. One is a sleek tall, glass office tower; another a masonry condominium tower in the post-Modern style; and the third—the McNeill Center—an interpretation of the Federal style.

The McNeill Center is devoted to study of and scholarly work about the history and culture of North America before 1850. The donor wanted a building that reflected the character of that period; the University of

411   K

Cira Centre, *2005*
2929 Arch St.
Pelli Clarke Pelli Architects and Bower Lewis
Thrower Architects

After the first tall skyscrapers were built in
the 1980s and 1990s, the area west of Penn
Center was considered the logical location
for additional office development. However,
no new office buildings were constructed
in downtown Philadelphia for 15 years and
when the first was completed it was west of
the Schuylkill River where no office buildings
had been built previously. Although this area
north of 30th Street Station had long been
the focus of planning and visionary designs,
Brandywine Realty Trust was the first to turn
visions into reality.

The Cira Centre is a 29-story steel frame
and semi-reflective glass curtain wall structure with an unusual sculptural form. At the
base, the building has four sides, while at the
top it has six. The northwest and southeast
sides taper, widening at the top as if the corners of the building had been sliced off. No
two floors have the same size or shape. The
roof of the building is also at an angle, giving

the silver building the appearance of a large
crystal.

The exterior skin is a gray semi-reflective
curtain wall that reflects sunlight by day.
At night, four facades are illuminated by
a pattern of individual LED lights set into
the grid of the window spandrels. Although
generally blue, the lights can be programmed
to produce a variety of designs, colors and
movement. Because of its location west of
the river, the building is seen from many
unexpected places; day or night it is a visually
impressive landmark.

Construction of the unusually shaped
structure presented many difficulties. The
building is located over operating rail tracks
and is isolated from adjacent streets that
carry normal utilities. One of the unusual
features of the building is the window
washing equipment, without which the all-
glass exterior would not have been feasible.
A slit in the roof allows an armature to
emerge, from which a window-washing cage
is hung. The cage runs on an east-west track
that lowers and pivots two window washers
over all sides of the buildings.

A bridge connects the two-story entrance
lobby directly to 30th Street Station.

415

416

Pennsylvania wanted a contemporary design. Stern's design attempts to balance both interests.

The two-story brick simplified Federal-style building is located prominently along 34th Street. A lecture hall and offices occupy the first floor, with the research library on the second. The overall form of the building resembles a large house. Traditional Federal elements include the Flemish-bond brick pattern, an entrance portico and a hipped roof surrounded by a raised parapet. The regular pattern of windows is reflected in openings in the parapet, intended to give the modest building added scale in its prominent setting.

415   L   PR
York Square, *2005*
305 Vine St.
Cecil Baker and Associates

In the early 2000s, Center City witnessed a surge in condominium construction encouraged by a 10-year tax abatement for new residential development. While many architects tried to insert taller, contrasting buildings into Philadelphia's historic districts, York Square is a remarkably restrained design that fits easily within the context of its Old City neighborhood.

Built on the site of a former service station and warehouse, the project provides 60 live/ work lofts in a six-story structure. The use of brick on a large structural frame with industrial scale and industrial style windows reflects the character of surrounding loft buildings. The simple mass is relieved by lower heights at the corners and by a central courtyard with projecting bay windows trimmed in a lighter color. The courtyard provides an entrance to the building without disrupting the pedestrian continuity along the street.

416   L   PR
Avenue North, *2006*
Broad Street and Cecil B. Moore Avenue
Erdy McHenry Architecture

Avenue North, created by the same architect/ developer team responsible for Hancock Square (413), consists of two buildings covering a full block adjacent to the Temple University campus. A two-story structure along Broad Street contains retail and restaurant space and a seven-screen movie theater that projects trailers on the south façade at night. The second floor consists of a folded plane wrapped around roof, sides and floor level. Within this wrapped plane angled floor-to-ceiling glass zig-zags back and forth to help relieve the block long façade.

To the west a 12-story apartment building cuts diagonally across the site so as to minimize shadows on the residences along 15th Street. A four-story brick corner building creates a transition in scale to the surrounding neighborhood. Known as "The Edge," the apartment building accommodates 1,200 students in flexibly arranged suite configurations based on a four-bedroom module. Student lounges are located on each floor and sky lounges on the upper floors.

The facade of The Edge is made of pre-fabricated metal panels that snap onto the structural system. The highly irregular window pattern reflects the interior flexibility of the plan and is a result of varying the placement of four types of exterior wall panels. On the west façade the window pattern is punctuated by the floor-to-ceiling glass openings for the student lounges.

417 L PR

Rag Flats, *2006*
1338–52 E. Berks Str.
Onion Flats/ Plumbob, LLC., with Minus
Studio and Cover
E Flats, *2006*
133–37 Laurel St.
Plumbob, LLC.
Berks/Hewson, *2008*
1317 Berks St. and 1318 Hewson St.
Onion Flats/ Plumbob, LLC./Jig

Since 2005, Onion Flats, Plumbob, LLC, and Jig—an inter-related development company, architectural firm and construction company—have worked together to produce a series of innovative residential developments in the Northern Liberties / Fishtown sections of Philadelphia. Although each project has its own distinctive character, they are united by a strong commitment to sustainable design.

Rag Flats (above, top), located on the site of a former industrial rag factory, is a residential garden community. Three-story houses modeled after the traditional Philadelphia "trinity" define a central courtyard.

Surrounding units in the form of row-houses and lofts create a complex environment with indoor and outdoor rooms at all levels. The exterior envelope combines stained cedar, stucco and metal panels. Environmental features include radiant floors, photovoltaic panels, a green roof and a 6,000-gallon cistern for rainwater collection.

E Flats (above, bottom) consists of 4 dwelling units in three-story twin row houses on a sloping site. A wood-frame structure is sheathed with stained cedar and concrete board. Color composite panels adorn the bay windows. Each structure contains a usable green roof.

Berks/Hewson is the first LEED-Gold residential project in Philadelphia. Two three-bedroom, infill row-houses are faced with stained cedar, stucco and metal panels. Each building is topped with a usable green roof and contains a rainwater collection tank and solar thermal panels for hot water. Each unit comes with a three-wheeled electric vehicle.

▼
2008
*Phillies win World
Series*

▼
2008
*Barack Obama elected
President*

418

419

---

418   OP

Leonard Pearlstein Art Gallery, *2007*
Drexel University
33rd St. and Lancaster Walk
Sandvold Blanda Architects

Although only 1,000 square feet, this modest art gallery on a tight site creates a notable landmark on the Drexel campus. The one-story building's unusual shape suggests a piece of sculpture rather than a building. Slate tiles line the base and support aluminum-clad sloping walls and a pitched roof. The corner of the building is angled, reflecting the similar treatment of the entrance to Furness's Centennial Bank (now the Paul Peck Center), diagonally opposite. Within, a single exhibit room provides space for student and professional art exhibitions.

419

Skirkanich Hall, *2007*
210 S. 33rd St.
Tod Williams Billie Tsien Architects

The eastern portion of Penn's campus contains many of the university's older buildings with little space for expansion and new facilities. When the School of Engineering and Applied Science wanted to add teaching and research labs for bioengineering, it had to accommodate over 50,000 sf of new facilities on an 18,000 sf site while also maintaining pedestrian access through the building. The resulting building is a bold departure from the traditional architectural character of the campus.

Skirkanich Hall is squeezed between Paul Cret's renovation of the Moore School and Cope and Stewardson's 1906 Towne School, both brick- and limestone buildings. To accommodate the program, the main block of the building projects well beyond the property line and its six stories dominate the adjacent buildings. The differences are further emphasized by the building's unusual materials. The slightly angled façade consists

of predominantly green glazed brick with vertical bands of "shingled" windows divided by acid-etched, zinc spandrel panels. Black granite paving lines the entrance, walkway and the public spaces of the first floor. Within the building, exposed vertical concrete surfaces have been bush-hammered to reveal the blue aggregate and give the feeling of stone.

Skirkanich Hall connects to the engineering complex formed by Levine Hall, placing the university's two most distinctive new buildings in direct juxtaposition with one another.

Significant buildings under construction in 2009

Annenberg Public Policy Center
University of Pennsylvania
202 S. 36th St.
Fumihiko Maki Associates with Ballinger

Hancock Square, Phase 2
2nd and Poplar Sts.
Erdy McHenry Architecture

Fox School of Business
Temple University
1800 Block North 13th St.
Michael Graves & Associates with Burt Hill Kosar Rittleman

National Museum of American Jewish History
5th and Market Sts.
Polshek Partnership Architects

Residence Hall, Drexel University
213 N. 34th St.
Erdy McHenry Architecture

10 Rittenhouse Square
130 S. 18th St.
Robert A.M. Stern Architects with PZS Architects

420   D,K

Comcast Center, *2008*
1701 John F. Kennedy Boulevard
Robert A. M. Stern Architects with Kendall
Heaton Associates

When Comcast Corporation became the
principal tenant in Liberty Trust's proposed
office tower, it transformed the original
Kasota limestone-clad building into a shimmering glass tower that became the tallest
building in Philadelphia. At 58 stories and
975 feet, the Comcast Center is a stunning
achievement in planning, architecture and
environmental design.

The plan of the building continues the
tradition created by Edmund Bacon at Penn
Center of linking the street level and the
Suburban Station concourse level with open,
light-filled spaces. From the 500-seat dining
court, visitors and employees ascend into a
120-foot high winter garden. The double-
skin clear glass curtain wall allows south light
to flood the entrance to the building, which
is enhanced by a 83-foot wide art video
screen designed by Niles Creative Group and

Jonathan Borofsky's sculptural figures fixed
to beams high above like tightrope walkers.
In front of the building a half-acre plaza contains an outdoor café that defines the street
edge along John F. Kennedy Boulevard.

The tapered tower is sheathed in double-
glazed-high-gloss glass panels so carefully
detailed that the walls appear seamless.
Reflected light and clouds blend with the
sky in a manner that almost makes the tall
building disappear. Clear Starphire glass at
the corners and the top relieve the reflective
surfaces, adding to the building's character.
High ceilings take advantage of the glass
facade to let natural light deep into each
floor.

When completed Comcast Center was
the tallest "green" building in the country. It
achieved LEED certification through the use
of heat deflecting glass and other features,
including floor-by-floor heating and air conditioning controls, waterless urinals and the
use of recyled materials.

Comcast Center is a both a dramatic and
understated addition to the city skyline.

Philadelphia Architects

Philadelphia architects have had national impact on the evolution of architectural styles since the late 18th century. The eleven individuals and firms described here have made unique contributions to American architecture well beyond the importance of their work in Philadelphia. Many other architects have contributed to the development of the city, however, and deserve mention.

Benjamin Latrobe, Robert Mills and John Haviland introduced classical details in the early 19th century and helped popularize the Greek Revival style. Samuel Sloan, working in the Gothic and Italianate styles, was one of the finest residential architects of his time and an important hospital designer. In the late 19th century The Wilson Brothers, one of the largest firms in the city, designed some of the most important railroad stations in the world. George and William Hewitt and Willis Hale created many outstanding houses in the High Victorian and Queen Anne styles.

There were also a number of fine residential architects in the early 20th century. Horace Trumbauer created fashionable mansions in addition to important civic buildings; outstanding suburban houses were built by Frank Miles Day, Edmund Gilchrist, Robert McGoodwin, Mellor and Meigs, and Duhring Okie and Zeigler. Ralph Bencker and Ritter and Shay were proponents of the Art Deco style of the 1930s. Oscar Stonorov introduced European housing concepts of the 1920s and 30s to the city.

Architecture in the 1950s and 60s was strongly influenced by Edmund Bacon, director of the City Planning Commission, and G. Holmes Perkins, dean of the School of Fine Arts at the University of Pennsylvania. They created a climate that encouraged many young architects in the city. Among the most influential firms were Vincent G. Kling, Bower and Fradley and Geddes Brecher Qualls Cunningham. These firms, the strength of Penn's architecture school and the presence of Louis I. Kahn, Robert Venturi and Romaldo Giurgola produced a subsequent generation of talented architects whose work has come to prominence in the past several decades. Included among them are Bolen Cywinski Jackson and Kieran Timberlake Associates, both recipients of the AIA National Architectural Firm Award, and others too numerous to list.

Margaret Esherick House drawing by Louis I. Kahn, 1958

Robert Smith
1722–1777

Robert Smith was born in Scotland into a family that included many masons. After an early apprenticeship in the building trades, he emigrated to America sometime before 1749, for in that year he was married in Philadelphia.

Most scholars consider Smith the foremost carpenter-architect of the colonial period. The carpenter-architect was primarily a builder. It was his responsibility to imitate the models of the past and adapt those to the modest building needs of the colonial city. Smith worked closely with his clients to determine the building design and to select details from the numerous architectural handbooks in the city and in his own collection. Once the design was agreed upon,Smith hired a team of men and acted as general contractor.

Smith's principal buildings in Philadelphia are the Christ Church steeple, St. Peter's Church and Carpenters' Hall. He designed the first building for the institution that would later become the University of Pennsylvania. His design for the Walnut Street Prison attracted attention for its use of fireproof vaults. Because of his fine reputation, Smith obtained commissions outside the city for Nassau Hall at Princeton University and for the first insane asylum in the colonies, at Williamsburg. His most prestigious patron was Benjamin Franklin, for whom he built a residence on Market Street while Franklin was in England.

Smith was active in cultural and political affairs. He was a member of the American Philosophical Society and the Carpenters' Company, serving on its Rule Book committee. He died a wealthy man; his estate included a country home, a tavern and at least thirteen rental properties.

Nassau Hall, Princeton University

William Strickland
1788–1854

William Strickland was born on a New Jersey farm. His family moved to Philadelphia, where his father worked as a carpenter for Benjamin Latrobe on the Bank of Pennsylvania. Strickland was apprenticed to Latrobe for two years before deciding to pursue a career as a painter. In 1815, however, he was catapulted to the front ranks of the architectural profession when he won the design competition for the Second Bank of the U.S. This design established the Greek Revival style in the United States.

Strickland was one of the foremost Greek Revival architects in the country. He relied completely on the illustrations in Stuart and Revett's *Antiquities of Athens* as the basis of his work, which combined the elegance and grace of Greek architecture with the practical requirements of new public buildings. In addition to the Second Bank, his outstanding work in Philadelphia includes the Merchants' Exchange and the U.S. Naval Home. Strickland worked in other styles, including Egyptian and Gothic Revival, and even used Georgian for his reconstruction of the Independence Hall steeple. Strickland was also a gifted engineer and one of the first to recognize the importance of the railroad. He predicted that railroads would supersede canals as a principal means of travel.

When the financial crisis of 1837 left a dearth of commissions in Philadelphia, Strickland was asked to design the new Tennessee State House in Nashville. It was his last major work and one of his most impressive. Strickland remained in Nashville until his death and is buried in a tomb beneath the State House.

Tennessee State Capitol Building, Nashville, Tennessee

Thomas Ustick Walter
1804–1887

As a young man, Thomas Walter followed his father's professional calling as a mason. He was twice apprenticed to William Strickland, from whom he received a sound training in architecture and engineering.

Walter established his own architectural practice in 1830. His first important commission was the Philadelphia County Prison, also known as Moyamensing, an early example of Gothic style. His national reputation was established when he won the competition for the design of Girard College in 1833, a project that occupied him for fourteen years.

Girard College was the high point of Walter's Philadelphia career. Soon after its completion he left the city to design the expansion of the U.S. Capitol Building in Washington, D.C. Walter was responsible for the extension of the Senate and House wings and the addition of the Capitol dome. Ill health forced his return to Philadelphia in 1865, where he worked as a consultant to John McArthur on the design of City Hall.

Walter taught at the Franklin Institute and was one of the founders of the first professional organization of architects; he was later a founding member of the American Institute of Architects and second president of the organization.

U.S. Capitol Building, Washington, D.C.

John Notman
1810–1865

John Notman was one of the most disinguished 19th-century American architects. Notman was born in Edinburgh, Scotland; it is believed members of his family were stonemasons. He probably was first apprenticed to a carpenter and then worked in an architectural office in Edinburgh before coming to the United States in 1831.

Although his first building for the Library Company was simple and ordinary, Notman's subsequent work introduced a succession of sophisticated English architectural styles to Philadelphia and to the United States. Notman's innovative design for Bishop George Washington Doane's house in Burlington, New Jersey, was the first Italianate house built in this country. It was highly publicized by Andrew Jackson Downing in his influential pattern books. Notman also designed the first Renaissance Revival building in America, the Philadelphia Athenaeum. He was also an important source of the Gothic Revival style. His patron, Bishop Doane, was the first American member of the Camden Ecclesiological Society, which advocated archaeologically correct Gothic design for church architecture. Notman used the Gothic style for Doane's Chapel in Burlington, but his finest Gothic building is St. Mark's Church in Philadelphia.

Notman had a national reputation, and his commissions ranged from churches in Delaware, Maryland and western Pennsylvania to cemeteries and garden designs in Cincinnati, Ohio, and Richmond, Virginia. He designed several picturesque villas still standing in Princeton, New Jersey. Notman was a founding member of the American Institute of Architects and the Pennsylvania Institute of Architects.

Guernsey Hall,
Princeton, New Jersey

The Wilson Brothers

Joseph M. Wilson
1838–1902

Joseph Wilson was born in Phoenixville, Pennsylvania, an iron and steel manufacturing center. After receiving a civil engineering degree from Rensselaer Polytechnic Institute in New York, he came to Philadelphia and worked for the Pennsylvania Railroad designing bridges, factories, depots and warehouses. In 1876 he founded an architectural and engineering firm with his older brother, John, who also graduated from Rensselaer and worked for the railroad.

Their first commission was the design of two major exhibition buildings at the 1876 Centennial Exposition. By the 1880s the firm had risen to a position of unquestioned authority in the architectural and engineering field. Although they are best known for their railroad terminals, the firm designed every type of building in Victorian society. The diversity of their commissions, the engineering accomplishments and extraordinary eclecticism of their designs rank them as one of the most important firms in the last quarter of the 19th century.

The Wilson Brothers undertook projects throughout the United States and in Mexico and Central America, but their best buildings were in Philadelphia. For Anthony J. Drexel, the prominent banker, they designed a house, his first bank and the main building of Drexel Institute. While completing the Reading Terminal, they also created the Pennsylvania Railroad's Broad Street station, one of the greatest train stations in the world, which featured a three-hinged, wrought-iron arched shed considerably larger than the Reading shed.

Joseph Wilson was a fellow of the AIA, a member of the American Philosophical Society and the British and American societies of Civil Engineers, and president of the Franklin Institute. After he died the firm continued, but it never achieved the prominence it had under his leadership.

Broad Street Station
(demolished)

Frank Furness
1839–1912

Frank Furness was born and raised in Philadelphia. He began his career as a draftsman for John Fraser, architect of the Union League. In 1859 he entered the New York atelier of Richard Morris Hunt, the first American architect to study at the École des Beaux-Arts. There Furness was exposed to John Ruskin's theories of architectural ornament and Viollet-le-Duc's structural concepts, the two principal influences on his own architectural style.

Furness joined the Union Cavalry in 1861 and earned the Congressional Medal of Honor. After the war, he established an office in Philadelphia, first with Fraser, then with George Hewitt. Furness and Hewitt became nationally prominent through their design for the Pennsylvania Academy of Fine Arts. Louis Sullivan worked briefly for Furness at this time.

After the firm dissolved in 1875, Furness practiced alone for the next six years. His personal style of Victorian Gothic design reached its pinnacle and most of his finest banks were completed during this time, including his masterpiece, the Provident Life and Trust Co.

In 1881, his assistant, Allen Evans, became his partner. During the next fourteen years they became one of Philadelphia's largest and most prominent firms. Much of Furness's residential work dates from this period as well as his great railroad stations. His remodeling of The Wilson Brothers' Broad Street Station made it the world's largest railroad passenger terminal.

Furness completed the widely acclaimed University of Pennsylvania Library in 1888. By the time it was finished, architectural tastes had turned to the Classical Revival. Furness's career declined, and his accomplishments were virtually ignored for fifty years; many of his most important buildings were demolished. Today Furness is recognized as one of Philadelphia's greatest architects.

Provident Life Trust Co., Philadelphia (demolished)

National Bank of the Republic, Philadelphia (demolished)

Wilson Eyre
1858–1944

Wilson Eyre was born in Florence, Italy. His family returned to the United States in 1869 and lived in a number of different places, including Newport, Rhode Island. Eyre's desire to be a painter was discouraged by his family. Instead, he chose a career in architecture, considered a more reputable profession. He studied at the Massachusetts Institute of Technology with Henry Van Brunt, and moved to Philadelphia around 1877 to work for James Peacock Sims. When Sims died, Eyre took over his practice.

Eyre maintained a small office, preferring to supervise the details of design himself. His only partner, John McIlvain, joined him in 1912. Most of their commissions came from Pennsylvania and New York.

Eyre traveled abroad, particularly in England, where he undoubtedly saw the work of Norman Shaw and C. F. A. Voysey, residential architects who designed in the Queen Anne and Arts and Crafts styles. Eyre's Philadelphia friends included Maxfield Parrish, Violet Oakley, Henry Mercer and the architects Frank Miles Day and Walter Cope. Eyre helped form the T-Square Club, which promoted Arts and Crafts principles through its annual exhibitions and catalogs. He was also a founder, with Frank Miles Day, of *House and Garden* magazine, and its editor from 1901 to 1905.

Eyre was one of the most imaginative residential architects of his generation. His work brought national attention to Philadelphia's fine suburban architecture. Eyre's playful, witty details made frequent use of sculptural ornament, enigmatic human figures and the reversal of traditional architectural motifs. Initially, Eyre was attracted to the complexities of the Queen Anne style, but as his practice evolved, his fondness for the Shingle style led him to simple yet sophisticated forms. By 1920, Eyre's career had virtually ended. When he died in 1944, his accomplishments were generally forgotten.

E. S. Sand Residence,
Southport, Connecticut

Paul Philippe Cret
1876–1945

Paul Philippe Cret was born in Lyons, France. He studied at the École des Beaux-Arts in Paris. Cret came to Philadelphia at the age of 27 to establish an École system at the University of Pennsylvania. He held his teaching position for 34 years, during which time he revolutionized the architectural program and established the most successful Beaux-Arts curriculum in the country.

Cret entered 23 competitions during his career, winning his first competition in 1907 for the design of the Pan American Building in Washington, D.C., which some judge to be his best work. Cret's interest in city planning involved him with groups devoted to improving Philadelphia's physical structure. He prepared the original plans for the Benjamin Franklin Parkway and redesigned Rittenhouse Square as part of a general improvement of the area.

Cret served in the French army during World War I. Afterwards he reestablished a thriving practice in Philadelphia and continued to devote himself to architectural education. Two of his major commissions of this period were the Federal Reserve Bank in Philadelphia and the Folger Shakespeare Library in Washington, D.C., which Cret considered to be his finest work.

Although Cret advocated an architecture which honored the past, he was strongly influenced by the International style. His 1933 design for the Hall of Science at the Century of Progress Exhibition in Chicago had International style elements and featured a 175-foot tower bristling with neoned fins and crowned by a Deco *torchère*. Cret also designed a series of streamlined trains in the 30s, including the Denver and Pioneer Zephyrs.

Cret continued to practice architecture despite failing health. He died of a heart attack during an air inspection of the site for a veterans' hospital.

Pan American Union Building, Washington, D.C.

George Howe
1886–1955

George Howe was born in Worcester, Massachusetts. He lived abroad with his mother and attended school in Switzerland. After further education at Groton and Harvard, Howe returned to Paris for architectural training at the École des Beaux-Arts.

Howe settled in Philadelphia in 1913, originally working for Furness, Evans and Co. Later he joined the fashionable firm of Mellor and Meigs in a partnership that lasted until 1926. The three partners often worked independently but shared a common regard for fine building materials and traditional English and French residential styles. Howe later referred to this style as Wall Street Pastoral because of the number of stockbrokers attracted to these houses.

The commission for the PSFS office building caused dissension over the firm's direction. Howe favored the International style. Mellor and Meigs preferred traditional architectural styles. Howe left the firm and entered into partnership with the Swiss architect William Lescaze. Together they designed a building for PSFS that is still one of the outstanding examples of modern architecture in this country.

PSFS was the pinnacle of Howe's career. During the Depression and Second World War, Howe formed brief partnerships with Norman Bel Geddes, the New York industrial designer, and with Philadelphia architects Oscar Stonorov and Louis Kahn. He also was supervising architect for the Public Buildings Administration in Washington and dean of the Architecture School at Yale from 1950–54.

As a sophisticated gentleman of aristocratic breeding, Howe was a unique advocate of the modern movement. He brought the International style to America, with a sense of its possibilities for richness despite its austerity. That he achieved this in conservative Philadelphia was astounding.

William Stix Wasserman House, Whitemarsh, Pennsylvania

Louis I. Kahn
1901–1974

Louis Kahn was born in Estonia and came to Philadelphia in 1906. His family, although poor, stressed the value of art, music and the Old Testament. Kahn studied architecture at the University of Pennsylvania, where Paul Philippe Cret was one of his teachers. His first job was for the city architect John Molitor, with whom he designed a Beaux-Arts plan for the 1926 Sesquicentennial Exposition.

Through most of the Depression and early 1940s Kahn was unemployed. He formed a research group with other architects to study city planning and housing. Here he met George Howe and Oscar Stonorov, with whom he later associated. From 1947 to 1957, Kahn taught at Yale. During this time he evolved a personal philosophy of design that was an almost Platonic search for fundamental principles, which he expressed in poetic, often obscure language. From 1957 on he taught at Penn, where he was influenced by two brilliant engineers: Robert le Ricolais and August E. Komendant. Kahn and Komendant worked together on the Richards Medical Building, the first unified expression of Kahn's structural and spatial concepts, and later on the Kimbell Museum in Fort Worth, Texas, which Kahn considered his finest work.

Kahn's use of heavy materials, elaborate structural solutions and natural light to form interior space offered dramatic contrast to the prevailing styles of modern architecture. Major projects outside Philadelphia include the Salk Institute in California, the Library at Phillips Exeter Academy in New Hampshire and the Yale Center for British Art in New Haven. After returning from a trip to one of his last projects, the new government complex in Dhaka, Bangladesh, Kahn died suddenly of a heart attack. His drawings and sketches are located in the Architectural Archives of the University of Pennsylvania.

Kimbell Art Museum, Fort Worth, Texas

Phillips Exeter Academy Library, Exeter, New Hampshire

Mitchell / Giurgola

*Romaldo Giurgola
1920–*

*Ehrman B. Mitchell, Jr.
1924–2005*

Romaldo Giurgola was born in Italy and received his architectural education at the University of Rome. He came to the United States in 1950 to study at Columbia, then taught at Cornell. Giurgola worked initially as a cover designer and editor of *Interiors* magazine. Because of his exceptional drawing skills, many architectural firms hired him to prepare renderings, including the Philadelphia firm Bellante and Clauss. There he met Ehrman Mitchell. Mitchell studied architecture at the University of Pennsylvania and had headed the firm's offices in London and Arizona. In 1958, when Giurgola came to teach at Penn, they established a partnership to design the Wright Brothers Museum at Kitty Hawk, North Carolina.

Mitchell / Giurgola's reputation was established by their competition entries. Their second-place entry in the Boston City Hall competition received considerable attention, and in 1968 they won the competition for the AIA headquarters in Washington, D.C. They also won competitions to renovate Louis Sullivan's Wainwright Building in St. Louis and the 1982 international competition to design the New Parliament House in Australia.

Mitchell / Giurgola's work is distinguished by a strong concern for urban context and for structural and design innovation. Many of the firm's best buildings are in Philadelphia. Other significant buildings include the Volvo headquarters in Gothenburg, Sweden, and the Anchorage Historical and Fine Arts Museum in Alaska. Both partners made important contributions to the architectural profession. Mitchell was national president of the AIA in 1979; Giurgola was chairman of the architecture department at Columbia. He received the 1982 AIA Gold Medal. In 1984, Giurgola moved to Australia to supervise construction of the New Parliament House. He established an architectural practice there and became an Australian citizen.

*Parliament House,
Canberra, Australia*

*Sherman Fairchild
Center for the Life
Sciences, Columbia
University*

Venturi, Scott Brown and Associates

Robert Venturi 1925–

Denise Scott Brown 1931–

Robert Venturi was born in Philadelphia, the son of a wholesale fruit grocer. He studied architecture at Princeton and then worked briefly for Eero Saarinen. As recipient of the 1954 Prix de Rome, Venturi traveled in Italy, developing an appreciation for historical styles that influenced his architectural theories.

Venturi worked briefly for Louis Kahn before establishing a his own practice first in partnership with William Short (1960) and then with John Rauch from 1964 to 1988. While in partnership with Rauch, Venturi completed his first significant buildings, including Guild House in Philadelphia.

Venturi also taught at the University of Pennsylvania, where he met his future wife and collaborator, Denise Scott Brown, who joined the firm in 1967. She was born in South Africa and studied architecture and planning in England and at Penn. Her interests in vernacular design, social planning and neighborhood organization reinforced Venturi's architectural theories.

The firm's publications and buildings were instrumental in turning attention away from the International style toward the current eclectic design attitudes referred to as "post modern" architecture. Venturi's *Complexity and Contradiction in Architecture* (1966) is considered one of the most important statements of contemporary architectural theory. *Learning from Las Vegas* (1972) drew attention to the popular use of ornamentation in the urban landscape and its application to architectural theory. Some of the firms most notable recent buildings are the Sainsbury Wing of the National Gallery in London, the Anlyan Center at the Yale School of Medicine, the Life Sciences Complex at the University of Michigan and the provincial Capitol Building in Toulouse, France. In 1991, Venturi was named laureate of the Pritzker Architecture Prize.

Wu Hall, Butler College, Princeton University

Building Chart

	Before 1700	1700 to 1739	1740 to 1779
Row house or block		Letitia House Elfreth's Alley	109–25 Kenilworth St. Workman Place Abercrombie House Shippen-Wistar House Powel House
Freestanding house	Wynnestay	Rittenhouse Homestead Bel Air Stenton Glen Fern Wyck	Grumblethorpe Mount Pleasant Cliveden Bartram Hall Deshler-Morris House
Apartments and hotels			
Retail stores and banks			Head House and Market Sheds Green Tree Tavern Man Full of Trouble Tavern
Office buildings			
Industrial buildings			

Religious buildings	Gloria Dei	Christ Church	St. Peter's Church
			Old Pine Presbyterian
			  Church
			St. George's Methodist
			  Church

Other institutional buildings			
Civic buildings		State House (Independence Hall)	Carpenters' Hall
Other			

1780 to 1799	1800 to 1834	1835 to 1849	1850 to 1869
Sansom's Row	York Row Franklin Row Girard Row Portico Row	1600 Locust St.	1800 Delancey Place 1500–2300 Green St. 2000–2100 Spruce St.
Hill-Physick-Keith House Reynolds-Morris House Woodlands Loudoun Upsala Lemon Hill			Gaul-Forrest Mansion Piper-Price House Watson House Mitchell House Burholme Ebenezer Maxwell House Woodland Terrace William Montelius House
			St. Charles Hotel
First Bank of the U.S.	Second Bank of the U.S.	PSFS	Farmers' and Mechanics' Bank Bank of Pennsylvania Lit Brothers PSFS
	Merchants' Exchange	Philadelphia Contributionship	
	Girard Warehouses Fairmount Waterworks Frankford Arsenal		Elliot and Leland Buildings Leland Building Smythe Buildings
	Arch St. Meeting House St. Stephen's Protestant Episcopal Church	Old St. Joseph's Church Church of St. James the Less Cathedral Basilica of SS. Peter and Paul St. Augustine's Church St. Mark's Church	Arch St. Presbyterian Church Tenth Presbyterian Church St. Clement's Episcopal Church Church of the Holy Trinity St. Timothy's Protestant Episcopal Church Second Presbyterian Church
Pennsylvania Hospital	Pennsylvania Institution for the Deaf and Dumb U.S. Naval Asylum Founders Hall, Girard College		Pennsylvania Hospital for Mental and Nervous Diseases Masonic Temple
Congress Hall U.S. Supreme Court	Franklin Institute (Atwater Kent Museum)	The Athenaeum	Union League
Fort Mifflin	Sparks Shot Tower Eastern State Penitentiary Walnut Street Theatre	Laurel Hill Cemetery	Academy of Music

|---|---|---|---|
Row house or block	Houses for a Moravian Community 1500 Block North 17th St. 4206–18 Spruce St. Bedell House	Clarence Moore House Neil and Mauren House Parkside Ave. Houses Joseph Leidy House 3500 Powelton Ave.	Benezet St. Houses
Freestanding house	Thomas Hockley House William Rhawn House Disston Mansion Anglecot Houston-Sauveur House Druim Moir Brinkwood Poth Mansion Charles Lister Townsend House	Kemble-Bergdol House Cummings House Overbrook Farms Fell–van Rensselaer House Oaks Cloister	100–102 West Mermaid Lane Adelbert Fischer House High Hollow Lincoln Drive Development Pepper House French Village Abraham Malmed House
Apartments and hotels	Wissahickon Inn	Divine Lorraine Men's Dormitories Nugent Home for Baptists St. James Apartments	Bellevue Stratford Hotel Robert Morris Hotel Alden Park The Drake Hotel
Retail stores and banks	Pennsylvania Co. for Insurance on Lives and Granting Annuities Centennial Bank Kensington National Bank Keystone National Bank		John Wanamaker's Department Store Jacob Reed's Sons Store Girard Trust Co. Packard Motor Car Co. Drexel and Co. Bldg.
Office buildings	Victory Building	Reading Terminal The Bourse Crozer Bldg. Land Title Bldg. Corn Exchange	Public Ledger Bldg. Fidelity Mutual Life Ins. Co. N. W. Ayer Bldg. WCAU Bldg.
Industrial buildings	Dobson Carpet Mills A. J. Holman Factory Navy Yard	Tutlemann Brothers and Faggen Bldg.	Reading Co. Grain Elevator Lasher Printing Co.
Religious buildings	Church of the Gesu St. Vincent's Parrish Hall Tabernacle Presbyterian Church First Unitarian Church Mother Bethel African Methodist Episcopal Church Baptist Temple	Mount Sinai Cemetery Chapel Church of the Advocate	Church of St. Francis de Sales Philadelphia Divinity School Rodeph Shalom Synagogue
Other institutional buildings	College Hall, University of Pennsylvania Pennsylvania Academy of the Fine Arts Ridgway Library Pennsylvania Institution for the Deaf and Dumb Fisher Fine Arts Library Drexel Institute Main Bldg.	Germantown Cricket Club University Museum Overbrook School for the Blind	
Civic buildings	City Hall Memorial Hall		Philadelphia Museum of Art Free Library of Philadelphia Rodin Museum
Other	Gravers Lane Station	Reading Terminal	Franklin Field 30th Street Station

1930 to 1969	1970 to 1984	1985 to 1999	2000 to 2008
Midvale Ave. Houses Society Hill Town Houses Franklin Roberts House		Latimer Street House	Delancey St. House E Flats Berks/ Hewson
Schofield Andrews House Charles Woodward House Margaret Esherick House Vanna Venturi House Dorothy Shipley White House Hassrick/Sawyer House		Gaither House	
Carl Mackley Houses Parkway House Hill Hall Guild House Society Hill Towers	International House Four Seasons Hotel University City Family Housing .	North Hall, Drexel Univ	One Hancock Square York Square Avenue North Rag Flats
Federal Reserve Bank	The Gallery	The Shops at Liberty Place	
One East Penn Square Bldg. PSFS Customs House Penn Center Complex Municipal Services Bldg. 500 Walnut St. Addition Police Administration Bldg. Rohm and Haas Bldg. United Fund Headquarters	Philadelphia Electric Co. Penn Mutual Life Ins. Co. Addition Federal Reserve Bank ISI Bldg Insurance Co. of North America Annex The Atrium One Logan Square	Graham Building / One Penn Square West Commerce Square One Liberty Place Two Logan Square Two Liberty Place Mellon Bank Center Bell Atlantic Tower	Cira Centre Comcast Center
			Module VII
Ukrainian Cathedral		St. Joseph's University Chapel	
Philadelphia Psychiatric Center Richards Medical Research Lab.	Shelly Ridge Girl Scout Center George D. Widener Memorial Tree House	Old Pine Community Center D'Angelo Pavilion, Magee Rehabilitation Hospital Skirkanish Hall Renfrew Center Center for Judaic Studies Mandell Futures Center Clinical Research Building LeBow Engineering Center Institute of Contemporary Art The Caring Center Vagelos Laboratories	Bossone Research Center Levine Hall McNeill Center Pearlstein Art Gallery
		Franklin Court Frankford Post Office Pennsylvania Convention Center	Kimmel Center Liberty Bell Center National Constitution Center Independence Visitor Center
University Parking Garage		Philadelphia Industrial Correction Center	NovaCare Complex Citizens Bank Park Lincoln Financial Field

The Tours

Philadelphia is a very easy and pleasant city to see. Center City, the area covered by Penn's original city plan, contains many interesting neighborhoods and significant buildings within close walking distance of one another. Other areas can be reached easily by public transportation or by beautiful drives along the Schuylkill River.

The 10 tours that follow were selected to represent significant concentrations of buildings described in the catalog and to draw attention to neighborhoods of different historic periods. Each tour follows a specific route that passes the most significant buildings in the area. However, each tour map indicates the location of all buildings listed in the catalog in the tour area, thereby enabling the tour to be tailored to fit individual interest and available time.

The tours assume that most people are starting from City Hall. Directions are given for public transportation or driving routes from that point. Tours A, B, C, D, F and G are walking tours; tours E, H and J are intended to be driven. The map below shows rapid transit and bus routes connecting Center City and West Philadelphia tours; the map to the right shows road access to the Fairmount Park, Germantown and Chestnut Hill tours.

In addition to the tours of individual areas, tour K is a highlights driving tour, which provides an overview of the city and many important buildings.

All maps throughout the book are oriented north-up.

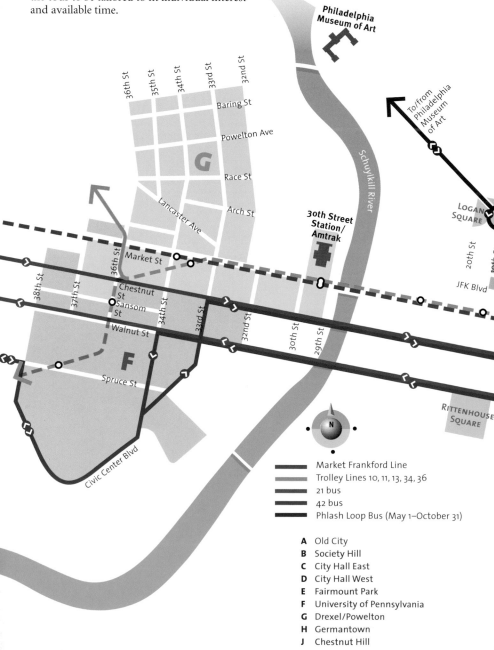

▬▬	Market Frankford Line
▬▬	Trolley Lines 10, 11, 13, 34, 36
▬▬	21 bus
▬▬	42 bus
▬▬	Phlash Loop Bus (May 1–October 31)

A Old City
B Society Hill
C City Hall East
D City Hall West
E Fairmount Park
F University of Pennsylvania
G Drexel/Powelton
H Germantown
J Chestnut Hill

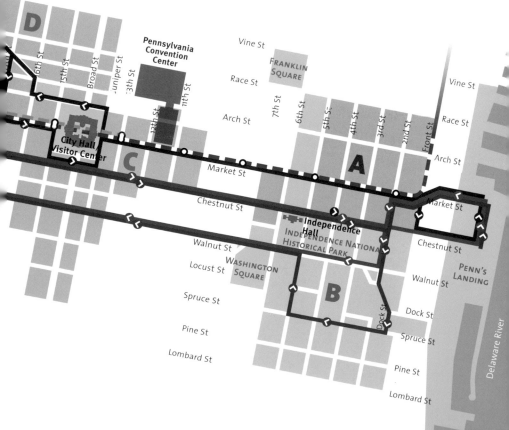

Old City

Old City, was the first residential area in Philadelphia and contained the city's earliest houses and religious buildings. In the 18th century, the city's principal markets were located along Market Street from Front to Third sheets, and there was a ferry terminal to New Jersey at the foot of Market Street. These activities encouraged commercial development in the blocks immediately north and south. By the 19th century, most of the houses had been displaced by commercial buildings. Now the area is noteworthy for its fine examples of 18th and 19th century commercial architecture of different styles and materials ranging from brick, terra cotta and marble to cast iron. Many of the buildings have been converted to apartments, as Old City has once again become a desirable residential neighborhood.

The Old City tour begins at Second Street, which can be reached by taking a Market Street bus or Market Frankford Line to the Second Street station, a good example of contemporary subway station design. The tour first proceeds north past the three major colonial landmarks in the area: Christ Church; Elfreth's Alley, the oldest continuously occupied street in the country; and the Arch Street Friends Meetinghouse. The route continues through Independence Mall from the National Constitution Center to the Liberty Bell Center and then along Chestnut Street, once the city's financial district.

The few remaining cast-iron fronted buildings are on Arch Street; commercial buildings of all eras may be seen on Third Street; and Chestnut Street has several outstanding examples of 19th-century Italianate banks as well as loft buildings, which were precursors of the late 19th- and 20th-century Commercial style.

Interspersed among the major streets are a number of small alleys with handsome commercial structures. It is worth wandering off the tour route to walk down Strawberry Street, Bank Street, Church Street or Letitia Street. There are also a number of unusual tourist attractions in the area, including the U.S. Mint, Betsy Ross's House and Benjamin Franklin's grave in the Christ Church Burial Ground.

107 **Christ Church**
22–26 N. 2nd St. OP

145 **Girard Warehouses**
18–30 N. Front St.

297 **Tutlemann Brothers & Faggen Building**
56–60 N. 2nd St. PR

220 **Smythe Buildings**
101–111 Arch St. PR

106 **Elfreth's Alley**
Between Front & 2nd, Arch & Race Sts. PR

a **Betsy Ross House**
239 Arch St. 1740 OP

211 **St. Charles Hotel St. Charles Court**
60–66 N. 3rd St. PR

141 **Arch Street Meeting House**
330 Arch St. OP

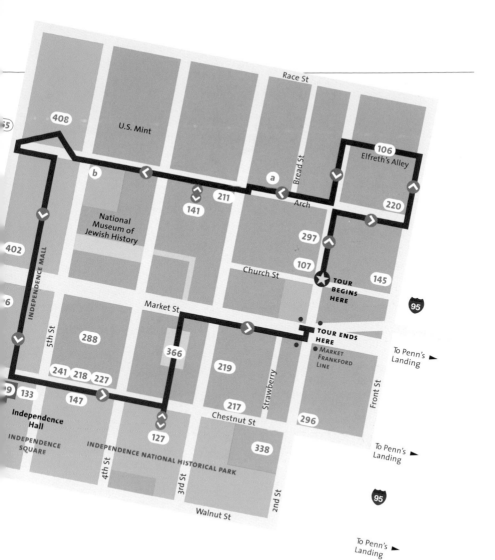

b **Chirst Church Burial Ground**
5th & Arch Sts. OP

408 **National Constitution Center**
525 Arch St. OP

365 **Federal Reserve Bank**
6th & Arch Sts.

402 **Independence Visitor Center**
6th & Market Sts. OP

406 **Liberty Bell Center**
501 Market St. OP

359 **Rohm & Haas Building**
6th & Market Sts.

151 **Franklin Institute Atwater Kent Museum**
15 S. 7th St. OP

318 **Public Ledger Building**
6th & Chestnut Sts.

131 **Congress Hall**
Chestnut St. at 6th St. OP

109 **State House Independence Hall**
Chestnut St. between 5th & 6th Sts. OP

133 **U.S. Supreme Court Building**
Chestnut St. at 5th St. OP

288 **The Bourse**
11–21 S. 5th St. OP

241 **Pennsylvania Company for Insurances on Lives & Granting Annuities American Philosophical Society, Richardson Hall**
431 Chestnut St.

218 **Farmers' and Mechanics' Bank American Philosophical Society, Franklin Hall**
427 Chestnut St.

147 **Second Bank of the U.S.**
420 Chestnut St. OP

227 **Bank of Pennsylvania The Bank Building**
421 Chestnut St.

127 **Carpenters' Hall**
320 Chestnut St. OP

366 **Franklin Court**
312–322 Market St. OP

219 **Leland Building**
37–39 S. 3rd St.

217 **Leland & Elliot Buildings Independence Park Hotel**
235–237 Chestnut St.

338 **U.S. Customs House**
100 S. 2nd St.

296 **Corn Exchange**
2nd & Chestnut Sts.

Society Hill

B

Sansom St

WASHINGTON
SQUARE

6th St

Society Hill contains the largest concentration of original 18th-century architecture of any place in the United States. As one of the principal residential areas of colonial Philadelphia, the neighborhood included homes of the wealthy and poor, prominent churches, markets and taverns. Most of the important 18th-century civic buildings were adjacent to the neighborhood, including Independence Hall and other buildings associated with the founding of the country.

When the population of the city moved westward in the 19th century, Society Hill deteriorated and became an area of dilapidated houses and commercial buildings, dominated by the city's wholesale food market. Today, as a result of a major urban renewal program begun in the 1950s by the city, state and federal governments, it is one of the most attractive and affluent neighborhoods in the city. All 18th-century buildings in the area have been restored, and parks and landscaped walkways were created to replace demolished buildings. Where sites were available for new construction, the best modern design was encouraged to contrast with the original colonial buildings. The neighborhood was renamed Society Hill after the 18th-century Society of Free Traders, which had its offices on the hill above Dock Creek.

Society Hill is one of the most pleasant areas of the city to walk through. The easiest way to reach the area is to take a Market or Chestnut Street bus or the Market-Frankford subway to Fifth Street. The walking tour begins at Independence Square and proceeds to Head House Square, passing the Society Hill Towers, the symbol of the neighborhood's transformation in the urban renewal period. The tour returns to Independence Square and Independence National Historical Park along St. Peters Walk, one of the many landscaped walkways in the area. The National Park Service gives tours of the Independence Hall area, which start at the Visitor Center.

There are many outstanding contemporary buildings on this tour, including the Penn Mutual Office addition, which incorporates the facade of an earlier Egyptian Revival building. Many buildings are open to the public: St. Peter's Church, the Hill-Physick-Keith House, the Powel House and the Independence Hall complex should not be missed.

The tour ends at the Curtis Building, the lobby of which contains *The Dream Garden,* a 49-foot-long, colored glass mosaic created in 1914 by Louis Comfort Tiffany from a design by Maxfield Parrish. It contains over 100,000 pieces of glass in 260 color tones.

109 **State House**
Independence Hall
Chestnut St. between
5th & 6th Sts. OP

131 **Congress Hall**
Chestnut St. between
5th & 6th Sts. OP

133 **U.S. Supreme Court**
Chestnut St. between
5th & 6th Sts. OP

a **American Philosophical Society**
104 S. 5th St.
1785–89, Samuel
Vaughan OP

147 **Second Bank of the U.S.**
420 Chestnut St. OP

127 **Carpenters' Hall**
320 Chestnut St. OP

135 **First Bank of the U.S.**
120 S. 3rd St. OP

338 **Customs House**
100 S. 2nd St.

156 **Merchants' Exchange**
143 S. 3rd St.

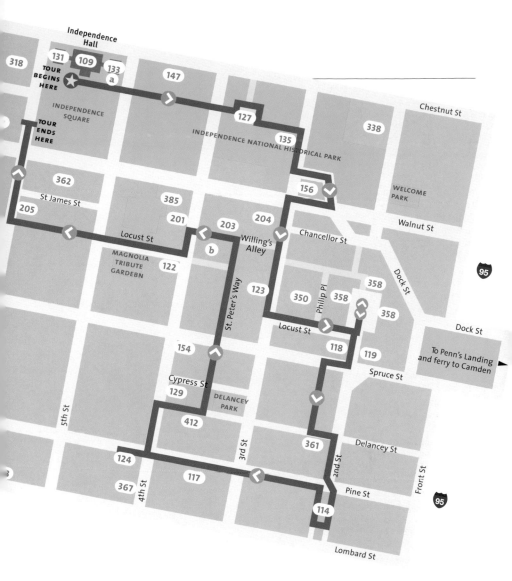

City Hall East

C

As the city grew farther west, the market sheds along High Street—as Market Street was known until 1859—followed, reaching 8th Street by the 1820s and 12th Street some years later. Other businesses located along the street adjacent to the markets, including the city's first department store founded in 1871. Even after the sheds were demolished in 1859, the market halls remained in the area, of which the Reading Terminal Market is the last surviving example. The concentration of retail shopping was reinforced by the construction of the Reading Railroad's new terminal at 12th Street in 1893 and by the decision to locate the new City Hall on Center Square in 1870.

Suburban growth in the 1950s along with new suburban shopping centers drew customers away from Market Street. To strengthen the retail area, the City supported the development of a new retail complex, The Gallery, with a three-block-long, enclosed pedestrian mall.

The tour should begin with a visit to the City Hall tower, which provides a magnificent view of the city, and a tour of the ornate public rooms of City Hall. From City Hall the tour proceeds east to the Reading Terminal train shed, then returns past the PSFS Building (now Loews Philadelphia Hotel) through the Grand Court of the Wanamaker Building to Broad Street. The southern portion of Broad Street is the Avenue of the Arts cultural district. At night, the principal buildings along South Broad Street are dramatically lit. The tour ends on the west side of City Hall where it connects to the City Hall West tour.

Many of the buildings along the tour are open to the public and contain exceptional interiors. In addition to City Hall, the Reading Terminal train shed and the Wanamaker Building, the most exceptional interiors are found in: the Masonic Temple, Loews Philadelphia Hotel (the PSFS Building), the Ritz-Carlton Hotel, the Academy of Music and the Kimmel Center.

243 **City Hall**
Broad & Market Sts.
OP

352 **Municipal Services Building**
1500 John F. Kennedy Blvd.
OP

237 **Masonic Temple**
1 North Broad St.
OP

333 **One East Penn Square Residence Inn by Marriott**
1–21 N. Juniper St.

280 **Reading Terminal & Shed**
Market St. between 11th & 12th Sts. OP

368 **The Gallery**
Market St. between 9th & 11th Sts. OP

397 **Pennsylvania Convention Center**
Arch St. between 11th & 13th Sts. OP

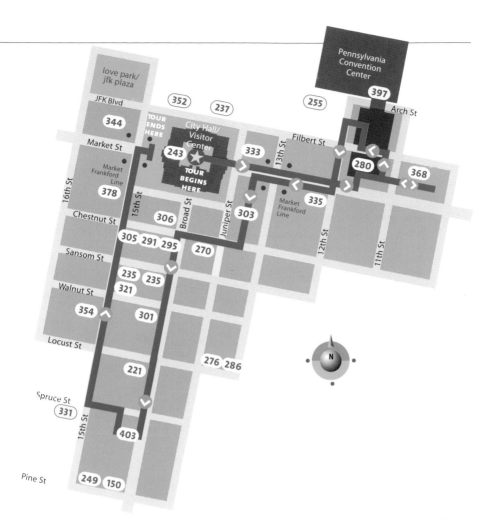

255 **A. J. Holman Factory**
1222–26 Arch St. PR

335 **PSFS Building**
Loews Philadelphia Hotel
12 South 12th St.

303 **John Wanamaker's**
Department Store
The Wanamaker Building
1300–24 Market St. OP

270 **Keystone National Bank**
1326 Chestnut Sts.

306 **Girard Trust Company**
Ritz-Carlton Hotel
34–36 S. Broad St. OP

295 **Land Title Building**
100–18 S. Broad St.

235 **Union League**
140 S. Broad St.

301 **Bellevue Stratford Hotel**
The Bellevue
Broad & Walnut Sts.
OP

276 **Clarence Moore House**
1321 Locust St.

286 **Joseph Leidy House**
1319 Locust St.

221 **Academy of Music**
232–46 S. Broad St. OP

403 **Kimmel Center**
Broad & Spruce Sts. OP

150 **Pennsylvania Institution**
for the Deaf and Dumb
Philadelphia College
of Art
University of the Arts,
Hamilton Hall
320 S. Broad St.

249 **Pennsylvania Institution**
for the Deaf and Dumb
Philadelphia College
of Art Addition
University of the Arts
320 S. Broad St.

331 **The Drake**
1512–14 Spruce St. PR

354 **1500 Walnut Street**
Addition
(On 15th St.)

321 **Drexel & Company**
Building
135–43 S. 15th St.

235 **Union League (Trumbauer**
addition)
Sansom & S. 15th Sts.

305 **Jacob Reed's Sons Store**
1424–26 Chestnut St.

291 **Crozer Building**
1420 Chestnut St.

378 **The Graham Building/**
One Penn Square West
30 S. 15th St.

344 **Penn Center Complex**
Market St. from 15th
to 18th Sts.

City Hall West

D

The 1870 decision to locate City Hall on Center Square—set aside for public buildings in William Penn's plan—shifted the center of the city away from 6th and Chestnut streets. At the time, Center Square was on the edge of the developed area of the city. However, the primary influence on the development of the area west of City Hall was the construction of the Pennsylvania Railroad's Broad Street Station in 1881. Its remodeling by Frank Furness in 1889 made it the largest railroad passenger station in the world. Office buildings were constructed adjacent to the station, but the "Chinese wall" of elevated railroad tracks extending west to 30th Street isolated the area to the north. The construction of the Benjamin Franklin Parkway beginning in 1907 transformed this area into a civic boulevard and the site of many cultural institutions.

The demolition of the Broad Street Station and the "Chinese wall" in 1953 launched the post-war transformation of Center City. It made way for the city's first new office buildings since the Depression, known collectively as Penn Center. Nearly all new office building construction has remained in the immediate area, including the city's tallest buildings.

The tour begins on the west side of City Hall and should include a visit to the City Hall tower, which has a magnificent view of the city, and a tour of the ornate public rooms in City Hall. The tour proceeds through the Penn Center complex past the city's major office buildings and connects to the beautiful Benjamin Franklin Parkway. Many of the buildings on the tour are open to the public and have distinctive interiors. In addition to City Hall, the most notable interiors are found in: the Shops at Liberty Place, the lobby of the Comcast Center, the Arch Street Presbyterian Church, the Cathedral Basilica of SS. Peter and Paul, the Pennsylvania Academy of the Fine Arts—designed by Frank Furness—and the Masonic Temple.

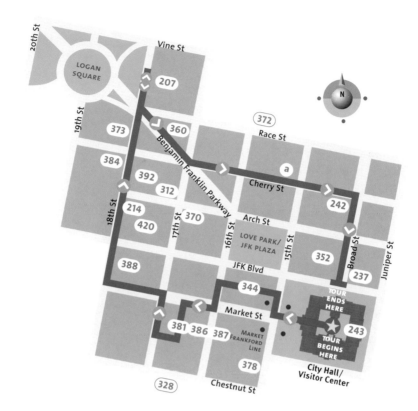

**214 Arch Street
Presbyterian Church**
1724 Arch St.

392 Bell Atlantic Tower
18th & Arch Sts.

384 Two Logan Square
100 N. 18th St.

**373 One Logan Square
& Four Seasons Hotel**
Race St. between
18th & 19th Sts.

**207 Cathedral Basilica
of SS Peter & Paul**
18th & Race Sts. OP

360 United Fund Building
Benjamin Franklin Pkwy.
between 17th & 18th Sts.

312 Robert Morris Hotel
1705 Arch St.

370 INA Building Addition
17th & Arch Sts.

**372 Magee Rehabilitation
Hospital**
1513 Race St.

**a Race Street Meetinghouse
and Friends Center**
15th & Cherry Sts.
1974, Cope & Lippincott
OP

**242 Pennsylvania Academy
of The Fine Arts**
Broad & Cherry Sts.
OP

**352 Municipal Services
Building**
1500 John F. Kennedy Blvd.
OP

237 Masonic Temple
1 North Broad St. OP

Fairmount Park

E

Fairmount Park is the largest park within city limits and one of the oldest in the country. Much of the area was originally occupied by the country homes and estates of colonial families. One of these, Lemon Hill, was acquired in 1844 to protect the city's water supply. In the years that followed, other estates were purchased, as was additional land on both sides of the Schuylkill River, to create the 3,000-acre park. In 1876 the park was the site of the Centennial Exposition. Most of the Exposition Buildings were demolished, but the Ohio House and Memorial Hall, now the Please Touch Children's Museum, remain. A detailed model of the Exposition is housed in Memorial Hall.

The demolition of temporary hotels built for the Exposition created the opportunity for developers to create large, ornate residential buildings along Parkside Avenue opposite the park.

Because Fairmount Park is so large, it must be seen on a driving tour. The tour starts at the Art Museum and proceeds along the beautiful Kelly Drive, past Boat House Row, a delightful collection of Victorian buildings housing the area's rowing associations. The tour through the east park passes the major colonial mansions, all of which are open to the public. In the west park are the Exposition buildings as well as a beautiful Japanese House, Shofuso. The park also contains an unusually fine collection of sculpture. The Philadelphia Zoo, oldest in the country, is adjacent to the park and contains many fine buildings. The tour returns to the Art Museum along the West River Drive, with a magnificent view of the Philadelphia skyline and the distinctive Cira Centre office building.

314 **Philadelphia Museum of Art**
26th St. & Benjamin Franklin Pkwy. OP

324 **Fidelity Mutual Life Insurance Co. Perelman Building**
2501 Benjamin Franklin Pkwy. OP

146 **Fairmount Waterworks**
Schuylkill River behind Art Museum OP

a **Boat House Row**
E. River Dr.

140 **Lemon Hill**
Lemon Hill Dr. OP

120 **Mt. Pleasant**
Mt. Pleasant Dr. OP

b **Rockland**
Mt. Pleasant Drive
1800

c **Ormiston**
Reservoir Rd. 1798 OP

d **Laurel Hill (Randolph House)**
Edgely Dr. 1748; 1760 OP

e **Woodford**
Strawberry Drive
1756; 1772 OP

f **Strawberry Mansion**
Strawberry Drive
1797, possibly by Summerville; 1825;
1870 OP

202 **Laurel Hill Cemetery**
3822 Ridge Ave. OP

342 **Philadelphia Psychiatric Center**
Ford Rd. & Monument Ave.

g **Belmont Mansion**
Belmont Mansion Dr.
1755 OP

h **Japanese House**
Lansdowne Dr. east of Belmont Ave.
1953, Junzo Yoshimura OP

i **Cedar Grove**
Lansdowne Dr. near Black Rd. 1748; 1752 OP

j **Sweetbrier**
Lansdowne Dr. 1797 OP

247 **Memorial Hall Please Touch Museum**
42nd St. at N. Concourse

281 **Parkside Avenue Houses**
4100 block Parkside Ave.
1897 PR

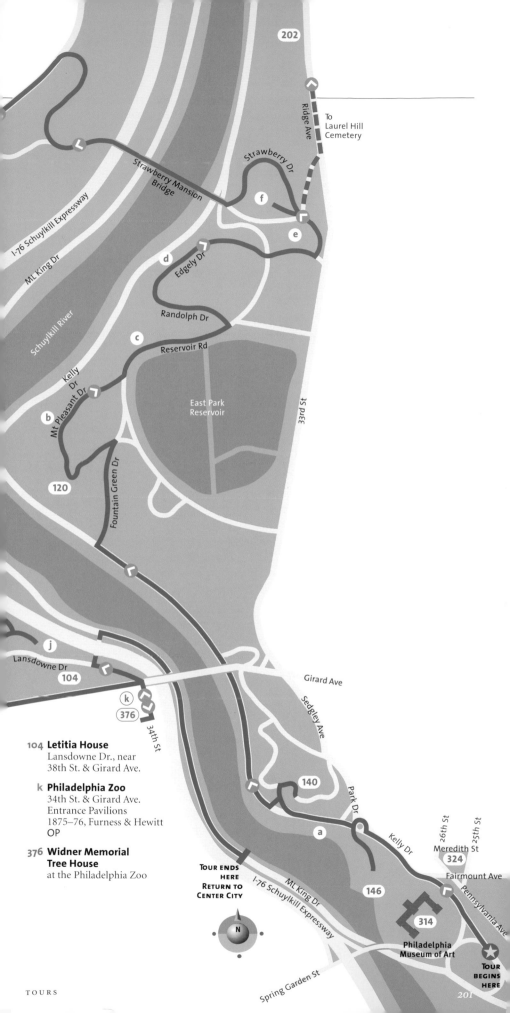

202

Ridge Ave

To
Laurel Hill
Cemetery

Strawberry Dr

Strawberry Mansion
Bridge

I-76 Schuylkill Expressway

ML King Dr

f

e

d

Edgely Dr

Randolph Dr

c

Reservoir Rd

Schuylkill River

Kelly
Dr

Mt Pleasant Dr

b

120

Fountain Green Dr

East Park
Reservoir

33rd St

j

Lansdowne Dr

104

k

376

34th St

Girard Ave

Sedgley Ave

140

a

Park Dr

Kelly Dr

26th St

25th St

Meredith St

324

Fairmount Ave

146

Pennsylvania Ave

314

Philadelphia
Museum of Art

TOUR
BEGINS
HERE

TOUR ENDS
HERE
RETURN TO
CENTER CITY

I-76 Schuylkill Expressway

ML King Dr

Spring Garden St

N

104 **Letitia House**
Lansdowne Dr., near
38th St. & Girard Ave.

k **Philadelphia Zoo**
34th St. & Girard Ave.
Entrance Pavilions
1875–76, Furness & Hewitt
OP

376 **Widner Memorial
Tree House**
at the Philadelphia Zoo

University of Pennsylvania

F

The University of Pennsylvania campus contains an impressive collection of outstanding buildings by local and nationally prominent architects. The university was founded in 1751. It was originally located at 4th and Arch streets and then moved to 9th and Market Streets. When the campus was moved to West Philadelphia in 1871, the area was still rural countryside with some scattered houses north and west of the campus.

The Penn campus has grown from its original setting around College Hall to a large urban complex covering many city blocks. Its buildings are representative of virtually every architectural style of the past 100 years and include examples of the work of Frank Furness, Louis I. Kahn, Mitchell / Giurgola, Eero Saarinen, Robert A.M. Stern and other nationally prominent architects. *The Campus Guide* by George E. Thomas contains a complete catalog of the University's Buildings.

Under the direction of Paul Philippe Cret, the Graduate School of Fine Arts, one of the finest architectural schools in the country, was an early advocate of the École des Beaux-Arts philosophy. In the 1960s, the school's faculty included many of America's leading architects. Penn's Architectural Archives, located in the Fisher Fine Arts Building, has an extensive collection of architectural documents including the papers, drawings and architectural models of Louis I. Kahn.

The easiest way to reach the University of Pennsylvania is to take the Market Frankford Line to 34th Street and walk south to Walnut Street, or take a bus on Walnut Street to 34th Street. The tour includes outstanding examples of the work of Frank Furness, Venturi Scott Brown and Associates, Tod Williams and Billie Tsien, and Louis I. Kahn's Richards Medical Building, one of the most influential buildings of the late 20th century. The tour returns to 34th Street along Locust Walk through the heart of the Penn campus.

Among the most interesting buildings open to the public are the University Museum and the Fisher Fine Arts Building.

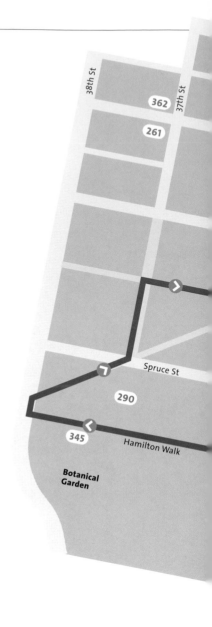

413 **McNeill Center for Early American Studies**
34th & Walnut Sts.

347 **Hill Hall**
Walnut St. between
33rd & 34th Sts. PR

356 **University Parking Garage**
3201 Walnut St.

271 **Anne and Jerome Fisher Fine Arts Building**
34th St. between Walnut
& Spruce Sts. OP

398 **Roy and Diana Vagelos Laboratories**
3340 Smith Walk

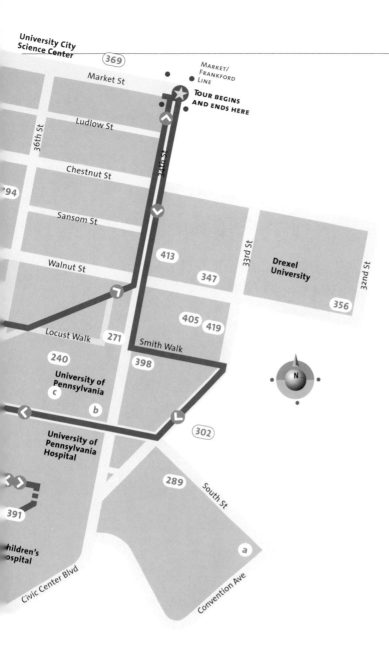

405 **Melvin J. and Claire Levine Hall**
3340 Walnut St.

419 **Skirkanich Hall**
210 S. 33rd St.

302 **Franklin Field**
33rd & South Sts.

289 **University Museum**
33rd & South Sts. OP

a **Parking Garage 2**
South St. & Convention Ave.
1968, Mitchell / Giurgola
Assocs.

b **Irvine Auditorium**
34th & Spruce Sts.
1929, Horace Trumbauer;
Renovated 1997, Venturi
Scott Brown and Assoc.

c **Perelman Quadrangle**
1998–2000, Venturi Scott
Brown and Assoc. OP

391 **Clinical Research Building**
35th St. South of Hamilton
Walk

345 **Richards Medical Research Building**
Hamilton Walk between
37th & 38th Sts.

290 **Men's Dormitories**
Spruce St. between
36th & 38th Sts. PR

240 **College Hall**
Locust Walk between
34th & 35th Sts. OP

394 **Institute of Contemporary Art**
36th & Sansom Sts. OP

261 **Tabernacle Presbyterian Church**
3700 Chestnut St.

362 **International House**
3501 Chestnut St. PR

369 **ISI Building**
3501 Market St.

Drexel University and Powelton Village

G

The eastern portion of West Philadelphia is the location of Drexel University and the adjacent Powelton Village neighborhood. The Drexel Institute of Art Science and Industry was founded in 1891 by financier Anthony J. Drexel to serve the needs of working-class students. In 1919, the Institute introduced one of the nation's first cooperative education programs, requiring students to combine their full-time study with professional employment. The co-op program has distinguished Drexel's approach to education ever since. By the mid-1960s, the Institute had the nation's largest private undergraduate engineering college, one of the largest graduate programs in library science and the largest private non-denominational home economics program. Drexel was designated a university by the Commonwealth of Pennsylvania in 2000.

Powelton Village was first settled in 1800. Most of its houses were built speculatively in the late 19th century after introduction of horse-drawn trolleys in the 1860s made it possible to commute easily to the city. Then there was a rapid growth of suburban houses with yards and tree-lined streets, in contrast to the dense row housing of the city. Most houses are twins or double houses in the Italianate style, usually of wood frame and stucco. There are a number of mansions, some built by prominent manufacturers of the period. There are also several blocks of distinctive and ornate Victorian row houses.

The tour can be reached from Center City by taking the Market-Frankford Subway or Market Street buses to 30th Street. The first buildings on the tour are the 30th Street Station, with its enormous waiting room, and the Cira Centre, which is dramatically lit at night. The tour proceeds west along Market Street to Drexel University, then through the Powelton Village neighborhood and ends at the Market Frankford Line station at 34th Street where it connects to the tour of the University of Pennsylvania campus.

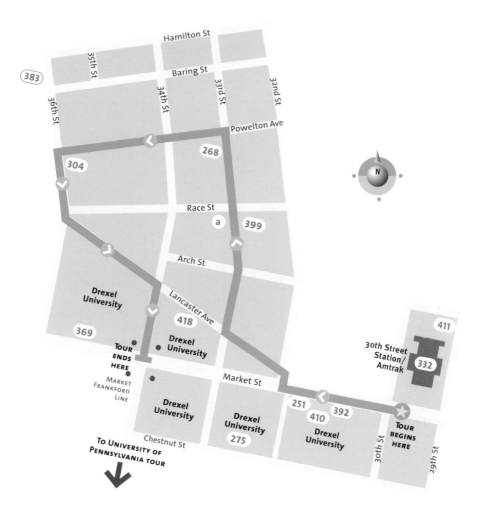

332 30th Street Station
30th & Market Sts. OP

411 Cira Centre
2929 Market St.

392 LeBow Engineering Center and Center for Automation Technology
Market St. between
31st & 32nd Sts.

410 Bossone Research Center
32nd & Market Sts.

251 Centennial Bank Paul Peck Alumni Center
3142 Market St.

275 Drexel Institute, Main Building
32nd & Chestnut Sts.
OP

399 North Hall
3200 Race St. PR

a Race Street Residences
32nd & Race Sts., Erdy
McHenry Archictecture,
2007 PR

268 Poth Mansion Alpha Pi Lambda
216 N. 33rd St. PR

304 3500 Powelton Avenue The Courts
3500 Powelton Ave.
PR

383 Gaither House
3601 Baring St. PR

418 Leonard Pearlstein Art Gallery
33rd & Lancaster Walk OP

369 ISI Building
3501 Market St.

Germantown

H

Germantown was founded in 1683, when Penn sold a large tract of land to Daniel Pastorius and a group of German-speaking Quakers. It was the largest early settlement outside the city having its own stores, businesses and even its own German newspaper. Most early buildings were located on Germantown Avenue, the original colonial road connecting to the city. After the yellow fever epidemics in the city in 1793 and 1796, Germantown became a popular location for summer homes. During the 19th century, Germantown grew rapidly after the commuter railroad was extended from the city in the 1840s. Many picturesque villas and Victorian mansions were built during this era for middle-class families eager to escape the noise and congestion of the city.

Germantown can best be seen by a driving tour, although it is possible to take the Chestnut Hill West train line to the Tulpehocken Station for a walking tour of most of the area. The driving tour reaches Germantown via the beautiful Lincoln Drive, along a natural wilderness area within the city. Germantown Avenue is the location of many of the oldest buildings and is an interesting driving tour in itself. Several blocks away, in the Walnut Lane area, is a fine collection of Victorian suburban houses. Most houses on the tour are private homes, and not open to the public. However, Cliveden, the Deshler-Morris House, Wyck and the Maxwell Mansion are open and provide excellent examples of both colonial and Victorian design.

The Germantown tour easily connects to the Chestnut Hill tour which begins on W. Allens Lane.

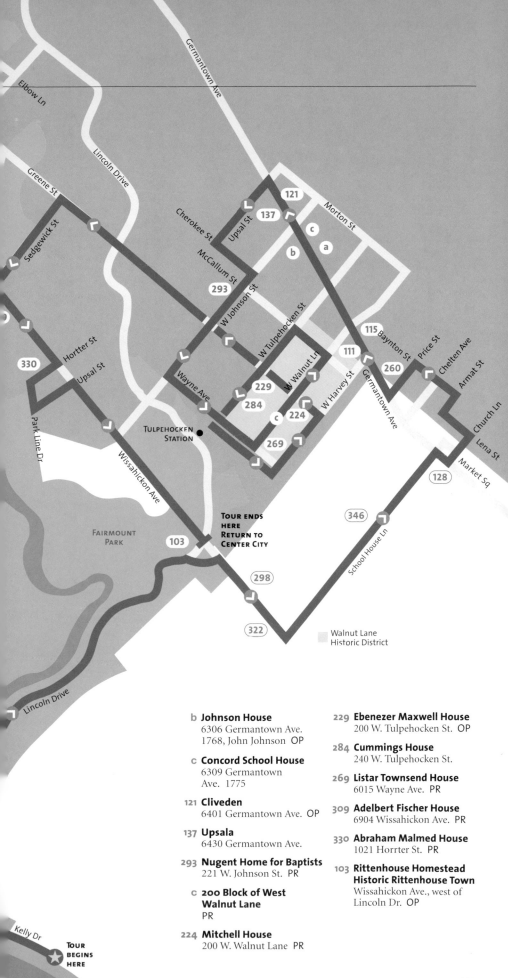

b Johnson House
6306 Germantown Ave.
1768, John Johnson OP

c Concord School House
6309 Germantown
Ave. 1775

121 Cliveden
6401 Germantown Ave. OP

137 Upsala
6430 Germantown Ave.

293 Nugent Home for Baptists
221 W. Johnson St. PR

**c 200 Block of West
Walnut Lane**
PR

224 Mitchell House
200 W. Walnut Lane PR

229 Ebenezer Maxwell House
200 W. Tulpehocken St. OP

284 Cummings House
240 W. Tulpehocken St.

269 Listar Townsend House
6015 Wayne Ave. PR

309 Adelbert Fischer House
6904 Wissahickon Ave. PR

330 Abraham Malmed House
1021 Horrter St. PR

**103 Rittenhouse Homestead
Historic Rittenhouse Town**
Wissahickon Ave., west of
Lincoln Dr. OP

Chestnut Hill

J

Chestnut Hill originally developed along Germantown Avenue. Early commercial and residential buildings were similar to those in Germantown. But Chestnut Hill's real growth and prosperity did not occur until the 19th century, with the extension of the commuter railroad. At that time, Henry Houston, a director of the Pennsylvania Railroad, undertook a number of real estate ventures designed to attract wealthy families to the area. He built an elaborate inn and church, gave land for a cricket club and constructed nearly 100 houses. Other residents built grand Italianate villas. The area contains a fascinating mix of elaborate mansions for the wealthy and small row houses originally built for their predominantly Irish servants. Houston's efforts were followed by those of his son-in-law, Dr. George Woodward, who developed many outstanding housing complexes in the early 20th century, most of which are still owned and rented by the Woodward family. These included some important early examples of grouped houses. Among the architects represented in the area are Mellor and Meigs, George Howe, Robert Venturi, Mitchell / Giurgola and Louis Kahn.

Chestnut Hill can best be seen by a driving tour, although it is possible to take the Chestnut Hill West train line to the Chestnut Hill station for a walking tour of the area. The driving tour reaches Chestnut Hill via Kelly Drive and the beautiful Lincoln Drive.

In Chestnut Hill the tour winds through residential streets containing some of the best examples of Victorian, early 20th century and contemporary houses in Philadelphia. Of particular interest are the early 20th century experiments in grouped housing, such as the Benezet Street houses, Winston Court, and the Lincoln Drive complex. Most of the buildings on the tour are private residences and not open to the public.

323 French Village
Elbow Lane & Gate Lane
off McCallum St. PR

a Krisheim
McCallum St.
& Mermaid Lane
1910, Peabody & Stearns PR

264 Druim Moir and Brinkwood
W. Willow Grove Ave.
& Cherokee St. PR

259 Wissahickon Inn Chestnut Hill Academy
500 W. Willow Grove Ave.

b St. Martins in the Fields
W. Willow Grove Ave.
& St. Martins Lane
1888, G. W. & W. D. Hewitt,
Renovated 2002, Kise Straw
Kolodner

353 Dorothy Shipley White House
717 Glen Gary Dr. PR

263 Houston-Sauveur House
8205 Seminole St. PR

341 Charles Woodward House
8220 Millman St. PR

351 Vanna Venturi House
8330 Millman St. PR

348 Margaret Esherick House
204 Sunrise Lane PR

257 Gravers Lane Station
Gravers Lane & Anderson St.

258 Angelcot
Evergreen Ave. & Prospect St. PR

223 Watson House
100 Summit St. PR

216 Piper-Price House
129 Bethlehem Pike PR

c Woodmere Art Gallery
9201 Germantown Ave.
1867 OP

313 High Hollow
101 W. Hampton Rd. PR

317 Pepper House
9120 Crefeld St. PR

334 Schofield Andrews House
9002 Crefeld St. PR

d Howe-Fraley House
10 W. Chestnut Hill Ave.
1921, George Howe PR

e Winston Court
7821–7909 Winston Rd.
1925, H. Louis Duhring PR

311 Benezet Street Houses
24–34 Benezet St. PR

315 Lincoln Drive Development
Lincoln Dr. & W. Willow Grove Ave. PR

315a Half Moon Houses
7919–25 Lincoln Dr. PR

315b Sulgrave Manor
200 W. Willow Grove Ave. PR

315c Unden Court
103–113 W. Willow Grove Ave. PR

315d Three Houses
8008–12 Crefeld Ave. PR

308 100–102 West Mermaid Lane PR

323 French Village
Emlen St. & W. Allens Lane PR

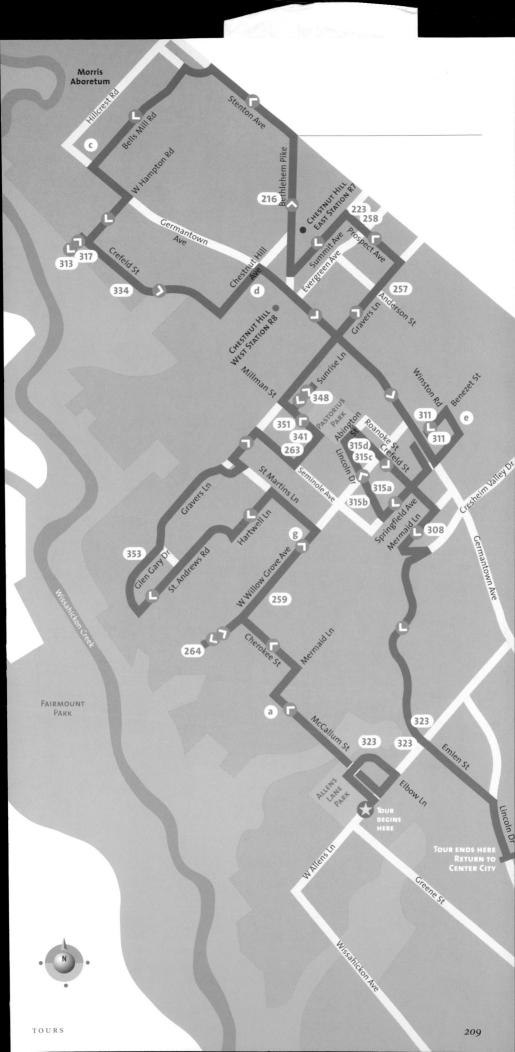

Morris
Aboretum

Hillcrest Rd

Bells Mill Rd

Stenton Ave

c

W Hampton Rd

Bethlehem Pike

216

CHESTNUT HILL
EAST STATION R7

223
258

Germantown
Ave

Summit Ave

Prospect Ave

313

317

Crefeld St

Evergreen Ave

334

Chestnut Hill
Ave

d

257

Anderson St

Gravers Ln

CHESTNUT HILL
WEST STATION R8

Sunrise Ln

Winston Rd

Benezet St

Millman St

348

PASTORIUS
PARK

Abington
St

Roanoke St

311

e

351

341

263

Crefeld St

315d

315c

311

Lincoln Dr

St Martins Ln

Seminole Ave

315a

315b

Gravers Ln

Hartwell Ln

g

Springfield Ave

Mermaid Ln

308

Cresheim Valley Dr

353

St. Andrews Rd

Glen Gary Dr

W Willow Grove Ave

259

Germantown Ave

264

Cherokee St

Mermaid Ln

FAIRMOUNT
PARK

a

McCallum St

323

Wissahickon Creek

323

323

Emlen St

ALLENS
LANE
PARK

Elbow Ln

Lincoln Dr

★ TOUR
BEGINS
HERE

TOUR ENDS HERE
RETURN TO
CENTER CITY

W Allens Ln

Greene St

Wissahickon Ave

N

Highlig

K

The Highlight[...]
those who want to see some of the city's
most important buildings and interesting
areas in a limited amount of time. The tour
takes approximately two hours. It begins at
Independence Hall, proceeds through most
areas covered by individual walking or driving
tours and encompasses portions of North
Philadelphia; it concludes at City Hall. The
buildings listed below are the most important
landmarks; other buildings along this route
can be identified by consulting the tours of
individual areas.

106 Elfreth's Alley
107 Christ Church
402 Independence Visitor's Center
406 Liberty Bell Center
230 Lit Brothers Mellon Independence Center
368 The Gallery
280 Reading Terminal
335 Philadelphia Saving Fund Society Loews Philadelphia Hotel

303 John Wanamaker's Department Store The Wanamaker Building
397 Pennsylvania Convention Center
237 Masonic Temple
242 Pennsylvania Academy of the Fine Arts
392 Bell Atlantic Tower
420 Comcast Center
373 One Logan Square & Four Seasons Hotel
360 United Fund Building
207 Cathedral Basilica of SS. Peter & Paul
316 Free Library
314 Philadelphia Museum of Art
343 Parkway House
277 Kemble-Bergdol Mansion
149 Eastern State Penitentiary
256 Disston Mansion
266 1500 Block North 17th St.
253 Church of the Gesu
158 Girard College
376 Philadelphia Zoo
304 3500 Powelton Ave. The Courts
347 Hill Hall
271 Fisher Fine Arts Building
398 Vagelos Laboratories
289 University Museum
290 Men's Dormitory

345 Richards Medical Research Laboratory
232 Woodland Terrace
267 4206–18 Spruce St.
320 Divinity School & Chapel
374 University City Family Housing
369 ISI Building
251 Centennial Bank Paul Peck Alumni Center
332 30th Street Station
411 Cira Centre
363 Philadelphia Electric Company
381 Commerce Square
371 The Atrium
388 Mellon Bank Center
381 One Liberty Place
387 Two Liberty Place and Shops at Liberty Place
331 The Drake
150, 249 University of the Arts
403 Kimmel Center
221 Academy of Music
307 Bellevue Stratford
235 Union League
295 Land Title Building
306 Girard Trust Company Ritz-Carlton Hotel
243 City Hall

18th St
17th St
16th St
15th St
19th St
Oxford St
Jefferson St
Master St
Thompson St
Girard Ave
Poplar St
Parrish St
Brown St
Wallace St
Ridge Ave
266
256
253

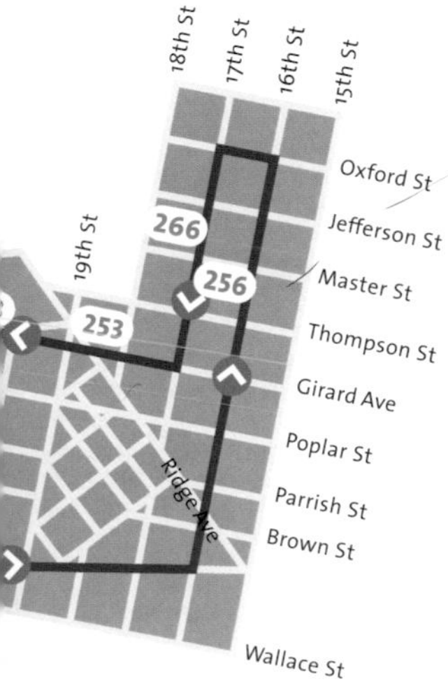

Hamilton St
Callowhill St

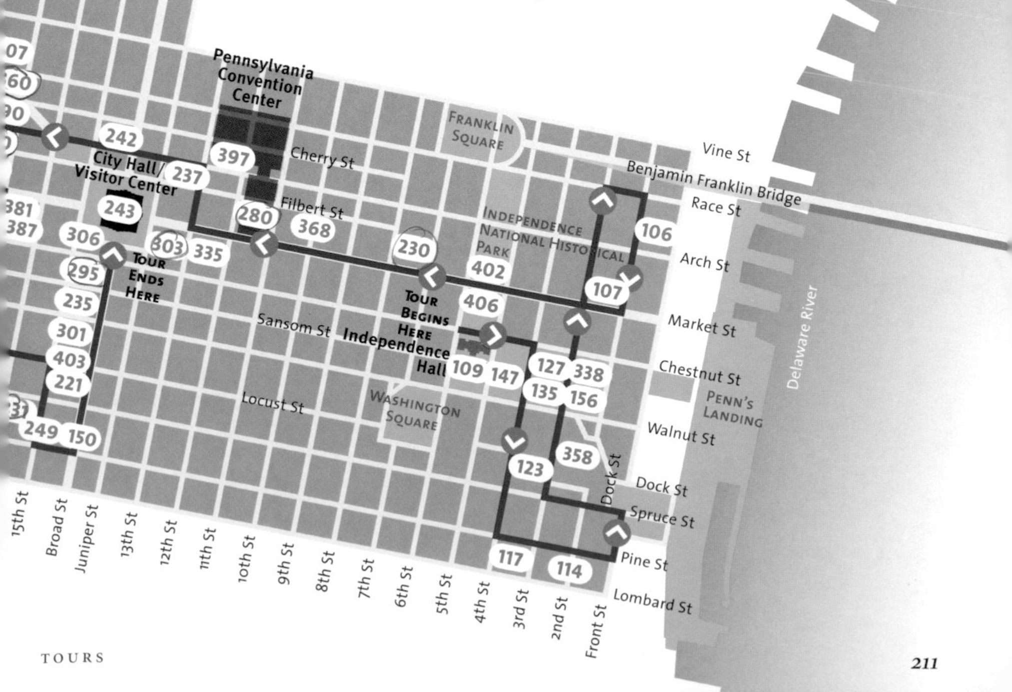

Pennsylvania Convention Center
Franklin Square
Vine St
Benjamin Franklin Bridge
Race St
Arch St
Market St
Chestnut St
Walnut St
Dock St
Spruce St
Pine St
Lombard St
Cherry St
Filbert St
Sansom St
Locust St
City Hall/ Visitor Center
Tour Ends Here
Tour Begins Here
Independence Hall
Independence National Historical Park
Washington Square
Penn's Landing
Delaware River
15th St
Broad St
Juniper St
13th St
12th St
11th St
10th St
9th St
8th St
7th St
6th St
5th St
4th St
3rd St
2nd St
Front St
Dock St
242
237
397
243
280
368
381
387
306
303
335
295
235
301
403
221
249
150
230
402
406
106
107
109
147
127
338
135
156
358
123
117
114

Buildings Not on Tours

L

Philadelphia
Museum of Art

Pennsylvania Ave

Benjamin Franklin Pkwy

Hamilton St

327

319

Callowhill St

I-76 Schuylkill Expwy

Schuylkill River

30th Street
Station/
Amtrak

LOGAN
SQUARE

389

225

32nd St

31st St

30th St

29th St

JFK Blvd

City Hall

262

272

24th St

23rd St

292

239 226

250

RITTENHOUSE
SQUARE

209
210

238

278

212 215

22nd St

21st St

20th St

19th St

18th St

17th St

16th St

15th St

Broad St

Juniper St

13th St

Numbers on maps refer to
building catalog numbers.

Places of Architectural Interest in the Region

501

502

[Map of the Philadelphia region showing numbered locations]

611
Doylestown
503
BUCKS CTY
476
MONTGOMERY CTY
276
95
504
501
508
73
1
76
426
76
509
502
510
PENNSYLVANIA
PHILADELPHIA
611
1
476
CHESTER CTY
1
676
NEW JERSEY
Camden
511
DELAWARE CTY
505
1
507
52
506
95
DELAWARE
Wilmington

The Philadelphia region contains a wealth of distinguished architecture ranging from colonial estates to historic Quaker Meetinghouses, elegant residences of the early-20th century, and distinctive civic and cultural buildings. The following are a few of the notable places of architectural interest within a reasonable distance of Philadelphia; most are open to the public. Additional information and directions can be found on the websites listed.

501   OP

Pennsbury Manor, *reconstructed 1939*
400 Pennsbury Memorial Road
Morrisville, PA 19067
R. Brognard Okie and Warren P. Laird

Penn offered first settlers in Pennsylvania large tracts of land in the countryside, as well as sites in the city of Philadelphia. He expected prominent landowners to live on country estates as was the case in England. For his own home he set aside 8.400 acres along the Delaware River 26 miles north of Philadelphia. Construction began before Penn arrived in 1682; he lived there for a few months before returning to England and then again during his second and final visit to Pennsylvania from 1699 to 1701. The house

503 The Mercer Museum   503 Fonthill

was demolished by the time of the American Revolution and the land passed out of the hands of the Penn family. In 1932, 10 acres of the original site, including the foundations of the manor house, were donated to the Commonwealth of Pennsylvania. The house was reconstructed by the Pennsylvania Historical and Museum Commission based on archeological evidence and correspondence between Penn and James Harrison, who built the house on his behalf.

A terraced promenade lined with poplar trees leads to the entrance to the house from the river, where Penn kept a barge that transported him to and from Philadelphia. The great hall in the front of the house was designed to accommodate large groups of visitors and connects via wide doorways to adjacent rooms for dining and family life. Each of these is furnished based on Penn's inventory and that of other colonial estates. In addition to the main house, 23 other structures have been reconstructed showing the type of outbuildings common to an estate of this magnitude.

Pennsbury is located about 45 minutes northeast of Center City Philadelphia. For directions and hours see www.pennsbury-manor.org.

---

502   OP

Andalusia, *1806/1834–35*
1237 State Road
Andalusia, PA 19020
Renovated, Thomas U. Walter

Andalusia, situated on a promontory overlooking the Delaware River, was originally the home of John Craig, a Philadelphia merchant. Nicholas Biddle, director of the Second Bank of the United States and one of the most prominent men in America, and his wife acquired the house and 100 acres from her parents. Biddle was a strong advocate of the Greek Revival style. He commissioned Thomas U. Walter to expand the house.

Walter added a double parlor with floor to ceiling windows opening onto a porch with a massive Doric colonnade. This transformed the house into one of the finest examples of domestic Greek Revival architecture in the country.

Andalusia contains 18th- and 19th-century furniture collected by the many generations of the Biddle family who lived here until 1980 when the family created a foundation to preserve the house and its spacious grounds for the benefit of the public.

Andalusia is located about 30 minutes northeast of Center City Philadelphia. For directions and hours see www.andalusiapa.org.

---

503   OP

Fonthill, *1908–10*
84 South Pine Street
The Mercer Museum, *1914–16*
East Court Street and Swamp Road
Doylestown, PA 18901
Henry Chapman Mercer

Dr. Henry Chapman Mercer was a renowned traveler, explorer, anthropologist and archaeologist. He devoted his life to the study of civilization. In 1897, he began to collect pre-industrial tools and artifacts. His collection, "Tools of the Nation Maker," contains 30,000 objects and is one of the most comprehensive of its type in the world. Mercer was also interested in Pennsylvania pottery and founded the Moravian Pottery and Tile Works, influenced by the Arts and Crafts movement. Mercer tiles became very popular; they were used in many prominent buildings and are still produced today.

In 1908, Mercer began to build a home, a building for his tile works, and one for his collections. All three structures were designed by Mercer himself; no architect was employed and no plans drawn. All three are built of poured-in-place reinforced concrete and are the earliest examples of the use of this material.

504 Cairnwood

504 Glencairn

Fonthill, Mercer's mansion, was built first; it contains 44 rooms, 18 fireplaces and 200 windows. It was designed from the inside out with workmen simply following Mercer's directions. The result is an unusual and striking building in which windows, doors and even rooms appear in no particular order. The tile works building followed after which Mercer built the museum to display his collection. This seven-story building contains a six-story central atrium to enable Mercer to hang such large objects as a whaling boat and stagecoach. Surrounding the atrium are rooms and alcoves with exhibits organized thematically by Mercer himself.

Mercer's organic approach to design and construction make Fonthill and the Mercer Museum among the most fascinating buildings in the Philadelphia region.

Fonthill and the Mercer Museum are located about a one hour northwest of Center City Philadelphia. For directions and hours see www.mercermuseum.org.

504 OP

Cairnwood, *1892–95*
1001 Cathedral Road
Carrère and Hastings;
Bryn Athyn Cathedral, *1913–55*
900 Cathedral Road
Cram, Goodhue and Ferguson/ Raymond Pitcairn;
Glencairn, *1928–39*
1003 Cathedral Road
Raymond Pitcairn
Bryn Athyn, PA 19009

John Pitcairn, co-founder of Pittsburgh Plate Glass, used his wealth to purchase land north of Philadelphia for his Swedenborgian religious community, the Church of New Jerusalem. Pitcairn built a home for himself (Cairnwood) and donated funds for the building of the Bryn Athyn Cathedral. His son, Raymond, built a home for him-

self (Glencairn) adjacent. Each of the three buildings is an exceptional architectural accomplishment.

Carrère and Hastings designed Cairnwood in the Beaux-Arts style. The sprawling L-shaped house sits on the ridge of a hill with dramatic views over lawns and protected woodlands. The main wing of the house, with an arched open porch, consists of two elements, one under a hipped slate roof, and the other with a gambrel roof of slate and metal. A central tower, with a chapel on the top floor, joins the main wing and east wing. Orange iron-spotted Roman brick is trimmed with rusticated buff-gray limestone. The elegant Beaux-arts interior focuses on a grand hall with elaborate ornamentation; large arched French doors open onto the terrace. The house is now used for social and corporate events.

The central portion of the cathedral, which houses the sanctuary, was designed by Ralph Adams Cram in a Gothic Revival style influenced by the early 20th-century Arts and Crafts movement. After 1917, Raymond Pitcairn took over responsibility for the project, particularly the north and south wings. Raymond was very interested in medieval architecture and attempted to duplicate both the form and method of early medieval buildings. Craftsmen and artists were organized into guilds that produced sample work before it was added to the building. There are no straight lines in the building; elements are often aligned deliberately off center and the cathedral floors are not level. Pitcairn felt this was consistent with medieval architecture and would soften the character of the massive building. The cathedral is decorated with exceptional stained glass windows, including a spectacular rosette window above the altar. It took 42 years to complete.

Glencairn, built by Raymond Pitcairn as his home, is designed in a Romanesque style with sculpture, stained glass and mosaics based on the teachings of the Church of New

506

507

Jerusalem. Pitcairn used no plans. Instead he relied on architectural models and full-size plaster models developed by craftsmen who worked in studios on the site. The house has 100 rooms on 11 floors. The main floor has been preserved in its original character, including the Great Hall; the other floors house a museum of Pitcairn's collection of about 8,000 works of religious art from diverse cultures and religions.

The Bryn Athyn Cathedral and Pitcairn houses are located about one hour north of Center City Philadelphia. For directions and hours see www.brynathyncathedral.org, www. glencairnmuseum.org and www.cairnwood. org.

505   OP

Longwood Gardens, *1907–30*
1001 Longwood Avenue
Kennett Square, PA 19348

In 1906, wealthy industrialist Pierre S. du Pont purchased the farm on which Quaker brothers Joshua and Samuel Peirce, had created an arboretum in 1798. du Pont wanted to save what had become the finest collection of trees in the nation and one of the first public parks. From this modest beginning he went on to create one of the country's great horticultural wonders.

From 1907 through the 1930s, du Pont designed and constructed a series of gardens based on his extensive travels to horticultural centers and gardens throughout the world. The first gardens were "old fashioned" in design, but later gardens drew on French and Italian influences. Today 350 acres of magnificently landscaped gardens are at the center of 1,000 acres of preserved land. Among the most outstanding features are the water gardens, derived from those at the Villa Gamberaia near Florence, Italy, and the spectacular fountains.

In 1914, du Pont enlarged the Peirce farmhouse and added a conservatory that was the first indoor garden. He subsequently built several huge glass conservatories, now open year-round, that contain 20 indoor gardens and seasonal displays. The Peirce-du Pont Mansion is also open to the public.

Longwood Gardens is located 45 minutes southwest of Center City Philadelphia. For directions see www.longwoodgardens.org.

506   C,J   OP

Nemours Mansion and Gardens, *1909–1910*
1600 Rockland Road
Wilmington, DE 19803
Carrère and Hastings
Restored 2008, John Milner Architects.

Nemours, the home of Alfred I. du Pont, is named after the town in France represented by Alfred's great-great-grandfather and founder of the du Pont dynasty. The mansion is located on a 200-acre estate that includes the largest formal French garden in North America. Designed by New York architects Carrère and Hastings in a modified French chateau style, the 47,000 sf house contains over 70 rooms on five floors. A three bay, colonnaded facade faces the formal gardens, behind which are magnificent rooms preserved and furnished just as they were when du Pont lived here. Among the exceptional collection of art and decorative objects are works by Charles Wilson Peale, Frederick Remington and Louis Tiffany.

The original estate was self-sustaining with its own orchards, dairy herd and greenhouses. A three year restoration, completed in 2008, revitalized the gardens following the model of the Petit Trianon at Versailles and restored such features as the 800,000-gallon reflecting pool.

Nemours is located approximately 30 minutes south of Center City Philadelphia. For directions and reservations see www.nemoursmansion.org.

508

---

507   OP

Winterthur Museum and County Estate,
1920s–1951
5105 Kennett Pike
Winterthur, DE 19735

When Henry Francis du Pont took over the management of his family's property, he began the creation of an American version of a European country estate. At its height, the estate covered 2,500 acres and contained romantic landscapes, 60 acres of naturalistic gardens, a prize-winning dairy farm and the du Ponts' home. It is still the greatest surveying example of its kind in the country.

du Pont and his father designed the initial house in the spirit of 18th- and 19th-century European country homes. Later, du Pont enlarged it to provide space for the installation of important American interiors, which he purchased and installed room by room, as well as his growing collection of 18th-century American antiques and artifacts. The museum contains more than 71,000 objects as well as 175 period rooms that have been restored and furnished in an historically complete manner. Winterthur also houses an important library and research center.

Winterthur is approximately 45 minutes southwest of Center City Philadelphia. For directions see www.winterrthur.org.

508   OP

Wharton Esherick Museum, *1928–66*
Near Valley Forge National Historical Park
Paoli, PA 19301
Wharton Esherick

Wharton Esherick was one of America's finest artists and wood craftsman. After training as a painter, Esherick began working in wood in 1926. His furniture, sculpture and architectural interiors were strikingly original and changed the way many designers thought about furniture design and the use of wood as a material.

Esherick's first major architectural interior was the home of Pennsylvania Supreme Court Justice Curtis Bok, constructed in 1937. Esherick began building a studio for himself in 1928, then later expanded it into his home, which he continued to modify until he declared it finished in 1966. The house looks deceptively small, but contains four levels set into the slope of Valley Forge Mountain. Esherick liked to avoid the use of traditional straight lines in both furniture and architecture; here, both the stone walls and roof ridge are curved. However, it is the interior of the house that shows Esherick's extraordinary talent.

The interior is designed as a single environment with architecture, building structure and furnishings fused into one continuous composition in wood. The central feature, and one of Esherick's most important works, is the spiral stair of hand-hewn red oak, which connects three of the four levels of the house. It was twice removed to be exhibited in New York.

The Esherick Museum is about 40 minutes west of Center City Philadelphia. It is open from March to December by reservation only. Call 610.644.5822 for reservations and directions.

509   OP

Beth Sholom Synagogue, *1959*

Old York and Foxcroft Rds.
Elkins Park, PA 19027
Frank Lloyd Wright

Beth Sholom Synagogue is the only major building by Frank Lloyd Wright in the Philadelphia area. Wright designed many religious buildings in his career, dating back to his 1906 Unity Temple in Chicago. His designs always incorporated the use of natural light to illuminate the sanctuary. In the 1930s he envisioned a church in the shape of a gigantic glass pyramid. Like many of his other early conceptual projects, this did not become an actual building until late in his career.

Wright found a sympathetic client in Rabbi Mortimer J. Cohen, who wanted a building that would make people feel "as if they were resting in the very hands of God." The pyramid form also had symbolic associations with Mt. Sinai. The synagogue consists of a temple seating 1,000 persons and a chapel below. The temple has a hexagonal plan with an inwardly sloping floor. It is brilliantly illuminated by the translucent roof, from the center of which hangs a colored-glass chandelier trimmed in incandescent lights. It is a spectacular and inspiring religious space. The pyramid structure, supported by a giant steel tripod, has double walls of plastic sheathed in glass. Along the spines of the pyramid are symbols of the menorah.

Wright's other significant project in this area is the Suntop Homes, on Sutton Road in Ardmore. Built in 1939, this complex is an early example of Wright's Usonian houses. Four houses are grouped together under a single roof, similar to the quadruple houses on Benezet Street. They were built as prototypes of moderate-income housing and used such innovative features as radiant heating in the floor slabs. Although several have been altered, they still retain Wright's distinctive style.

Beth Sholom Synagogue is about 45 minutes north of Center City Philadelphia. For directions and hours see www.bethsholomcongregation.org.

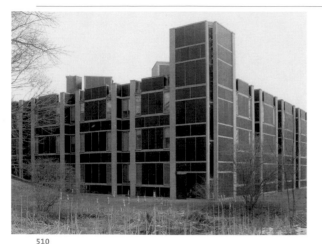

510

511

510 PR
Erdman Hall, *1960–65*

Bryn Mawr College
100 N. Merion Avenue
Bryn Mawr, PA 19010
Louis I. Kahn
Restored 2003, 1:1:6 Technologies Incorporated

Bryn Mawr is one of the country's finest educational institutions for women. One of the most notable buildings on its campus is the Erdman Hall dormitory, designed by Louis I. Kahn from 1960–65. The dormitory consists of three diamond-shaped units, each of which focuses around an inner court illuminated by natural light, in Kahn's distinctive manner. Although the exterior is exposed concrete and slate, its scale and siting make it part of the more traditional campus.

In 2003, Bryn Mawr College extensively restored Erdman Hall, removing all 1,735 slate panels to install new stainless-steel securing straps and to correct other problems. Today it is one of the Philadelphia regions important landmarks of mid-20th century modern architecture.

Bryn Mawr College is located about 30 minutes west of Center City Philadelphia. For directions see www.brynmawr.edu.

511 C,J
One Port Center, *1996*

Delaware River Port Authority Headquarters
2 Riverside Drive
Camden, NJ 08101
Michael Graves Associates

The Delaware River Port Authority (DRPA) resulted from the decision in 1919 of Pennsylvania and New Jersey leaders to construct a bridge over the river, now known as the Benjamin Franklin Bridge. DRPA went on to create four additional bridges and become a bi-state transportation and economic devel-opment authority with responsibility for regional rail and ferry services.

In 1996, DRPA built a headquarters for itself with office space for other organizations in an effort to revitalize downtown Camden and contribute to the development of the Camden waterfront. The 11-story building is located adjacent to the Thomas Kean New Jersey State Aquarium. The lower portion of the building consists of a large frame of blue and white brick; the upper floors, containing executive offices, are located behind three-story tall yellow aluminum composite columns. At the building entrance similar three-story columns on the lower level suggest a traditional colonnade. The building is a prominent and colorful landmark on the Camden skyline.

The DRPA headquarters building is located directly opposite Center City Philadelphia on the Camden waterfront and can be easily reached by public transportation. For directions see www.dvrpa.org.

Bibliography

American Philosophical Society.
Historic Philadelphia from the Founding until the Nineteenth Century.
Philadelphia, 1953.

Brownlee, David B., and David G. Delong.
Louis I. Kahn: In the Realm of Architecture
New York: Rizzoli International Publications, 1991.

Brownlee, David B.
Building the City Beautiful
Philadelphia, 1989.

Cohen, Jeffrey A., Michael J. Lewis, George E. Thomas.
Frank Furness: The Complete Works (Revised Edition).
Princeton Architectural Press, 1996.

Gallery, John Andrew.
The Planning of Center City Philadelphia: From William Penn to the Present.
Philadelphia: Center for Architecture, Inc., 2007.

Gallery, John Andrew, ed.
Sacred Sites of Center City.
Philadelphia: Paul Dry Books, 2007.

Garrison, James B.
Houses of Philadelphia: Chestnut Hill and the Wissahickon Valley, 1880-1930.
Acanthus Press, New York, 2008.

Greiff, Constance M.
John Notman, Architect: 1810 – 1865.
Philadelphia: Athenaeum of Philadelphia, 1979.

Keel, Thomas H.
Forgotten Philadelphia, Lost Architecture of the Quaker City.
Philadelphia: Temple University Press, 2007.

Laverty, Bruce, Michael J. Lewis, Michele Taillon Taylor.
Monument to Philanthropy, The Design and Building of Girard College, 1832-1848.
Philadelphia: Girard College, 1998.

Lewis, Michael J.
Frank Furness: Architecture and the Violent Mind.
New York: W.W. Norton, 2001.

Maas, John.
The Glorious Enterprise: The Centennial Exhibition of 1876 and H. J. Schwarzmann, Architect-in-Chief.
Watkins Glen, N.Y.: American Life Foundation, 1973.

Mellor Meigs and Howe.
Boulder, Colo.: Graybooks, 1991.

Miller, Fredric M., Morris J. Vogel, and Allen F. Davis.
Still Philadelphia: A Photographic History, 1890 – 1940.
Philadelphia: Temple University Press, 1983.

Mitchell, Ehrman and Romaldo Giurgola.
Mitchell / Giurgola.
New York: Rizzoli International Publications, 1983.

Moss, Roger W.
Historic Houses of Philadelphia.
Philadelphia: University of Pennsylvania Press, 1998.

Moss, Roger W.
Historic Sacred Places of Philadelphia.
Philadelphia: University of Pennsylvania Press, 2005.

Moss, Roger W.
Historic Landmarks of Philadelphia.
Philadelphia: University of Pennsylvania Press, 2008.

Nash, Gary.
The First City, Philadelphia and the Forging of Historical Memory.
Philadelphia: University of Pennsylvania Press, 2002.

O'Gorman, James F.
The Architecture of Frank Furness.
Philadelphia: Philadelphia Museum of Art, 1973.

Philadelphia Museum of Art.
Philadelphia: Three Centuries of American Art.
Philadelphia: Philadelphia Museum of Art, 1976.

Schwartz, Frederic, ed.
Mother's House.
New York: Rizzoli International Publications, 1992.

Silent Witness: Quaker Meetinghouses of the Delaware Valley, 1695 to the Present.
Philadelphia: Philadelphia Yearly Meeting of the Religious Society of Friends, 2002.

Stern, Robert A. M.
George Howe: Toward a Modern American Architecture.
New Haven: Yale University Press, 1975.

Tatum, George B.
Penn's Great Town: 250 Years of Philadelphia Architecture.
New Haven: Yale University Press, 1975.

———.
Philadelphia Georgian: The City House of Samuel Powel and Some of Its 18th-Century Neighbors.
Middletown, Conn.: Wesleyan University Press, 1976.

Teitelman, Edward and Richard W. Longstreth.
Architecture in Philadelphia: A Guide.
Cambridge, Mass.: MIT Press, 1974.

Thomas, George E.
The Campus Guide, University of Pennsylvania.
New York: Princeton Architectural Press, 2002.

Tinkcom, Harry M., Margaret B. Tinkcom, and Grant Miles Simon.
Historic Germantown.
Philadelphia: American Philosophical Society, 1955.

Venturi, Robert.
Complexity and Contradiction in Architecture.
Cambridge, Mass.: MIT Press, 1967.

Warner, Sam Bass, Jr.
The Private City: Philadelphia in Three Periods of Its Growth.
Philadelphia: University of Pennsylvania Press, 1968.

Webster, Richard J.
Philadelphia Preserved: Catalog of the Historic American Buildings Survey.
Philadelphia: Temple University Press, 1976.

Weigley, Russell F., ed.
Philadelphia: A 300-Year History.
New York: W. W. Norton and Company, 1982.

White, Theo B.
Paul Philippe Cret.
Philadelphia: The Art Alliance Press, 1973.

———.
Philadelphia Architecture in the 19th Century.
Philadelphia: University of Pennsylvania Press, 1953.

Wolf, Edwin 2nd, ed.
Philadelphia: Portrait of an American City.
Harrisburg: Stackpole Books, 1975.

Wurman, Richard Saul and John Andrew Gallery.
Man-Made Philadelphia: A Guide to the Physical and Cultural Environment.
Cambridge, Mass.: MIT Press, 1972.

Photography Credits

All black and white photographs by Peter B. Olson, courtesy of the Peter B. Olson Collection of The Athenaeum of Philadelphia, except those noted below, which are used with the permission of the individual or organization indicated and listed by page number.

All color photographs, including the front and back cover, by Wyatt Gallery except for the following: *75* bottom, Graydon Wood; *91* top left, Tom Crane; *98R* Jeffrey Totaro; *116-117* Philadelphia Museum of Art / Graydon Wood; "Diana," Gift of the New York Life Insurance Co.; Reception Hall from a Nobleman's Palace, Gift of Edward B. Robinette. *123* bottom right, Graydon Wood; *165R* Jeffrey Totaro. *168* Tim McDonald; *171-72* middle, J. Randall Cotton; and *219* Historic American Buildings Survey (HABS), Library of Congress; right, Lawrence S. Williams Collection Inc., The Athenaeum of Philadelphia.

On pages with more than one photograph, the credit for the photograph on the left or on the top is given first; the credit for the photograph on the right or bottom is given second after a semicolon. When further clarity is need, R,L,T,B are used to indicate right, left, top, bottom.

Every attempt has been made to give proper credit and obtain appropriate permission for each illustration. The Center for Architecture apologizes for any omissions.

CATALOG 1

10 Historical Society of Pennsylvania. *11* The Library Company of Philadelphia. *12* The Library Company of Philadelphia. *13* The Philadelphia Museum of Art (PMA); PMA, Given by Titus C. Geesey. *14* PMA, Given by Mrs. Rodolphe Meyer de Schauensee and Mrs. James M. R. Sinkler in memory of Mrs. Lewis Audenried. *15* PMA, Thomas Skelton Harrison Fund; Richard Saul Wurman / GEE, Inc. *16* PMA, Thomas Skelton Harrison Fund; PMA, Bequest of Elizabeth Gratz. *17* PMA, Given by Mrs. Francis B. Gummere and Mrs. Thomas F. Branson. *20R* Wyatt Gallery. *24* HABS. *25L* Wyck Association. *28L* HABS. *31L* Tom Crane. *35* HABS / Jack E. Boucher. *36* Wyatt Gallery. *39R* Tom Crane.

CATALOG 2

48 PMA, Given by Mr. and Mrs. John Mulford. *49* PMA, Given by Agnes Davisson Loughran / Will Brown; Richard Saul Wurman / GEE, Inc. *50* PMA, Given by Mrs. Walter S. Detwiler; PMA, Given by the heirs of Mr. and Mrs. James Dobson. *51* PMA, Given by George Wood Furness. *52* PMA, Given by Charles T. Shenkle in memory of his mother, Edna H. Shenkle. *53* PMA, Given by the executors of the estate of Mary T. W. Strawbridge / Will Brown; PMA, From the Edgar V. Seeler and Marie Josephine Rozet Fund. *57L* Tom Crane. *58* HABS. *59* Tom Crane. *60R* HABS. *61* Tom Crane; Wyatt Gallery. *62L* Bower Lewis Thrower. *63R* J. Randall Cotton. *64* Wyatt Gallery; Tom Crane. *68L* Wyatt Gallery. *69* Tom Crane; HABS / Jack E. Boucher. *71* John Andrew Gallery. *75T* Philadelphia City Archives. *76R* Wyatt Gallery. *77* Wyatt Gallery. *84R* HABS / Joseph Elliot. *91R* Wyatt Gallery. *92L* Wyatt Gallery. *93R* HABS/ Joseph Elliott. *94L* Kise Straw Kolodner. *96* John Andrew Gallery; HABS / Jack E. Boucher. *97L* John Andrew Gallery. *99L* Ross O'Neal.

CATALOG 3

102 PMA, Gift of COLLAB: The Contemporary Design Group for the Philadelphia Museum of Art (COLLAB) in honor of Elisabeth L. Fraser. *103* PMA, Gift of Mr. Bayard H. Roberts and Mrs. John Wintersteen; Richard Saul Wurman / GEE, Inc. *104* PMA, Gift of COLLAB / Eric Mitchell; PMA, Gift of Adeline Edmunds / Will Brown. *105* PMA, Gift of Atelier International Ltd. *106* PMA, Given by Dr. Morton Beiler; PMA, Given by Knoll International. *107* PMA, Given by Habitat, Inc.; PMA, Gift of COLLAB. *110R* John Andrew Gallery. *112R* HABS. *113L* Paul Warchol. *119L* Jeffrey Totaro. *120R* Wyatt Gallery. *121* John Andrew Gallery. *122* Wyatt Gallery. *125* HABS / Jack E. Boucher; James B. Garrison. *129L* Tom Bernard. *129R* John Andrew Gallery. *131* Wyatt Gallery. *135L* Venturi Rauch and Scott Brown / George Pohl. *137L* Rollin R. La France. *139R* John Paskovich. *141L* Mark Cohn. *145* Otto Baitz Inc.; Matt Wargo. *146* James Oesch; Paul Warchol. *147* Nathaniel Lieberman courtesy of Pei Cobb Freed & Partners; Tom Bernard. *150* Jeffrey Totaro; GBQC. *151* H. Durston Saylor. *152* Matt Wargo; C. Geoffrey Berken. *153* Matt Wargo; Barry Halkin. *155* Venturi, Scott Brown and Associates / Matt Wargo; Matt Wargo.

CATALOG 4

158 PMA, Gift of COLLAB. *159* PMA, Gift of Ralph Rucci; PMA, Gift of Fury Design, Inc. *160* John Andrew Gallery. *161* Peter Aaron/ Esto; Roman Viñoly. *162* Matt Wargo; Barry Halkin. *163* Peter Aaron/ Esto; Wyatt Gallery. *164* Jeffrey Totaro. *165* Timothy Hursley. *167* Barry Halkin; Timothy Hursley. *169* Jon Perlmutter; Michael Moran Photography.

PHILADELPHIA ARCHITECTS

172 Louis I. Kahn Collection, University of Pennsylvania and Pennsylvania Historical and Museum Commission. *174* Princeton University. *175* Free Library of Philadelphia; Tennessee Tourist Development Office. *176* The Athenaeum of Philadelphia. *177* The Athenaeum of Philadelphia; Otto Baitz. *178* From Moses King, "Philadelphia and Notable Philadelphians," Philadelphia Historical Commission. *179* Collection of Hyman Myers; Historical Society of Pennsylvania. *180* E. Teitelman, Photography. *181* Blank and Stoller; Rittase. *182* Howe Archives, Columbia University. *183* Louis I. Kahn Collection, University of Pennsylvania and Pennsylvania Historical and Museum Commission / Lautman Photography; Kimbell Art Museum, Fort Worth, Texas / Bob Wharton; John Ebstel / Louis I. Kahn Collection, University of Pennsylvania and Pennsylvania Historical and Museum Commission. *184* Copyright by Wendy Reid; Engineering News-Record photo; John Pottle; John Gollings. *185T* Venturi, Scott Brown and Associates/ Frank Hanswick. *185B* Tom Bernard.

PLACES OF ARCHITECTURAL INTEREST IN THE REGION

214 Tom Crane. *215L* Mercer Museum of the Bucks County Historical Society. *215R* Don Pearson Photographers Inc. *216* Don Pearson Photographers Inc.; Glencairn Museum. *217* Grace Gary; Winterthur Port Royal Parlor/Gavin Ashworth. *218* James Mario. *220* Barry Schnoll; Matt Wargo.

Index